It's a Complement

Color Palettes in Graphic Design

SANDU

It's a Complement

Color Palettes in Graphic Design

First published in 2025 by Sandu Publishing Co., Ltd.

SANDU PUBLISHING

Edited and produced by Sandu Publishing Co., Ltd.
Editor: Joann Chung, Anton Tan
Designer: Wu Yanting
Cover Design by Wu Yanting

Sandu Publishing Co., Ltd.
Address: 2/F, Yau Tak Building, 167 Lockhart Road,
Wanchai, Hong Kong, China
info@sandupublishing.com
www.sandupublishing.com

Size: 190 mm × 250 mm
First Edition: 2025

ISBN: 978-988-70752-5-7

Printed and bound in China.

Contents

Preface

Color could be described as a fusion of light and perception, a dance between physics and psychology. It's how our eyes interpret reflected light, creating an infinite palette of shades that shape our environment.

In physics, color is the manifestation of light, a fascinating interaction between the different wavelengths that compose the electromagnetic spectrum. When the white light passes through a prism, it breaks down into a spectrum of colors ranging from red to violet, passing through orange, yellow, green, and blue. Each of these colors corresponds to a specific wavelength, a unique vibration of light, which our eyes interpret and process to shape our visual perception of the world.

Other than physics, color is a powerful catalyst for emotions, memories, and communication. Whether it's the calming effect of blue in healthcare environments or the urgency conveyed by red in warning signs, color choices are deliberate and impactful, shaping our perceptions and influencing our behaviors. Thus, a simple glance at a landscape or a work of art not only evokes a feeling of nostalgia but also communicates volumes of information, guiding us through our surroundings and enriching our experiences.

Color also serves as a critical tool in information design and wayfinding. Color has indeed been codified in various ways across different cultures, shaping our understanding and perception of the world around us. For instance, the symbolism of red in Western cultures where it commonly represents passion, danger, or even love, contrasting with its association with luck and prosperity in some Eastern cultures like China. Similarly, the color white can symbolize purity and innocence in Western contexts, while in some Eastern cultures, it's associated with mourning and death.

Despite these variations, certain color codes remain universal, transcending cultural boundaries. Traffic lights provide a clear example of how color can convey essential information across diverse cultures, ensuring efficient communication and safety on roads worldwide. Understanding these nuances is essential for designers seeking to create inclusive and effective visual communication across diverse cultural landscapes.

Accessibility adds another layer to the significance of color. Individuals with vision impairments, such as color blindness or low vision, may have difficulty perceiving certain colors or distinguishing between similar shades. Therefore, when choosing color palettes, it's essential to consider vision impairments to ensure that information is accessible to everyone. This may include using strong contrasts between text and background, as well as avoiding relying solely on color to convey important information.

Isa Lloret Fernandez

Independent Designer

In today's digital landscape, where attention is fleeting and impressions are made in split seconds, the strategic utilization of color has become more crucial than ever before. Whether you're crafting a logo, designing a website, or conceptualizing a brand identity, the ability to comprehend and effectively apply the principles of color psychology, theory, and practical application is indispensable.

As you navigate through the pages of this book, you'll be introduced to a plethora of inspiring examples sourced from the industry's leading designers and studios. These exemplary works serve as beacons of creativity, illuminating the diverse ways in which color can be harnessed to captivate, communicate, and inspire action.

Beginning with an exploration of color theory, delving into fundamental concepts such as hue, lightness, and saturation, designers gain invaluable insights to inform their decisions when selecting color palettes for their projects.

Secondly, we pause to glean insights from esteemed collectives or studios from all over the world, such as ESTUDIO ALBINO, Forma, Humana Studio, MAUM STUDIO, Spatio Studio, and Tiquismiquis.club. They will share with us some of their case studies, unique perspectives, and experiences, offering invaluable tips for the ever-evolving landscape of graphic design.

The chapters that follow, encapsulate a distinct mood or aesthetic. Chapter 1 invites you to immerse yourself in the tranquility of serene hues, exploring the soothing nuances of the calm, quiet, secret, and deep palettes. Here, we discover the art of creating compositions that exude serenity, mystery, and introspection.

Chapter 2 beckons you to bask in the purity and elegance of sweet, pure, natural, and clear palettes. Within these pristine color schemes, innocence meets sophistication, and simplicity reigns supreme. From the soft sweetness of pastels to the timeless allure of neutral tones, this chapter celebrates the understated beauty of simplicity and refinement.

Finally, in Chapter 3, we dig further into the dynamic energy of refreshing, smart, bright, and hot palettes. These vivid color combinations pulsate with life, offering a spectrum of creative possibilities to ignite passion and spark innovation.

Whether you're an experienced designer seeking fresh inspiration or a beginner aiming to learn the basics, this book serves as a magnificent and valuable resource in the field of graphic design.

The Principle of Color Palettes

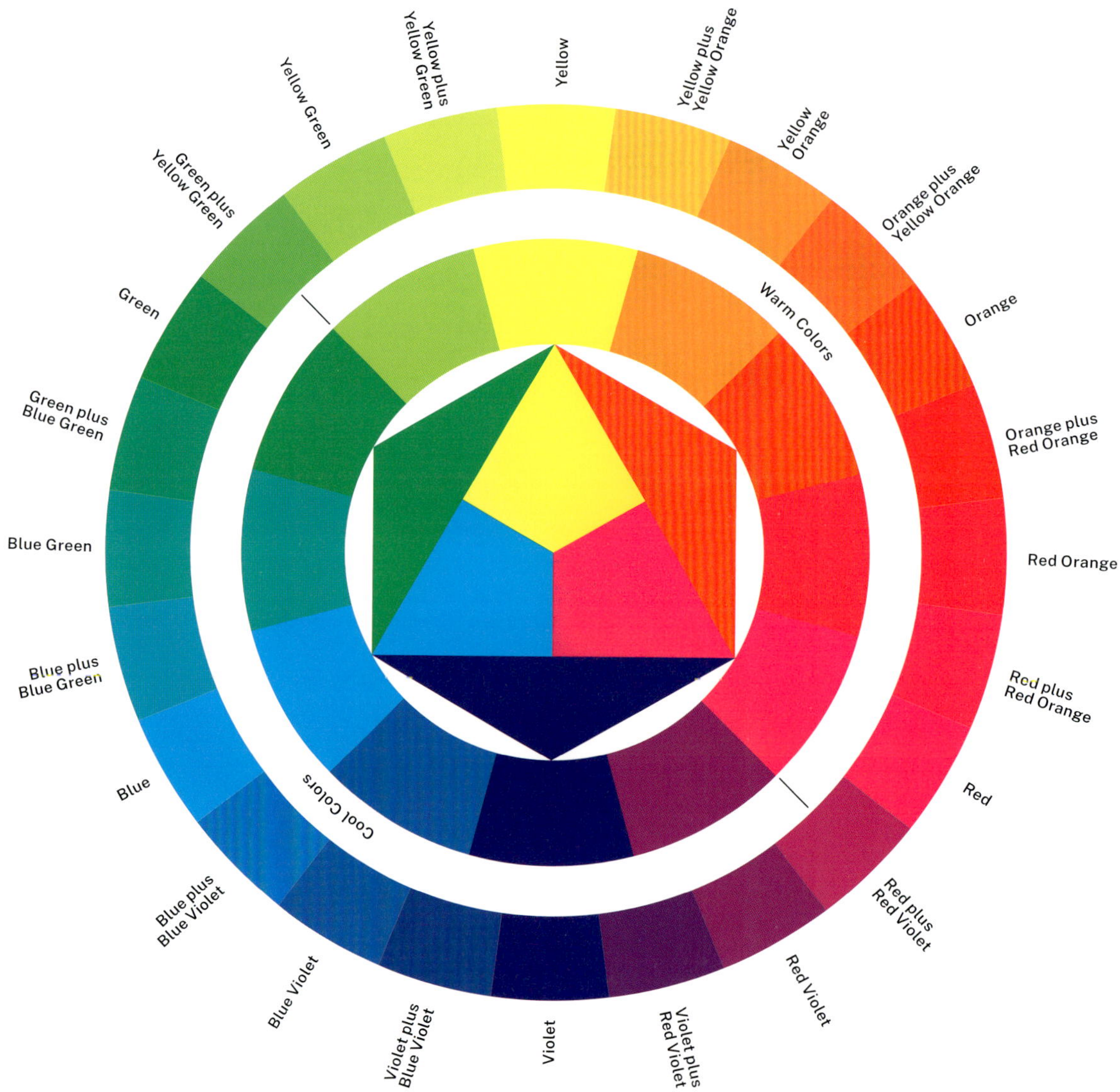

Color matching is the practice of combining different colors to create visually appealing effects. It plays a crucial role in influencing people's emotions and perceptions across various contexts of art and design. Let's explore some common concepts in color matching, starting with contrast, harmony, and the psychological effects of colors.

The primary colors—red, yellow, and blue—form the foundation of the color wheel. These colors can be combined to create the secondary colors; orange, purple, and green. The secondary colors are produced by mixing two primary colors together.

Additionally, there are mixed colors on the wheel, which are combinations of primary colors and adjacent secondary colors. For example, orange is a mix of yellow and red, while cyan combines yellow and green.

Hue is the primary characteristic of color, representing its essential identity. Any color besides black, white, and gray possesses a hue, which is derived from primary and secondary colors. Each hue presents a unique appearance, ranging from purple-red to orange-yellow.

Lightness refers to the perception of how light or dark a color appears. It's mainly influenced by the intensity of light—a stronger light source results in a brighter appearance, while weaker light creates a darker effect. Value also denotes the lightness or darkness of a color. Even colors with the same hue may vary in brightness; for instance, magenta appears darker than pink despite both containing red.

Saturation indicates the vividness of a color. It's one of the three attributes in the hue-saturation-value (HSV) color model, alongside hue and lightness. Primary colors typically exhibit the highest saturation, with colors becoming progressively darker as saturation decreases until they become achromatic.

Color matching based on hue involves selecting colors within a similar hue range for a cohesive and harmonious feel. Using contrasting colors from opposite ends of the hue circle can create a striking contrasting effect. Matching colors with similar hues can evoke a unique impression, striking a balance between commonality and variation.

Similarly, medium-difference color matching balances brightness and contrast, offering a popular choice for its vibrant yet non-conflicting appeal.

Primary Colors

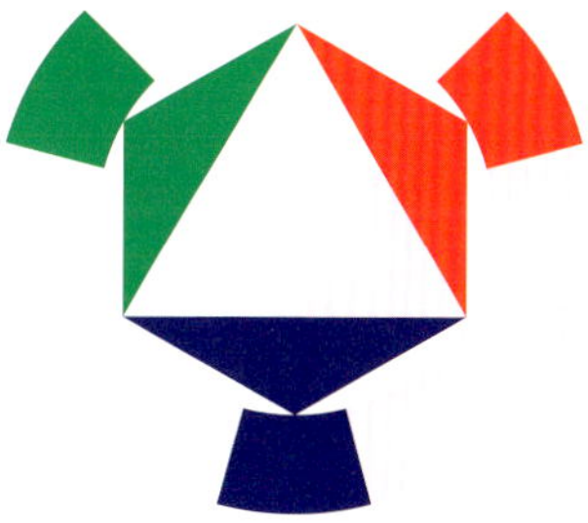

Secondary Colors

Tertiary Colors

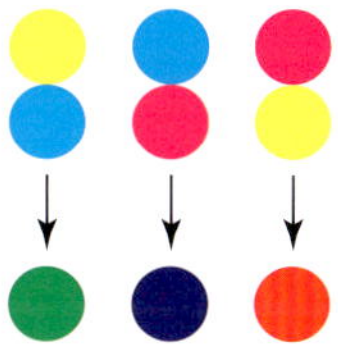

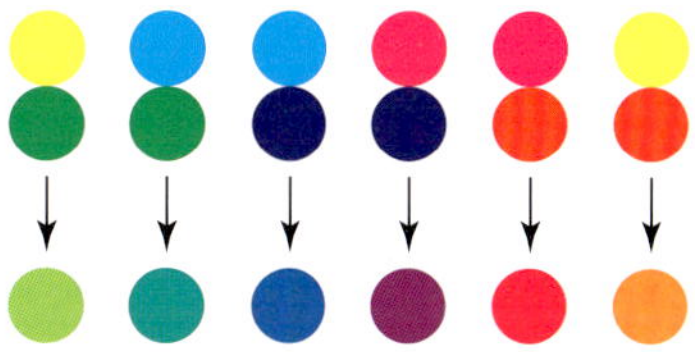

Hue-Saturation-Value

Minimum Saturation

Maximum Saturation

Hue and Lightness

Maximum Lightness

Minimum Lightness

I. Contrast of Colors

1. Contrasting Color

Contrasting colors are pairs of colors that are distinctly different, typically positioned around 120 degrees apart on opposite sides of the color wheel. These pairs include hue contrast, lightness contrast, saturation contrast, cold-warm contrast, complementary color contrast, and color-achromatic contrast. They play a vital role in creating visually striking effects and enhancing the expressiveness of colors.

They can be categorized into simultaneous contrast (occurring when colors are viewed together) and successive contrast (occurring when colors are viewed one after the other). For example, yellow and blue, purple and green, red and cyan, and any color with black, white, gray, dark, or light colors all demonstrate contrasting effects.

In design, contrasting colors are often utilized between text and background to ensure legibility and to enhance visual impact. They help in distinguishing different elements, guiding users' attention, and highlighting important information.

2. Complementary Colors

Complementary colors are pairs of colors positioned opposite each other (180 degrees apart) on the color wheel, forming a straight line. Examples include yellow-purple, orange-blue, and red-green.

Complementary colors exhibit strong color contrast, particularly when saturation is high, resulting in distinctive visual effects that evoke excitement and dynamism.

In design, complementary colors can be used to emphasize specific elements, attract attention, and add balance and interest to the overall composition.

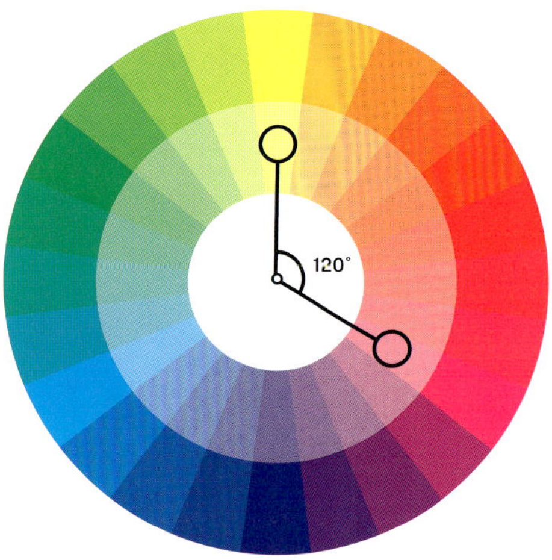

Contrasting Colors

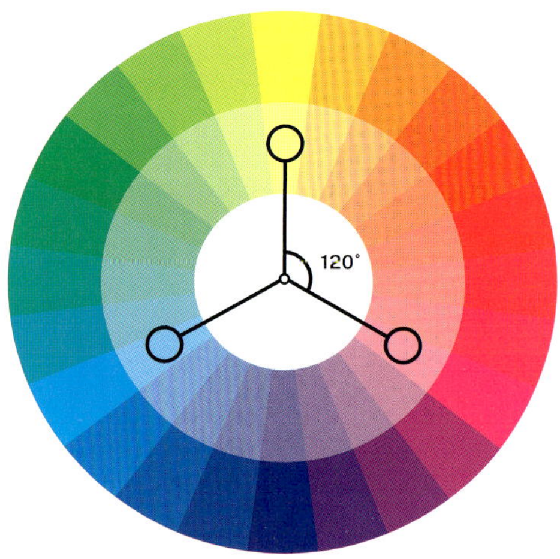

Triad Colors

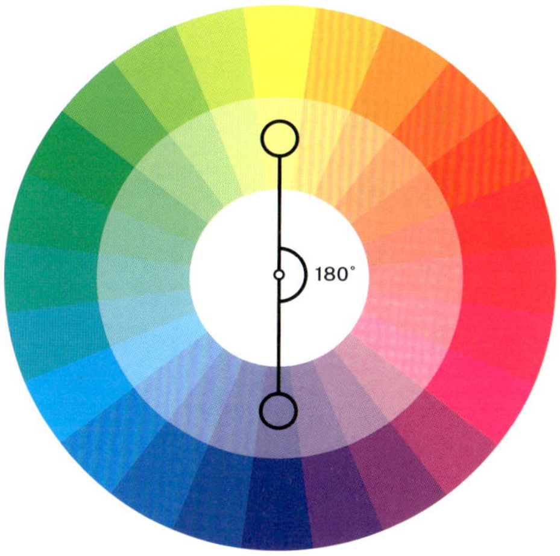

Complementary Colors

Split-complementary Colors

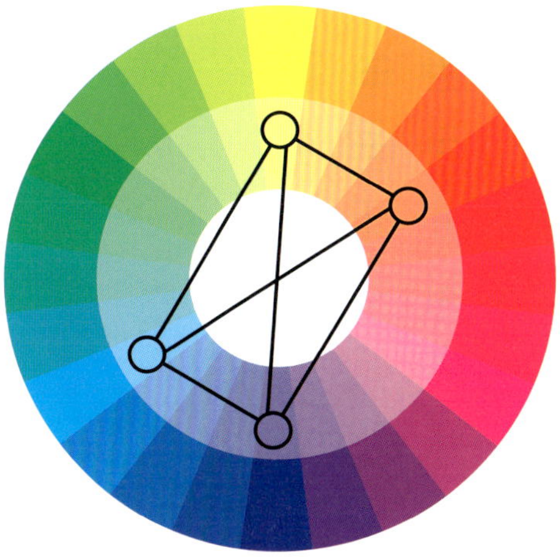

Rectangle (Tetradic) Complementary Colors

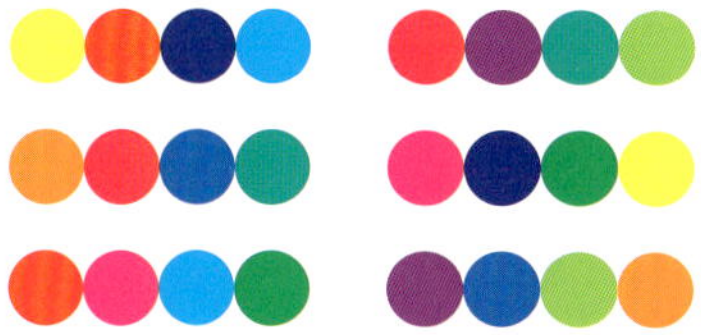

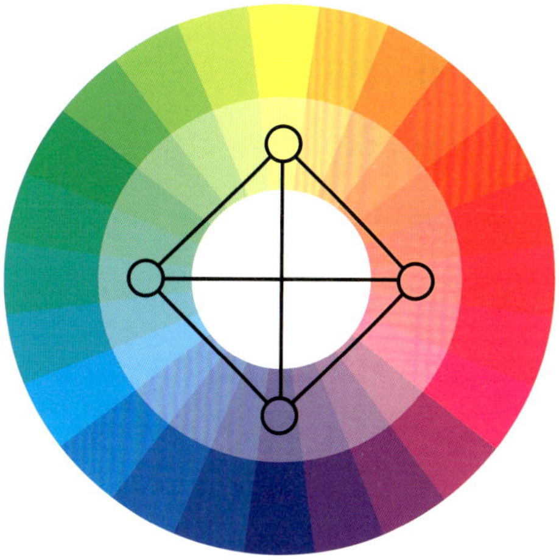

Square Complementary Colors

3. Medium Colors

Medium colors are pairs of colors approximately 90 degrees apart on the color wheel, falling between similar colors and contrasting hues. Examples include red-orange, orange-yellow, yellow-green, green-blue, blue-purple, and purple-red.

These colors offer a medium level of contrast, appearing fresh, bright, soft, and elegant. While they are widely used in color design, they may appear less dynamic compared to complementary colors and require attention to adjusting differences in brightness, saturation, and coverage.

II. Harmony of Colors

1. Monochromatic colors

Monochromatic colors consist of variations of the same main color, typically located adjacent on the color wheel with slight differences in brightness. They offer consistency in hue, brightness, and saturation, creating a cohesive and visually appealing palette.

Adjusting brightness and saturation can introduce gradients, enhancing the overall richness and vividness of the color scheme.

2. Similar colors

Similar colors, also known as analogous colors, are colors adjacent within a 90-degree angle on the color wheel. They offer a balance between unity and variability in design, with the middle color serving as the main color and the surrounding colors as secondary colors.

Analogous colors provide a calm and harmonious feel due to their minimal contrast and shared pigments between primary and secondary colors.

3. Adjacent colors

Adjacent colors are pairs of colors positioned 60 degrees apart on the color wheel or within three positions of each other. They offer a medium level of contrast, with similar hues, consistent cold-warm properties, unified tones, and emotional characteristics.

Examples include red and yellow-orange, blue and yellow-green, among others.

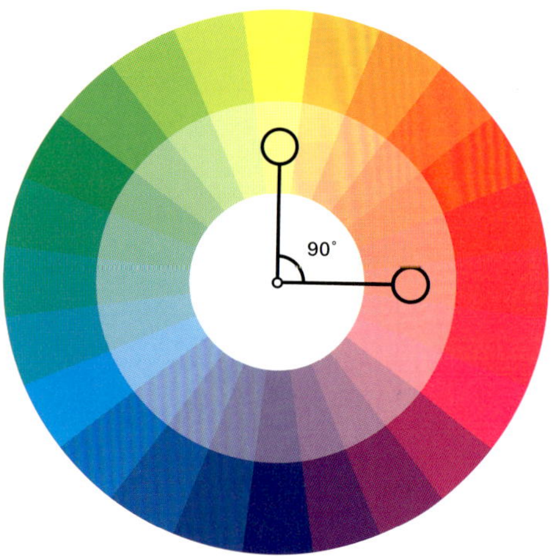

Medium Colors

Monochromatic Colors With Different Brightness/Purity

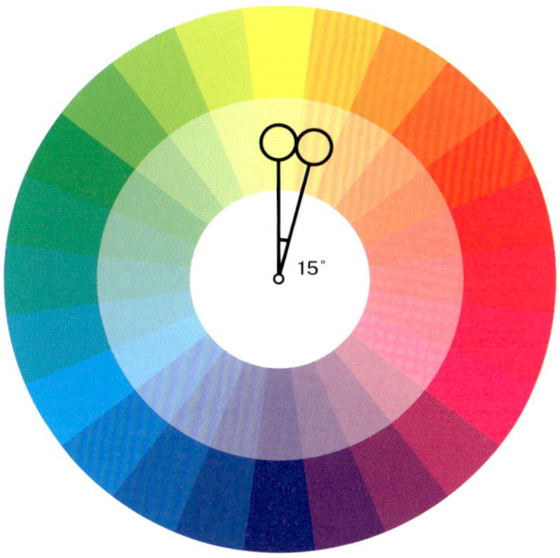

Monochromatic Colors

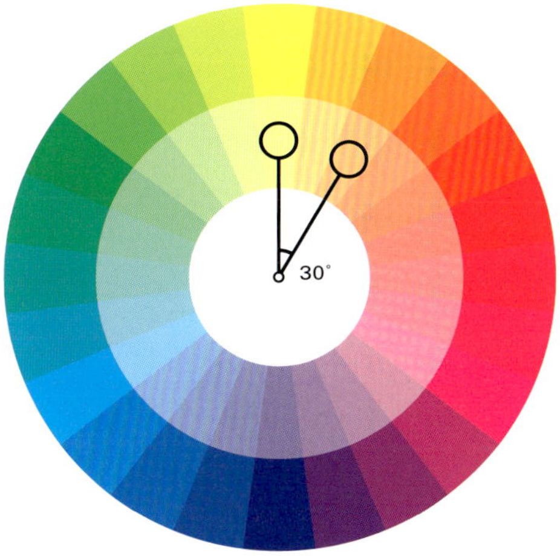

Similar Colors

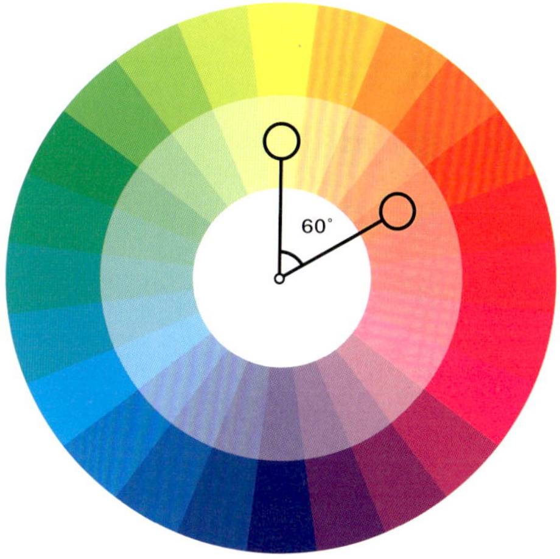

Adjacent Colors

III. Color Psychology

Color psychology is a significant field that explores how colors affect human perception, emotions, and behavior. In art and design, colors serve as both stimuli and symbols, evoking subjective reactions and behaviors. This psychological process unfolds from visual perception to emotional responses, memory associations, cognitive thoughts, and symbolic meanings. The interplay of these factors makes color psychology a complex and multifaceted area of study.

The application of color in various contexts underscores the importance of understanding this cause-and-effect relationship. It involves recognizing how different colors can evoke specific emotional and psychological responses, shaping people's perceptions and behaviors. For instance:

- Low-key and subdued colors may create a calming and refreshing atmosphere.
- Bright and vibrant colors can grab attention and convey energy and vitality.
- Light and pastel shades evoke feelings of warmth, cleanliness, and innocence.
- Dark and somber colors may convey a sense of seriousness or solemnity.

In the market, products often come in a variety of colors, each chosen strategically to evoke specific consumer responses. Different industries and products utilize color psychology in graphic design, product development, and marketing strategies to influence consumer perceptions and behaviors.

In the following sections, we'll delve into the psychological reactions and practical applications of commonly used color correspondences.

Low-key & Quiet

C0	M10	Y10	K10
R237	G223	B214	
C20	M0	Y10	K30
R167	G187	B186	

C0	M10	Y35	K0
R254	G234	B180	
C5	M0	Y10	K10
R230	G234	B222	
C10	M20	Y0	K0
R231	G213	B232	

C10	M0	Y10	K10
R220	G230	B222	
C10	M0	Y0	K20
R203	G213	B220	
C0	M10	Y0	K20
R218	G207	B212	
C20	M0	Y10	K30
R167	G187	B186	

Deep & Solemn

C0	M40	Y50	K30
R193	G138	B99	
C70	M30	Y30	K20
R67	G128	B145	
C70	M40	Y40	K40
R59	G94	B102	

C25	M60	Y100	K0
R198	G121	B21	
C40	M100	Y100	K0
R167	G33	B38	
C90	M50	Y80	K20
R0	G94	B70	

C30	M40	Y60	K0
R191	G157	B109	
C50	M30	Y55	K15
R130	G145	B113	
C80	M60	Y100	K35
R52	G74	B37	
C55	M65	Y70	K30
R108	G79	B63	

Light, Sweet & Clean

C35 M5 Y0 K0
R174 G215 B243

C0 M10 Y0 K0
R253 G239 B245

C0 M0 Y55 K0
R255 G247 B140

C30 M0 Y60 K0
R193 G219 B129

C50 M10 Y100 K0
R144 G184 B33

C25 M0 Y25 K0
R202 G229 B205

C40 M0 Y45 K0
R166 G211 B162

C70 M15 Y45 K0
R68 G165 B152

C70 M35 Y60 K0
R88 G138 B115

Refreshing & Smart

C0 M0 Y40 K0
R255 G249 B177

C20 M25 Y0 K0
R209 G196 B224

C20 M0 Y100 K0
R219 G224 B0

C0 M0 Y50 K0
R255 G247 B153

C0 M20 Y80 K0
R253 G210 B62

C50 M0 Y25 K0
R132 G204 B201

C80 M20 Y45 K0
R0 G151 B148

C0 M0 Y100 K0
R255 G241 B0

C0 M40 Y100 K0
R247 G171 B0

C0 M80 Y10 K0
R233 G82 B142

C70 M75 Y0 K0
R101 G77 B157

Eye-catching, Energetic & Vigorous

C0 M100 Y75 K0
R230 G0 B51

C0 M15 Y90 K0
R255 G218 B1

C100 M0 Y100 K30
R0 G124 B54

C50 M0 Y0 K0
R126 G206 B244

C0 M10 Y85 K0
R255 G227 B41

C0 M100 Y20 K0
R229 G0 B110

C0 M15 Y100 K0
R255 G217 B0

C0 M80 Y0 K0
R232 G82 B152

C100 M100 Y0 K0
R29 G32 B136

Questions and Answers

① ESTUDIO ALBINO ② Forma
③ Humana Studio
④ MAUM STUDIO ⑤ Spatio Studio
⑥ Tiquismiquis.club

01. How do you decide the brand's color scheme when designing a full case for a brand?

ESTUDIO ALBINO

All our projects narrate a story, where each one of the elements tells part of it. Color is usually the first element with which the audience has contact, so knowing how to convey the right sensations is necessary to guide the audience to a mood where they can begin to discover and connect with the proposed concept. Depending on the project, we can follow established codes in the category or look for something contrary to generate contrast and a unique personality that makes our client stand out.

Forma

Color selection can be driven by concept or by mood. Concept-chosen colors can be too straightforward—you make a project for something sustainable, you choose green—, but they work nicely and communicate an idea properly. Choosing by mood means to focus on what sensations a color or a color combination can convey. Everything becomes more subtle, and aspects like saturation, contrast, intensity, or vibrancy have a key role.

Humana Studio

Every brand design starts with research to understand its core values and how to translate them into visuals. The selected color scheme is a reflection of these values. It ensures an effective communication of the brand's personality to its audience.

MAUM STUDIO

Depending on the nature of the brand, we strive to achieve completeness with minimal colors. First, we create the color by specifying the primary color and adjusting the saturation and brightness.

Spatio Studio

When working on a brand, the color palette is a primary way to instantly capture people's attention. Choosing the right colors is crucial, as it can lead to love at first sight or total failure. The industry context is the first and most critical factor in selecting a color palette for a brand. Each industry has common color schemes associated with specific emotions.

For example, designers often use pure, warm colors like red, orange, and yellow for fast food products, conveying the product's purpose of providing quick satisfaction and short-term pleasure. Industries have unwritten rules that help people subconsciously understand a product's intent and compare it to their personal goals.

However, sometimes it's more beneficial to emphasize the main colors within the niche and choose a palette completely different from competitors. This approach suits bold brands aiming to set trends, inspire change in perception, and rewrite market rules.

In any case, the crucial first step in selecting a color palette is market research. Depending on the brand's personality and goals, we can follow existing trends, go against them, or combine both approaches to complement the brand's overall intentions.

Tiquismiquis.club

When designing a color palette for a visual identity, we begin by evaluating the initial impressions generated by the project. The very essence of the brand conveys its values and personality, which will determine the suitability of certain colors over others. However, we always start from this premise and proceed to experiment with how the brand interacts. Subsequently, it is crucial to ensure that these colors work in harmony with each other as well as within current trends and differentiate from competitors. Additionally, this palette needs to be effective in real contexts, both online and physical environments, ensuring the necessary readability and contrast for clear understanding. This constant evaluation and adjustment allow us to refine the color palette to faithfully reflect the brand's identity and values, as well as to ensure its practicality and effectiveness in various applications.

---

02. In design, the color selection is a crucial step. Do you usually conduct special research on color matching? Where does your color inspiration come from?

ESTUDIO ALBINO

As Mexicans, we have a rich cultural heritage, where color has played an important role; we find it in textiles, crafts, architecture, food, and general art. We are used to being surrounded by many colors in our environment, we just need to go out in the street to discover color combinations that we would never have imagined would work together. All this information is stored in us, we just have to know how and when to use it to generate the color palette that will help us to transmit what our project is asking for.

Forma

As for inspiration, I guess that we have a sociocultural bias, as does everyone. We define colors assuming the public will perceive them the way we think they will.

Humana Studio

Our decisions are based on preliminary research, but we also turn inward to our emotions. We aim to understand how the colors make us feel before we make a final decision. Inspiration comes from a lot of places, different cultures, industries, art, and illustrations. We try to avoid getting direct inspiration from graphic design.

MAUM STUDIO

I think the color selection step in design is a very important part of improving completeness. The inspiration for the color is nature. We believe that the colors expressed by nature are ultimately all the colors we can see.

Spatio Studio

There are strict and non-strict rules in choosing a color palette. The previous one we discussed is rather flexible, and breaking it may even be advantageous in the long run.

However, some rules should not be ignored. One of these fundamental points is the contrast. It sets the dynamic relationship between typography, images, and background. If the color palette does not include at least two shades with a sufficient level of contrast, it will be difficult to read and perceive the final design. The base of any color palette should include a pair of neutral colors used in all elements with an informative function, like text blocks on the background, iconography, etc.

Another rule is the rule of accents. Accents add character and flair to a design and usually consist of one or more colors. They act as pointers and signal what you need to pay special attention to.

As for inspiration, it is simple. If we look at everything that surrounds us, we will see that the whole world is a set of colors. The majority of them are neutral, frequently occurring shades. Accent colors are a rare sight in the appearance of pretty much everything—be it products, interiors, bird plumage, botanical gardens, or seashores. These colors are what make things stand out. Looking around, it becomes clear that everything operates on the same principles of contrast and accents.

Tiquismiquis.club

Color plays a fundamental role in our work, as it can have a significant impact on the outcome of any project. We focus on understanding how colors affect the visual perception of design and how they interact with each other to achieve the desired effect.

Our inspiration for color selection comes from a wide range of sources. We explore the worlds of cinema, art, photography, and fashion for ideas. Additionally, we find inspiration in everyday objects and elements such as traffic signs, furniture, or urban signage. We like to distill an image to its essence, stripping it of shapes and embellishments to appreciate only its color harmony.

By integrating these diverse influences, we aim to create coherent and captivating color palettes that reflect the identity and objectives of the project at hand. This approach allows us not only to visually stand out, but to effectively communicate the desired message through the intelligent use of color.

---

03. Do you have your own color preferences? How to rationally avoid personal color preferences in design?

ESTUDIO ALBINO

In the studio, we all have our favorite colors; but the advantage lies in having a very clear story that we want to tell in each project, so it can guide us to explore the graphic style and of course, the color palette. This has helped us to discover new color combinations that we didn't have in our minds.

Forma

We do! And we do not try to rationally avoid them. Don't get us wrong: a designer must adapt to each project's needs, but what makes this job wonderful is that everyone has their own way to approach a problem. The fun part is finding the balance between what one likes and what the project needs.

Humana Studio

Yes, of course. Our color preferences always influence us. That's what makes us unique. We adapt our preferences to what needs to be transmitted, and how to communicate each brand effectively.

MAUM STUDIO

We prefer primary colors C, M, Y, and K at 100% each. We strive to make color perception easy for our clients and the public. It is a special case when multiple colors are used in one project, and usually, one or two colors are used as the main colors.

Spatio Studio

I have some favorite colors that I like to use in my projects, but I understand that they may not always be the best choice. To avoid making decisions based purely on my personal preferences, I have a few tricks. These tricks are quite funny, and you may also find them useful in your everyday life.

So the first trick. We need to take the design layout. Close your eyes slightly to blur the image and see the general color spots of the main design elements. Step back for a better perspective. So what should we see here? The design always communicates something. And there are fundamental elements, like a slogan or brand name—that should catch your eye first. If not, the color palette or accents may need adjustment.

The second trick is to make sure that the color palette works. We have to take a blank sheet of paper. Place our design in the middle of it and surround it with similar designs from competitors in the niche. The main point is to combine different designs from the same category together. Next, let's look at our composition from a slightly detached perspective. Our design should stand out, indicating a strong color palette and the right accents.

Tiquismiquis.club

Yes, we have our own color preferences that influence our designs. For example, we tend to work with vibrant and saturated color palettes which are often a distinctive feature in our work and part of our brand identity. It's natural for our work to reflect some of our own creative DNA. In fact, this can be an advantage as it contributes to the coherence and uniqueness of our brand.

If we take, for example, the works of specific artists like Pedro Almodóvar, whose distinctive use of color palettes in his films has become an integral part of his artistic brand. When you watch one of his films, it's easy to identify his style and vision through the colors he chooses to use. This way of using color is a source of inspiration for us, as we are interested in how it is present in all his works. Our designs may carry that unique imprint that defines us as creators. Although it's important to maintain a balance and not allow our personal preferences to completely dominate the design process, letting our own style shine through the use of color can add a layer of authenticity and coherence to our work.

---

04. Can you share a project that you find particularly successful or interesting in color palettes?

ESTUDIO ALBINO

We really like our project "Garcés", where the color palette was selected to transport us to an era where romanticism had another meaning; there was more detail, more intensity and, of course much more drama. All those concepts are represented in the identity but the color takes on a great importance to convey those feelings.

Forma

Maybe "Dimension 70." It was a never-ending back-and-forth with the client, they were not sure about our first color proposals and we kept evolving it until we were all happy. Without this process, we would not have ended there, as it is a quite rare color palette.

Humana Studio

The branding we designed for the electronic music artist James Flower. We combined a total of 14 colors to create different gradients that capture the emotional connection of his music.

MAUM STUDIO

Many people liked the recently conducted project "Korea Public Design Awards 2023." (P188) Because it is a key visual design project for a public design contest, we were concerned about publicness. Based on the colors that people with normal color vision and color vision deficiency can see, the representative colors were set in the palette and applied to the graphics.

Patterns (textures) that help people with color vision impairment recognize shapes were applied to the graphics. It was a meaningful project using design colors for everyone.

Spatio Studio

The project we want to share is a classic in the design world. It belongs to the industry titans Chermayeff & Geismar & Haviv. We are referring to the color palette they created for the National Geographic (NatGeo) brand guidelines. And it's brilliantly simple—just two colors: yellow and black. It might seem too basic for some projects, but it's perfect for NatGeo. Why?

NatGeo is known as a massive television network with various commercial and volunteer projects. However, NatGeo first became recognizable because of the bright yellow frame highlighting color photographs on their magazine covers. NatGeo excels in producing wildlife graphic content, capturing amazing photographs and videos that evoke empathy. The magazine layout typically uses white and black for text fields.

This is a great example where just one color is so strongly associated with a company that it needs no companions other than black and white. Sometimes, a color palette just needs one strong color with a compelling story.

Tiquismiquis.club

We would like to share details about our work for FESTEME (P168), a musical theater festival in Córdoba, Spain. Our project is distinguished by its visual approach, highlighting the creative use of typography, vibrant colors, and graphic elements such as the musical staff, as well as the representation of movement through asymmetrical horizontal lines that add dynamism to the visual identity.

In this context, we have created a color palette composed of four main shades: blue, red, brown, and sky blue. These colors coexist and are combined in a specific way, aiming to convey particular sensations and generate striking contrasts. This choice is based on classical theatrical tradition, which we have reinterpreted to adapt to a contemporary context.

As it is the first edition of the festival, we aimed to make it stand out through color and make it recognizable from the outset. For this purpose, we selected a color palette in which neutral colors do not appear, and all colors have brightness and saturation adjustments to make them work and contrast with each other.

---

05. Do you think there has been a change in the selection of color schemes when brand communication has shifted from offline to online, and design has more kinds of dynamic forms than the past?

ESTUDIO ALBINO

Definitely yes, digital media and new printing techniques have opened the possibility of achieving colors and tonalities that could not be achieved before, allowing us to expand the possibilities of the projects.

Forma

Obviously, online has a broader range and is not restricted by printing techniques. In our case, however, we usually have to find color solutions that can work both in digital and print. So, we try to be careful when playing with this extra freedom that screens can give you.

Humana Studio

Oh yes, definitely! Brands gained life when they shifted online, and so did their color schemes. Nowadays they are dynamic, and colors can shift indefinitely. This opens the door for more experimentation and infinite possibilities.

MAUM STUDIO

We think there is more autonomy in using color online because the colors that can be expressed are infinite. We think the preference for fluorescent or stimulating colors has also increased.

Spatio Studio

The field of design is currently experiencing significant shifts, making it a fascinating time to be part of this industry. The world is constantly accelerating, and the amount of consumed content is also growing. People are learning how to communicate more effectively due to information overload. It has led to shorter attention spans. To grab attention in this new world, brand design is adapting.

When design went digital and shifted from paper to screens, the matrices of our monitors coped with the human need for innovation. Modern screens display the contrast between white and black much more clearly than paper ever could. Thanks to RGB profiles that are more vivid than CMYK, now we have a set of brand-new colors that can only be recreated on a monitor. This has led to a revolution in the world of design.

Yet, people crave novelty, and the initial revolution has slowed. New monitor technologies slightly expand the color range, but our eyes' ability to see the spectrum of colors is still limited. We've hit a point where simply adding more colors isn't possible, and inventing something entirely new is a challenging task. Now is the time for qualitative rather than quantitative changes. I believe we're on the brink of a new revolution in the perception of colors.

Tiquismiquis.club

Certainly, there has been a notable shift in the selection of color schemes as brand communication has shifted from offline to online, and design has evolved towards more dynamic forms than in the past. In the digital environment, where user interaction is essential, colors play an even more crucial role in creating an attractive and coherent visual experience. Unlike the offline world, online design tends to be more dynamic and adaptable, with interactive elements and animations that can influence color perception. This shift has led to greater experimentation with more vibrant and saturated color palettes, aimed at capturing the user's attention and effectively communicating the brand's identity.

---

06. What is your opinion on the future color trends?

ESTUDIO ALBINO

Trends, in general, have been recycled time and time again; we are already in the third wave of grunge when that happened only 30 years ago. It's the same with the colors we now see in some films; they're returning to the saturation tones of the early 2000s. We think that by correctly selecting a color palette, we can make a project timeless and relevant for many years, regardless of trends.

Forma

We try not to think about them too much. We constantly see all kinds of color solutions in great projects from designers we admire, so they are not that important, after all.

Humana Studio

As the world becomes more interconnected, we will see influences from a variety of cultures emerge. Despite all the advancements in technology, we believe that people will turn more and more to nature in the upcoming years. It's leading to more organic and natural color palettes that resonate more with humans and less with machines.

MAUM STUDIO

To be cautious, We think the color trend will lose much of its meaning in the future. Because various color expressions are becoming more freely available, many people seem to have a significantly higher level of awareness of color. That's why we think it's important to have an essential meaning to the colors used in a project rather than following trends.

Spatio Studio

I believe the trend for natural palettes in brand design is set to rise. In the past five years, we have seen the dominance of bright colors and bold shapes from the Bauhaus movement, followed by a return to the neon phase. However, the trend for vibrant colors seems to have peaked.

Influenced by current global concerns, color choices are shifting towards palettes inspired by natural textures and materials. We see a growing popularity of colors like ocher, marsh, and eggshell. There is also a growing interest in Eastern culture, religion, and philosophy, particularly the concept of "kaizen," which advocates gradual improvement without sudden leaps. We are interested in exploring new ways to perceive colors and live happier and more conscious lives. Minimalism and respect for the natural environment are also influencing design principles. As Europe becomes more concerned about ecology and responsible consumption, the trend for organic forms and natural color palettes are expected to become more relevant as well.

Tiquismiquis.club

In our opinion, future color trends will continue to evolve to reflect the growing importance of visual design and the need to stand out in an increasingly digitized world. The "color block" technique is an example of how colors can be used boldly and strategically to create vibrant and eye-catching compositions. We believe we will see a continuation of this trend, with greater experimentation in color combinations to achieve striking visual effects. Additionally, the combination of color and motion opens up a range of possibilities that we can explore and delve into regarding how to convey this. In this sense, color will not only accompany but communicate and evoke emotions more deeply and effectively in the digital world.

Chapter 1

Calm and Serene

Through the combination of low value and low saturation colors and the matching of different hues with middle to high value and saturation, a calm and quiet atmosphere is presented in this chapter.

C10	M10	Y11	K0
R216	G215	B215	
C29	M27	Y29	K4
R172	G164	B163	
C21	M20	Y21	K1
R191	G185	B185	
C37	M44	Y56	K31
R122	G104	B91	

PEARLSTIGE Branding

The PEARLSTIGE brand design process is a journey full of unknowns. The designers tried to explore the possibilities of pearl packaging and develop a unique packaging language. For the brand identity, they used the most intuitive classic serif font as the expression of the logo. The neutral gray color close to gypsum and the brownish red color of the freshwater pearl shell surface are used as embellishments, highlighting the natural and real attitude that the brand wants to convey.

PEARLSTIGE proudly holds the distinction of being China's first B Corp in the jewelry industry. They are committed to promoting sustainable development in both society and the environment. The packaging material is made from sugarcane residue, which gracefully returns to nature in a mere 90 days, free of any synthetic or harmful substances. Their philosophy is simple but profound: to take from nature, give back to nature, and promote a regenerative cycle of life.

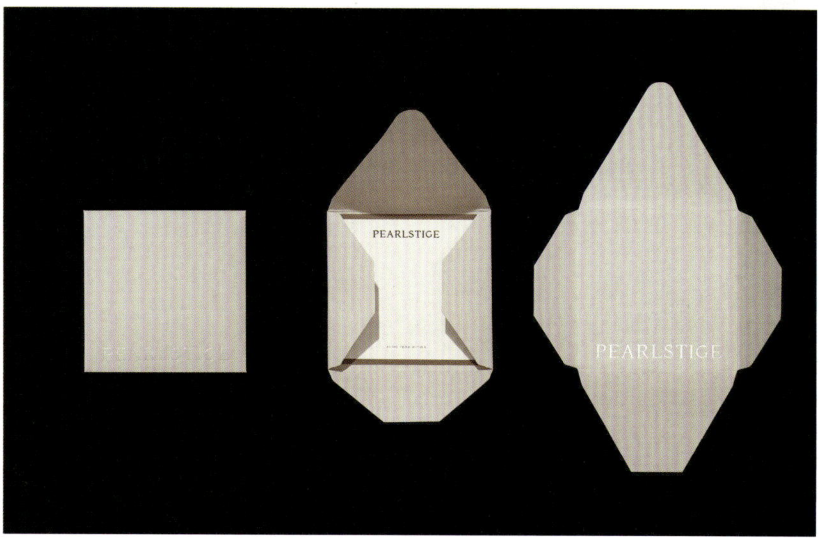

Agency/
ONNFF™

Design/
Hu Zhengrui

Photography/
DAZHI

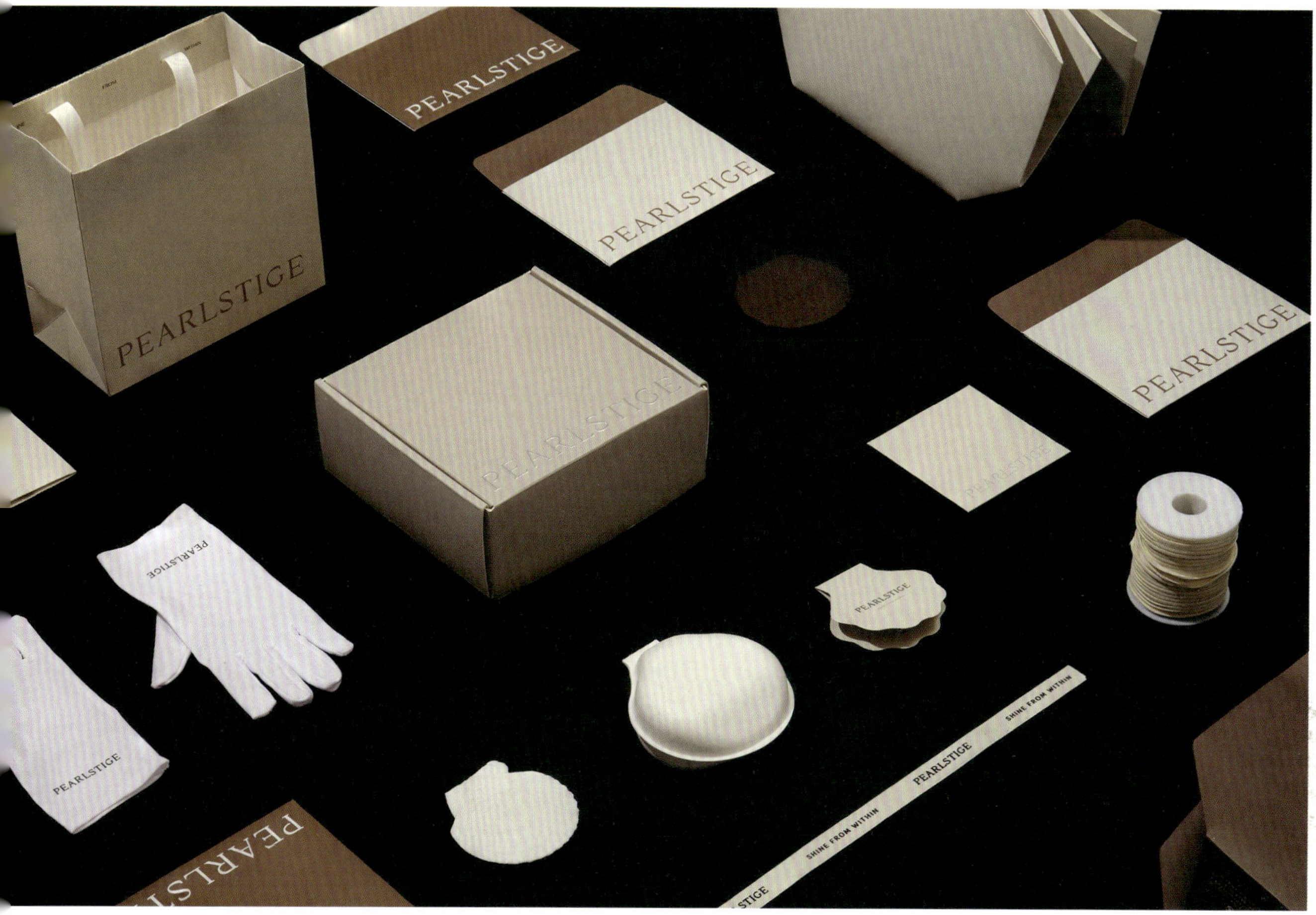
PEARLSTIGE
PEARLSTIGE
PEARLSTIGE
PEARLSTIGE
PEARLSTIGE
PEARLSTIGE
PEARLSTIGE
PEARLSTIGE
SHINE FROM WITHIN
PEARLSTIGE
SHINE FROM WITHIN

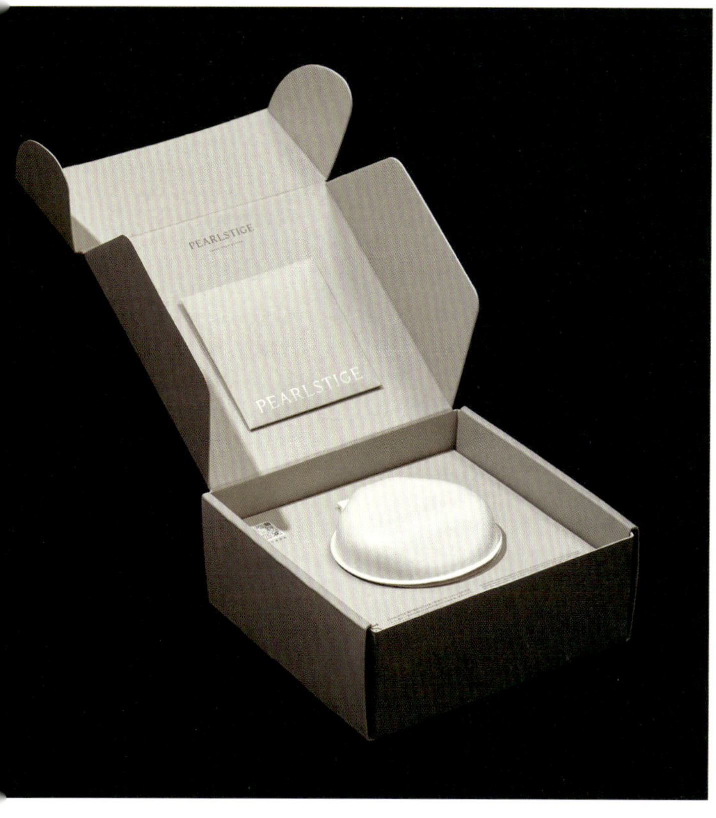
PEARLSTIGE
PEARLSTIGE

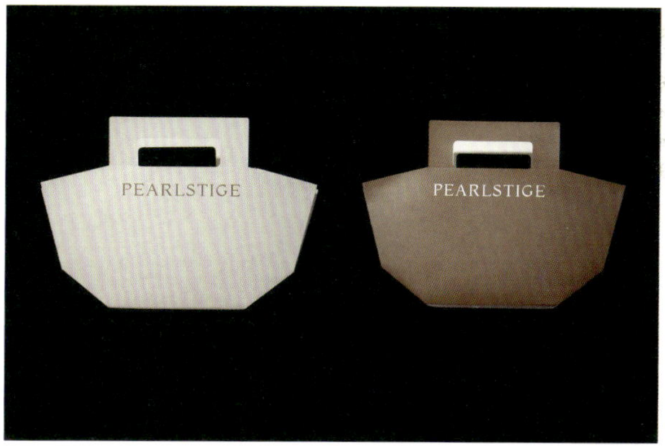
PEARLSTIGE
PEARLSTIGE

PEARLSTIGE

C	M	Y	K
C45	M43	Y47	K25
R130	G119	B107	
C18	M16	Y21	K0
R216	G211	B200	
C15	M15	Y15	K90
R53	G47	B46	
C38	M57	Y67	K53
R103	G71	B48	
C16	M30	Y51	K9
R207	G174	B124	
C13	M18	Y26	K0
R227	G211	B189	
C10	M10	Y11	K0
R234	G229	B225	

Nubia Lopes Architecture

The mission of Nubia Lopes Architecture and Interiors is to provide an exceptional architectural experience committed to values such as responsibility, dedication, objectivity, and sensitivity, always seeking to meet the needs and expectations of clients. The visual strategy of Nubia Lopes Architecture and Interiors focuses on creating a unique and memorable identity with distinct and carefully selected elements. The brand uses strategic colors and shapes to reflect its values and personality, maintaining a refined, minimalist, and modern aesthetic that emphasizes sophistication and professionalism. The visual identity highlights the Egyptian origin of the name Nubia, with a monogram based on the Egyptian alphabet and colors that evoke the deserts, creating a bold and minimalist visual appearance. The strategy combines historical and contemporary elements, generating a cohesive, consistent, and impactful visual identity.

Agency/
LOTIPA STUDIO

Creative Direction/
Antoniel Felaînne

Núbia Lopes®
PROJETOS
ARQUITETÔNICOS
RESIDENCIAIS
COMERCIAIS
MULTIFAMILIARES
INTERIORES
Arquitetura
& Interiores

Núbia Lopes

Núbia
Lopes®
PROJETOS DE ARQUITETURA
PARA AMBIENTES RESIDENCIAIS
E COMERCIAIS QUE VÃO ALÉM DAS
SUAS EXPECTATIVAS.

Núbia Lopes
INTERIORES
PARA SE VIVER.
Arquitetura
& Interiores
(86) 9 9644-1308
@NUBIALOPES.ARQUITETA
Núbia
Lopes®
CONTEMPORÂNEA
ELEGANTE
SOFISTICADA
SINGULAR
Núbia Lopes®

C0	M42	Y55	K24
R193	G111	B86	
C6	M0	Y4	K23
R185	G197	B189	
C0	M8	Y17	K7
R237	G218	B196	

Bkd. by Gemini

Bkd. by Gemini is a bakery and coffee house based in the United Arab Emirates. The designer was reached out to create a brand strategy and identity to showcase the cafe as a place for work, meeting with friends, and fun events.

The concept is rooted in the cafe's name—Gemini, which is the zodiac sign of the founder. Thus, it was decided to include all the signs to tell a story. The designer identified and manifested verbally, visually, and physically the brand's DNA, positioning, and tone of voice—what, eventually, made a distinctive brand out of the coffee place.

Studio/
Kate Zest Studio

BKD. BY GEMINI
The universe of own bakes and coffee. Soon.
IT'S PISCES SEASON
Pisces special bite: Ice cream with peanuts. Come try.
Find your sign.
BKD. BY GEMINI
MASTERCLASS
Latte Masterclass at Bkd. by Gemini
Al Safia Park, Ajman
BKD. BY GEMINI
Smart, but Aries

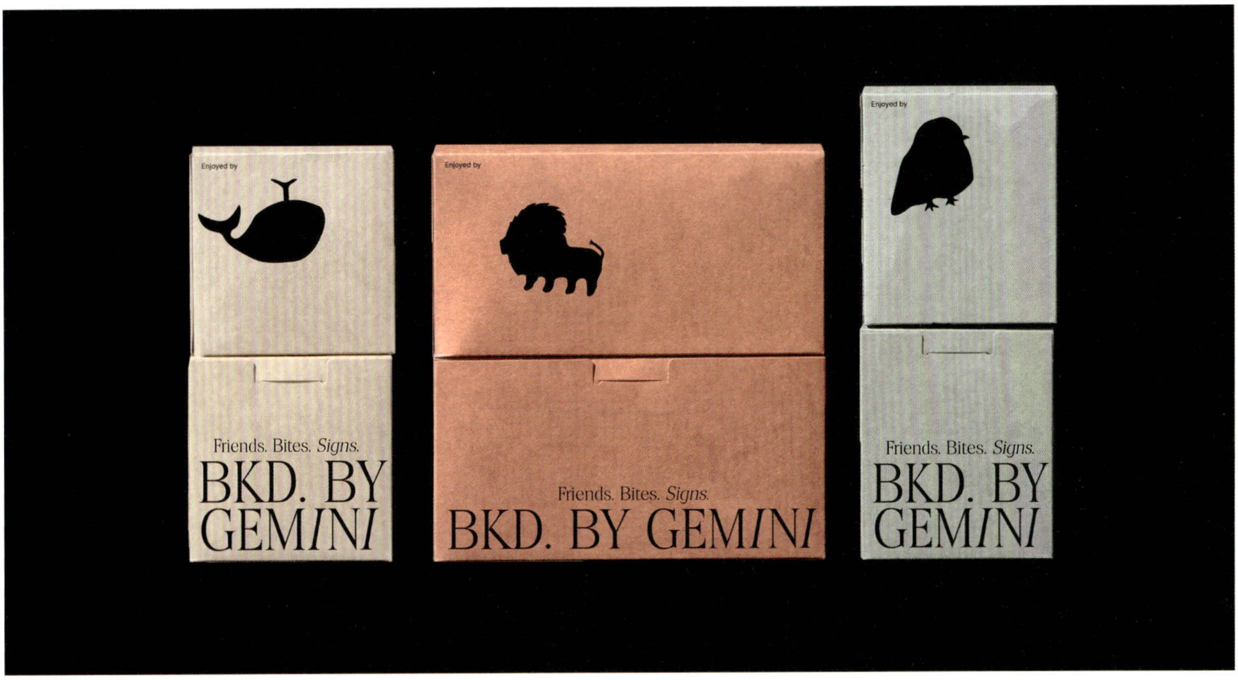
Enjoyed by
Friends. Bites. Signs.
BKD. BY GEMINI
Enjoyed by
Friends. Bites. Signs.
BKD. BY GEMINI
Enjoyed by
Friends. Bites. Signs.
BKD. BY GEMINI

Friendly, but Scorpio

BKD. BY GEMINI
Find your sign.

C70 R77	M64 G73	Y87 B46	K33
C24 R202	M9 G219	Y7 B230	K0
C35 R180	M44 G147	Y62 B103	K0
C7 R240	M7 G237	Y8 B234	K0

Glow

The design team worked with Tim Ellis and Yahnay Pointon from Melbourne-based architecture practice, Glow, to refresh their brand identity and website. Previously known as Glow Building Design, the company name was shorten by the design team as "GLOW."

The Glow logo is a result of carefully-crafted typography, where each serif character is tailored to sit perfectly abreast its opposing letterform.

Agency/
Studio Romanes

Village House
Woodend

Site-orientation maximises
northern sunlight and eastern
views of Mount Macedon

GLOW
MENU
Contact
General Enquiries
123.456.789
info@glowdesignstudio.com
instagram @glowdesignstudio.com
Visits by appointment only
Studio, 25 Aitken street Williamstown,
VIC, Australia
Start your project
Name
Email
Phone
Message
Submit
Upload Attachments
Siteplans, Photos, Council Documents etc.
Studio
Projects
Contact
ELEVATED Country LIVING
0438192155, Email
Instagram
Studio, 25 Aitken St.
Williamstown, Melbourne
9am-5:00pm M-F
by appointment

C96 R0	M76 G25	Y52 B45	K67
C35 R176	M16 G198	Y9 B218	K0
C21 R210	M20 G201	Y25 B189	K0
C31 R188	M39 G159	Y54 B120	K21
C9 R236	M7 G236	Y7 B235	K0

Juliana de Souza Photography

Juliana de Souza has been a photographer for over three years and her mission is to immortalize quality moments through photography. Through design, a striking and delicate visual identity was created for Juliana to convey more professionalism and personality. For this, the main resource explored were the colors: more neutral and delicate in pastel shades of blue and brown to convey harmony, refinement, and welcome.

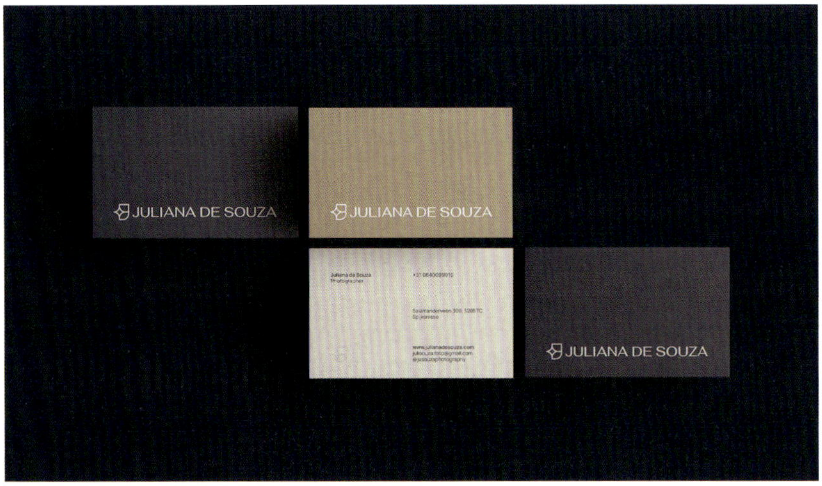

Design/
Lucas Barreira

Telling stories
through
photography
JULIANA DE SOUZA

Telling stories
through
photography

Telling stories
through
photography

C0	M19	Y19	K0
R255	G206	B206	
C0	M10	Y21	K15
R216	G194	B170	
C0	M10	Y36	K0
R255	G229	B162	
C7	M0	Y35	K0
R237	G255	B165	
C12	M22	Y0	K0
R225	G200	B255	
C0	M11	Y13	K14
R220	G195	B191	

C0	M3	Y12	K1
R253	G246	B223	
C0	M7	Y26	K6
R240	G223	B117	
C5	M0	Y12	K15
R207	G217	B190	
C9	M1	Y0	K13
R202	G221	B223	

Simplexidade

Agency/
ESTUDIO CRU

Creative Direction/
Bernardo Winitskowski

Design/
Victoria Carvalho

Project Management/
Maria Alice Leal, Clarisse Svaiter

Simplexidade is a consultancy in complexity management for organizations. Developing mind maps and evolutionary processes, Simplexidade starts from the premise that the complex is not complicated. Complexity theory states that complex systems can arise from simple interactions between their components. This approach was applied in the creation of the visual identity. The design team used graphics that are based on the idea of the potency of relationships when integrated, and that explore the organic/digital duality.

sim—
como trabalhar complexidade enquanto gestão
Como linguagem, a complexidade permite descrever e compreender siste
complexos, como os mencionados acima, que envolvem uma grande variedade de
interdependentes e interconectados. Além disso, a complexidade também pode s
estratégia útil para lidar com um tempo de transições, como o que vivemos atual
sim—
plexidade
LINGUAGEM LINGUAGEM LINGUAGEM LINGUAGEM
interdependência e coevolução
sim—
Rio de Janeiro
contato@simplexidade.com

A gestão de empresas sob a ótica da complexidade requer a criação de ecossistemas organizacionais dinâmicos e interconectados, que favorecem o surgimento de comportamentos emergentes e a inovação contínua, em detrimento da estrutura hierárquica rígida e inflexível.
→ LINGUAGEM → ABORDAGEM → LINGUAGEM → ABORDAGEM
como trabalhar complexidade enquanto gestão
ABORDAGEM ATRAVÉS DO MODELO
SISTÊMICO
COMPLEXO

COS NÃO-LINEARES → SISTEMAS DINÂMICOS

A gestão de empresas sob a ótica da complexidade requer a criação de *ecossistemas* organizacionais dinâmicos e interconectados

Aproximar
o complexo com
uma mentalidade
não-complexa o faz
parecer complicado.
LINGUAGEM → LINGUAGEM → LINGUAGEM → LINGUAGEM → LI
Não é de A
para B. É de A
para processo
evolutivo.

sim —
LINGUAGEM → LINGUAGEM → LINGUAGEM → LINGUAGEM →

SOS PROJETOS → CONHEÇA NOSSOS PROJETOS → CO
Complexidade
enquanto
linguagem e
estratégia para
um tempo de
transições
como trabalhar complexidade
enquanto gestão
roberto@simplex.com
21 98790 8786
Rio de Janeiro
sim-plexidade.com
sim —

C60 R105	M40 G119	Y70 B81	K20
C0 R137	M0 137	Y0 B137	K60
C0 R253	M10 G237	Y10 B228	K0
C20 R209	M25 G196	Y0 B224	K0
C10 R234	M10 G229	Y15 B218	K0

1545 Branding

To relieve the stress of daily work the 1545 brand set 15:45 as the tea time. Tea is an important form of traditional cultural heritage. To promote tea culture to more young people, the designer uses products as a carrier to connect the younger generation and tea culture. 1545 has four flavors, including black tea, oolong tea, green tea, and white tea, all of which were packed with whole original leaves and suitable for different tea-making methods.

The designer uses the defined tea time at 15:45 in digital form to create the logo and utilizes the form of an analog clock as the super symbol to emphasize the concept of time. 1545 encourages consumers to focus more on their health. Stay healthy and drink tea. 15:45 is the tea time.

Agency/
CB Design

Art Direction/
Jackie Price

到●喝茶
TEA TIME
●Black ●Oolong ●Green ●White
四种冷泡茶/紅青綠白
Cold Brew Tea* 4 Flavors
群芳最
Qun Fang
Most
紅茶
不知春
Unknown
Spring
烏龍茶
霧里青
Foggy
Blue
綠茶
月光白
Moonligh
White
白茶
15:45
www.1545.com
15:45

到●喝茶
TEA TIME
霧里青
Foggy Blue
15:45
TEA 到●喝茶 TIME

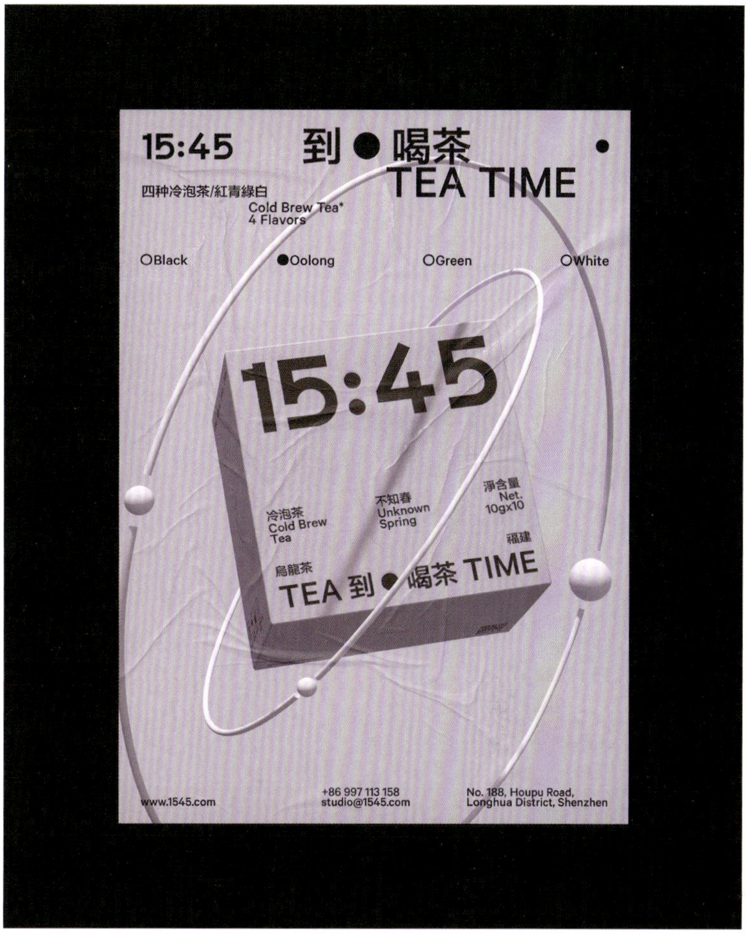
15:45
到●喝茶
TEA TIME
四种冷泡茶/紅青綠白
Cold Brew Tea*
4 Flavors
○Black
●Oolong
○Green
○White
15:45
冷泡茶
Cold Brew
Tea
不知春
Unknown
Spring
淨含量
Net.
10gx10
福建
烏龍茶
TEA 到●喝茶 TIME
www.1545.com
+86 997 113 158
studio@1545.com
No. 188, Houpu Road,
Longhua District, Shenzhen

15:45
冷泡茶
Cold Brew
Tea
TEA 到●喝茶 TIME
15:45
冷泡茶
Cold Brew
Tea
組合裝
Mix
Pack
淨含量
Net.
10gx10
群芳最
不知春
霧里青
月光白
TEA 到●喝茶 TIME
15:45
四种冷泡茶
紅青綠白
Cold Brew Tea* 4 Flavors
TEA 到●喝茶 TIME

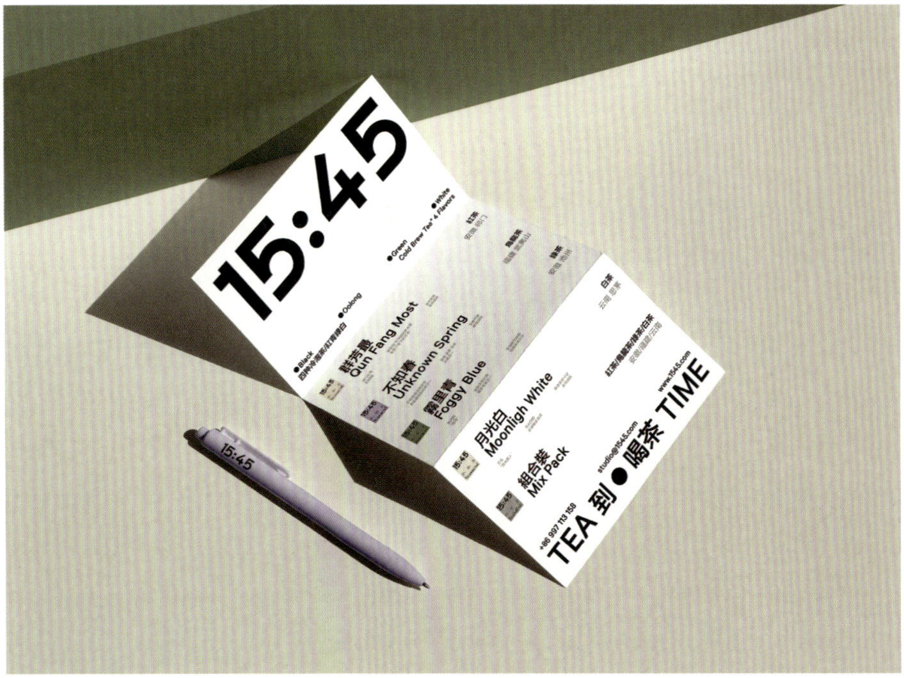
15:45
群芳最 Qun Fang Most
不知春 Unknown Spring
露里青 Foggy Blue
月光白 Moonligh White
組合裝 Mix Pack
TEA 到●喝茶 TIME
www.1545.com
studio@1545.com
+86 997 113 158

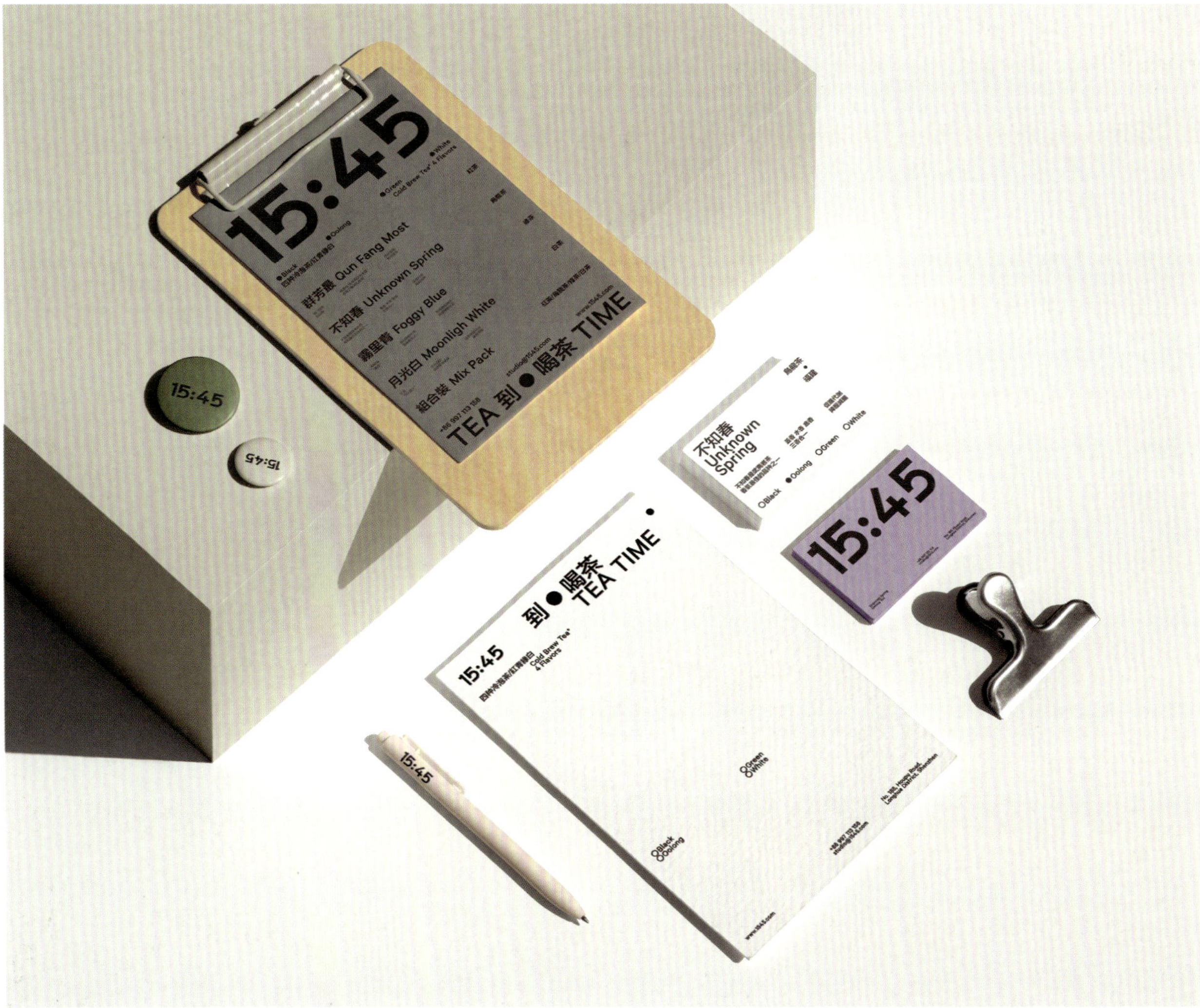
15:45
群芳最 Qun Fang Most
不知春 Unknown Spring
露里青 Foggy Blue
月光白 Moonligh White
組合裝 Mix Pack
TEA 到●喝茶 TIME
15:45
15:45
不知春
Unknown
Spring
15:45
15:45 到●喝茶 TEA TIME
Cold Brew Tea*
4 Flavors
15:45

15:45
到●喝茶 TEA TIME
Zoe Wang
15:45

15:45
冲泡指南
Brewing Guide

15:45
冷泡茶
Cold Brew Tea
TEA 到●喝茶 TIME

C6	M53	Y66	K0
R230	G154	B99	
C18	M18	Y12	K0
R215	G210	B214	
C46	M26	Y26	K0
R158	G174	B181	
C52	M44	Y100	K0
R169	G147	B52	
C67	M63	Y77	K22
R91	G85	B67	
C0	M44	Y42	K0
R240	G176	B145	
C33	M84	Y100	K0
R175	G77	B20	
C21	M22	Y28	K0
R210	G201	B186	

THREE GIRLS

THREE GIRLS is a home life brand dedicated to curtains, and the design inspiration comes from the perception of life, with "feeling the beautiful moments" as the core. In the visual system, based on the linear structure of the Chinese "三 (three)," the concepts of time, scenery, and color have been integrated. Through the injection of bold and poetic colors, those touching moments in life, full of small warmth and surprise, just like to appear.

Design/
Daqing, KimYeonhee

三千金 THREE GIRLS©
拉开理想生活的帷幕
Unveiling The Curtain Of An Ideal Life
三千金 THREE GIRLS
THREE GIRLS©
如何利用小样来决定面料
How to Use Samples to Determine Fabrics
THREE GIRLS

Pantone 555 U / 5555 C
C65 M29 Y57 K7
R97 G140 B120

Pantone 2444 U / 2338 C
C8 M37 Y28 K0
R229 G171 B163

Pantone 3599 U / 3599 C / 871 C (for metallic shine)
C13 M26 Y52 K0
R222 G186 B135

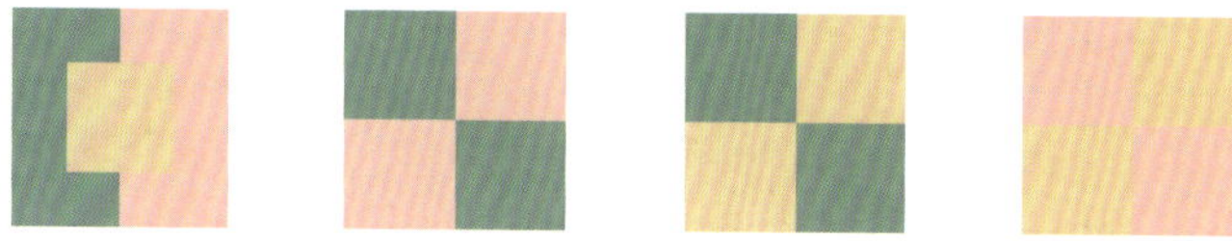

The Royal Hotel

The Royal Hotel has been lovingly restored by a local family, reimagined for today's travelers while honoring its strong roots in the community and situated at the heart of Prince Edward County.

The design team worked alongside the architects of GPAIA from day one to ensure every detail was considered. Influenced by the layers of materiality to its full visual language, the design team created an identity that weaves the history and the unique sense of place together. The logo was inspired by the cross-stitching and connection to Prince Edward County's heritage. Along with designing the visual identity for The Royal Hotel, the design team was involved in the design of the website, photography, menu systems, packaging, signages, and architectures.

Art Direction, Design & Strategy/
Blok Design

Architecture/
GPAIA

Photography/
Graydon Herriott

Client/
The Royal Hotel, Sol Korngold

THE
ROYAL

THE COUNTER BAR
PICTON
PRINCE EDWARD COUNTY

ROYAL
always here
3202
3201
ROYAL
3090
3090
ROYAL
always here
ROYAL

PIZZA
red
ROYAL

unwind
gone out
1608

still here

THE
ROYAL

C	M	Y	K	R	G	B
C10	M9	Y15	K0	R224	G221	B210
C9	M34	Y32	K0	R217	G170	B157
C8	M51	Y77	K0	R212	G137	B89
C45	M52	Y11	K0	R142	G129	B175
C47	M36	Y100	K13	R123	G124	B64

DUSK Candles

Design/
Mariia Terebenina

DUSK, a hand-poured soy wax candle brand, draws inspiration from tranquility. The packaging system evokes pure bliss with its psychedelic typography and dusk-inspired color palette. Stunning core elements and captivating photography showcase each candle's scent, engaging multiple senses.

DUSK
SAGE • LAVENDER
AMBER • SMOKE
OZONE • MOSS

DUSK
VERBENA • LEMONGRASS
VIOLET • VANILLA
PALO SANTO • SUEDE

DUSK
OZONE • MOSS

DUSK
DAWN
soy wax candles
infused with essential oils
hand-poured
scented candles
AMBER • SMOKE

C3	M10	Y11	K0
R247	G234	B226	
C43	M7	Y29	K0
R159	G201	B190	
C4	M58	Y37	K0
R234	G136	B136	
C16	M58	Y78	K4
R209	G124	B66	
C84	M64	Y59	K75
R25	G36	B38	

Golba

Golba is a Brazilian architecture firm focusing on interior projects. The inspiration for this project came from Brazilian architect Lina Bo Bardi, who became known for her large international projects incorporating geometric forms and colors.

With a minimalist and pragmatic logo, the designer could convey the lightness and timelessness of the project. The brand's color palette consists of five contrasting colors. Orange represents energy and warmth; pink conveys sensitivity and delicacy; blue brings serenity and reliability; beige offers balance and lightness; gray represents seriousness and stability.
The combination of colors reflects the entire universe of Golba.

Design/
Nathalia Ultramar

quitetura
GOLBA
GOLBA
BÁRBARA GOLBA
GOL
BA
arqui
tetura

GOLBA

GOL
BA
arqui
tetura

C16 R210	M50 G140	Y94 B25	K5
C0 R236	M73 G102	Y88 B36	K0
C43 R78	M77 G31	Y90 B5	K66

POUR

POUR was founded in Rome in 2022 as a distributor of beer/craft beer and cider. The design called for a flat approach that would depart from the language usually used for this kind of activity. The path taken is characterized by a concise and eye-catching approach. The logo built on a linear typeface hides the power of synthesis in the letters "O" and "U", which are used separately to refer to the silhouette of a bottle and a wineglass.

Design/
Michelangelo Greco

Craft Beer & Cider Distribution
Based in Rome
Pour Bar Coming Soon
info.pour.roma@gmail.com

C0	M73	Y93	K0
R236	G102	B24	
C58	M59	Y98	K13
R121	G100	B42	

Laicup Cafe

This project is a store-within-a-store business model that continues the colors of the main brand and adds a color to match each other. This brand benchmarks against other chain coffee brands and has been rejuvenated to enhance brand differentiation. The concept of sharing is used in the brand, and the design principle is simple, advanced, popular, and elegant.

Agency/
Batoer Studio

Laicup
Cafe
The cup for you
Laicup
Cafe
Laicup
Cafe
Laicup
Cafe
Laicup
Cafe

来杯给你
夏日来咖
THE CUP
FOR YOU
SUMMER
LAICUP
www.laicup.com

取餐
1640
Laicup
Cafe
TAKE MEALS
冰美式
Laicup
Cafe

The cup for you
Laicup
Cafe
Laicup
Cafe
Laicup
Cafe

Laicup
Cafe

C27	M93	Y76	K0
R189	G49	B58	
C82	M78	Y78	K61
R32	G32	B30	
C45	M54	Y71	K0
R159	G125	B84	
C18	M13	Y16	K0
R217	G217	B212	

I Congrés Internacional d'Espectadors de Teatre

Agency/
Forma

Organized by Àfora Focus, the International Congress of Theater Spectators is an event that celebrates and debates over the spectator and its role in the creation of art. We were commissioned to design the visual identity and communication campaign for the first edition. The diversity of audiences was the inspiration behind the creation of a geometric and flexible pattern that could be used in many ways through the application system.

Teatre Romea
Barcelona
24 – 26 OCT 2022
I Congrés
Internacional
d'Espectadors
de Teatre

I Congrés
Internacional
d'Espectadors
de Teatre
#congresespectadorsbcn
Teatre Romea
Barcelona
24 – 26 October

I International
Congress
of Theater
Spectators
I Congrés
Internacional
d'Espectadors
de Teatre
I Congreso
Internacional
de Espectadores
de Teatro

Pantone	C	M	Y	K	R	G	B
Pantone 165 C	C0	M68	Y96	K0	R255	G103	B39
Pantone 2715 C	C52	M47	Y0	K0	R140	G132	B227
Pantone 1815 C	C2	M97	Y72	K52	R125	G39	B45
Pantone 9226 C	C3	M5	Y17	K0	R235	G227	B215
Pantone 291 C	C38	M4	Y0	K0	R156	G205	B251
Pantone 10347 C	C24	M26	Y43	K7	R177	G163	B139

THE CAFE DECO

THE CAFE DECO's hardcover gift box has two design versions: the neat block patterns printed with six Pantone colors, overcoming the difficulty of the printing accuracy, and elaborately intersecting each square. The design team chose Bvlgari paper from Daya Paper, a high-quality art paper that offers an excellent texture and presents vibrant, eye-catching colors under UV printing. Photography reflects continuous totems with mirrored surfaces, making flat color blocks extend into 3D space. The hard light and shadow present a clean and confident atmosphere, without unnecessary decoration, allowing the product to tell its own story.

Agency/
Transform Design

Creative Direction/
Leo Huang

Art Direction/
Celine Shen

Design/
Celine Shen, Wan Yu Cheng

Project Management/
Vivia Wang

CAFE DECO
THE CAFE DECO
CAFE
DECO
LESS IS A BORE

C	M	Y	K
C65	M40	Y15	K0
R100	G137	B179	
C0	M80	Y65	K0
R234	G85	B72	
C0	M10	Y50	K0
R255	G232	B147	
C20	M40	Y60	K0
R210	G163	B108	
C0	M30	Y20	K0
R248	G198	B189	
C0	M40	Y70	K0
R246	G174	B84	

KOKO

Envisioned by the team behind Ryuko, KOKO is a casual Japanese eatery situated at the Calgary Farmers' Market West. Rooted in the visual language of Japanese convenience store culture (Konbini), the design serves as a nostalgic nod to the elements that ground people in the familiarity of their daily lives. In Japanese, KOKO can be translated as "baby tiger"—since "ko" means both "tiger" and "child"—which inspired the playfulness of the identity system, brimming with small moments of unexpected joy.

Agency & Photography/
Blok Design

Client/
KOKO

KOKO
KOKO
KOKO
KOKO

KOKO

いつもの
KOKO

KOKO

いつもの
KOKO
Tonkatsu Sauce
500ml
いつもの
KOKO
500ml

KOKO

Welcome!
KOKO
いらっしゃいませ!

KOKO
TONKOTSU
HALF BOILED
CHASHU ADD
UDON 11
SHRIMP TEMPURA 2PCS 4
SOFT OPENING :D
KOKO

KOKO

KOKO
Black Milk Tea
500 ml

C	M	Y	K
C89	M40	Y58	K42
R0	G83	B80	
C0	M34	Y82	K0
R250	G180	B60	
C0	M72	Y64	K0
R250	G100	B80	
C79	M0	Y86	K0
R0	G170	B81	
C2	M19	Y32	K0
R248	G215	B182	
C0	M45	Y44	K0
R249	G165	B137	

Compadre Boteco

Art Direction & Design/
Andreza Soares

Compadre Boteco is a Brazilian eatery specializing in regional fare. Alongside refining the brand, a language strategy was crafted for an authentic, cozy ambiance.

UM BRINDE
A saideira

UM BRINDE
A saideira
DESCE A ÚLTIMA
rodada
SAÚDE!
COM PADRE

caldinhos
SURURU R$ 0,00
FEIJÃO R$ 0,00
CAMARÃO R$ 0,00
CALDO VERDE R$ 0,00
cervejas
COM PADRE
BOTECO
entradinhas
BATATA RÚSTICA R$ 0,00
LINGUIÇA COM CREME DE ALHO R$ 0,00
BOLINHO DE MACAXEIRA R$ 0,00
refeições
CARNE DE SOL NA MANTEIGA DE GARRAFA R$ 0,00
CAMARÃO CROCANTE COM ARROZ CREMOSO R$ 0,00
pra rachar
FEIJOADA R$ 0,00
ASINHA DE FRANGO APIMENTADA R$ 0,00
COSTELA AO MOLHO DA CASA R$ 0,00

caldinhos
SURURU R$ 0,00
FEIJÃO R$ 0,00
CAMARÃO R$ 0,00
CALDO VERDE R$ 0,00
cervejas
BRAHMA R$ 0,00
DEVASSA R$ 0,00
HEINEKEN R$ 0,00
BUDWEISER R$ 0,00
ORIGINAL R$ 0,00
SKOL R$ 0,00
CERVEJA
COMPADRE
COMIDA REGIONAL
DESCE A ÚLTIMA
BRASILEIRO COMIDA REGIONAL
geladaaa!
um brinde A AMIZADE
BOTECO BRASILEIRO COMIDA REGIONAL
rodada

C	M	Y	K	R	G	B
C13	M10	Y14	K0	R227	G225	B219
C22	M18	Y29	K2	R205	G198	B183
C35	M71	Y77	K47	R113	G61	B41
C29	M9	Y30	K0	R195	G210	B189
C50	M23	Y54	K6	R138	G161	B128
C63	M41	Y62	K33	R88	G102	B83
C0	M0	Y0	K16	R225	G225	B224
C0	M0	Y0	K64	R127	G127	B127
C0	M0	Y0	K100	R0	G0	B0

Efad

Efad understands furniture as a tool to elevate the interaction and experience between users and the workspace. Designers believe that through simplicity they could design a visual identity capable of transmitting everything that Efad represents. Based on the timeless and minimalist style of the products, they designed a clear but dynamic and flexible graphic system. The logo was designed with exclusive typography, aligning the precision of the straight lines with the flexibility of the curves. The result is a bold, robust, and memorable logo. The typography is the central focus of all applications, interacting with product images in a dynamic, joyful, and unmistakable way.

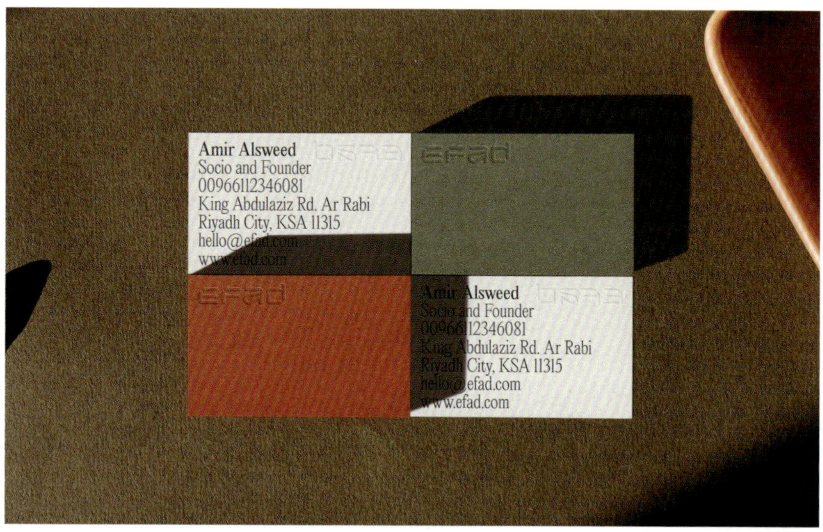

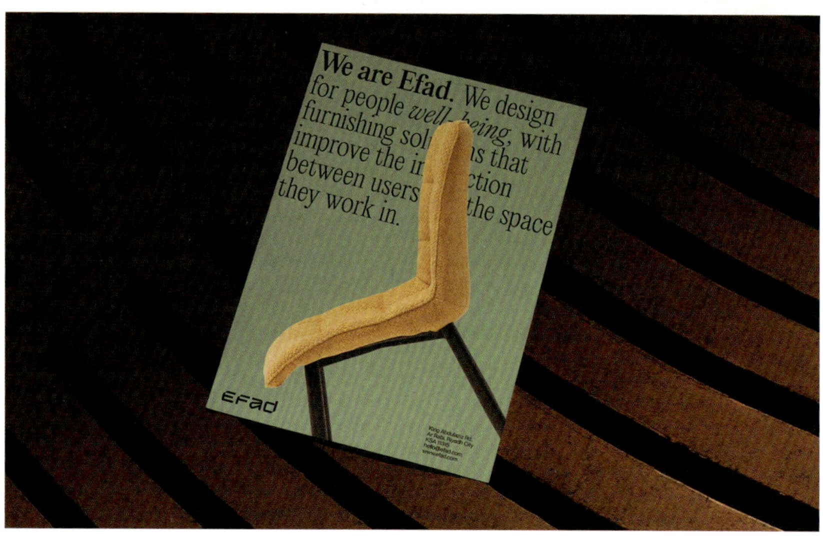

Agency/
Sérgio Fonseca Studio

We are Efad. We design for people *well-being*, with furnishing solutions that improve the interaction between users and the space they work in.
Efad
Efad

We design for people *well-being*.
Efad
Efad

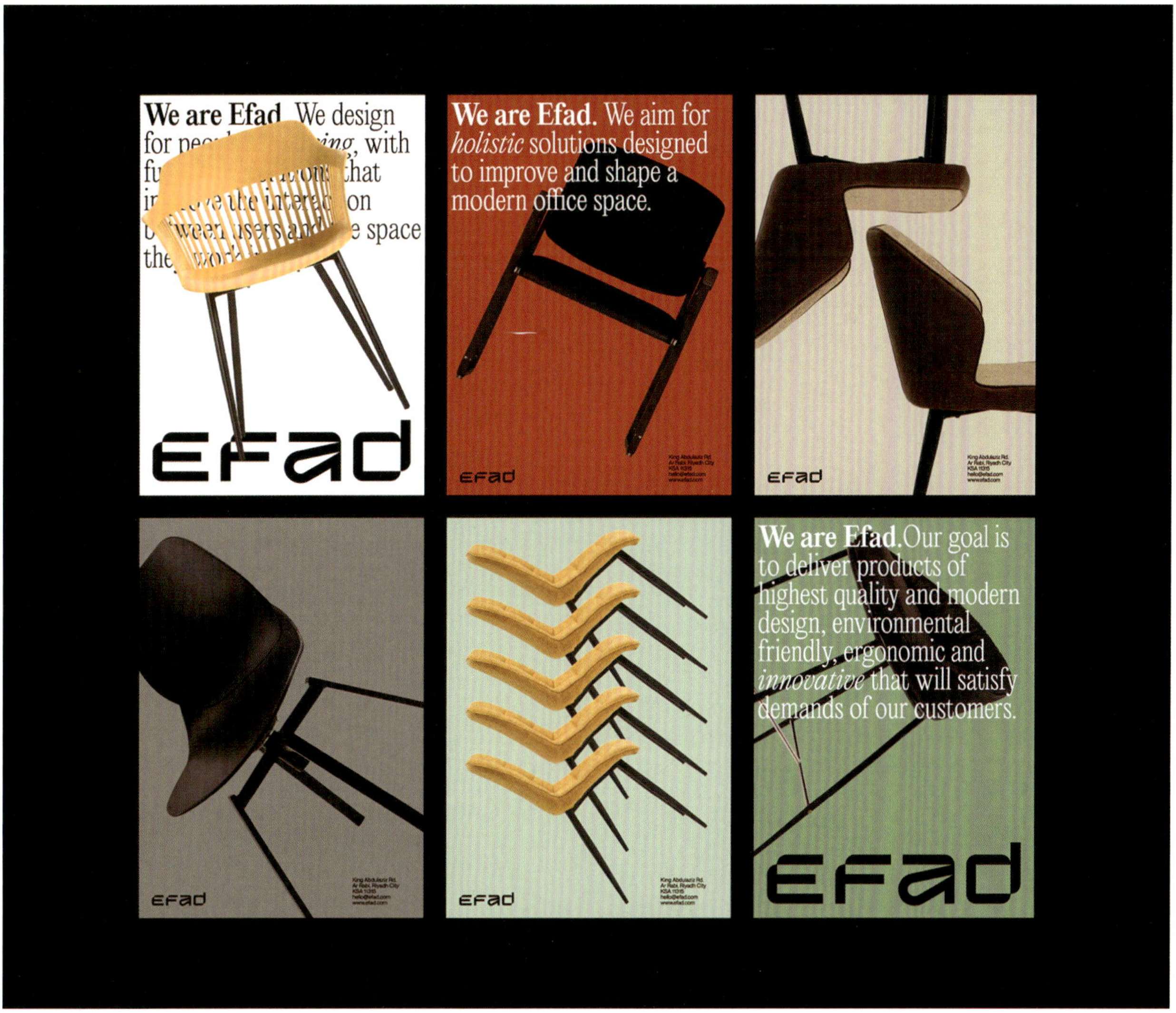
We are Efad. We design
Efad
We are Efad. We aim for *holistic* solutions designed to improve and shape a modern office space.
Efad
Efad
Efad
Efad
We are Efad. Our goal is to deliver products of highest quality and modern design, environmental friendly, ergonomic and *innovative* that will satisfy demands of our customers.
Efad

●	C70	M50	Y80	K0
	R97	G117	B78	
●	C40	M90	Y80	K0
	R167	G58	B58	

Klara Bistro & Charcoal Bar

Klara is a restaurant located in Singapore. The boss has a lovely daughter called Klara. Therefore, the designer decided to use the prototype of Klara as the brand design image. The overall color scheme of the brand is mainly olive green. Olive green is often used as a protective color, a metaphor for the boss's love for his daughter. In addition, olive green brings people a feeling of intimacy, low-key vibes, and calmness, and soothes people's hearts.

Design/
Isabelle Lin

A moment of joy
KLARA
9 Jasmine Road,
Adelphi Park Estate,
Singapore 576582
88707622
hello@kinfoods.sg
Bistro AND Charcoal Bar
TO START
BITES
CHARCOAL GRILL
Klara
Bistro & Charcoal Bar

C87	M63	Y97	K46
R28	G61	B34	
C87	M56	Y93	K27
R30	G84	B51	
C10	M38	Y21	K0
R233	G180	B182	
C6	M11	Y15	K0
R241	G229	B217	

Motsa Pizzeria

Agency/
Nord Brands

Design/
Pamela Picoli

Motsa is a Brazilian pizzeria, but it's actually much more than a pizza option; it's a celebration of the culture it brings into people's lives. From the name, which evokes the phonetics of mozzarella, Motsa is a conceptual and immersive gastronomic experience. Between a bit of tradition and fun calls to action, the design team created an identity to enjoy one of the foods they love the most.

TOO GOOD
TO BE TRUE
TOO GOOD
TO BE TRUE
good times
good food
good drinks
PARTNERS IN pizza
MOTSA
PIZZERIA
A MOSTA EVERYONE DESERVES

EVERYONE
DESERVES
A MOTSA
MOTSA
PIZZERIA
good times
good food
good drinks
PARTNERS IN pizza

TO BE TRUE
TOO GOOD
TO BE TRUE
good times
good food
good drinks
TOO GOOD
TO BE TRUE
TOO GOOD

MOTSA
PIZZERIA
DON'T
TOUCH
MY PIZZA
DON'T
TOUCH
MY PIZZA
A MOSTA EVERYONE
MOTSA

C	M	Y	K	C	M	Y	K
C69 R88	M61 G86	Y85 B56	K24	C29 R196	M43 G155	Y58 B112	K0
C59 R95	M87 G43	Y75 B47	K39	C16 R221	M17 G212	Y19 B203	K0
C2 R249	M20 G219	Y11 B217	K0	C27 R199	M70 G104	Y66 B83	K0
C4 R248	M6 G243	Y8 B237	K0	C72 R61	M75 G48	Y78 B42	K49

BUCI

Nestled in the heart of the vibrant Saint Germain neighborhood in Paris, BUCI offers a unique blend of homey intimacy and eclectic design. The design team deliberately mixed various typefaces, papers, colors, and textures to evoke the feeling of entering a beloved personal space, stepping away from traditional, predictable branding to mirror the distinct comfort of a home rich with stories.

They wanted the hotel's print materials to be experienced as if they were carefully curated stationery items, feeling timeless, personal, and Parisian. This was enhanced by creative papers with varied colors and textures. This transforms the brand into a living, breathing entity, with each interaction revealing layers of sophistication, intrigue, and a whiff of the unexpected, all told through touch, texture, and type.

Agency/
ABMO

Art Direction & Strategy/
Sonia Cordier, Dez Gusta

Design/
Arthur Alazard, Dez Gusta

Photography/
Dez Gusta

BUCI

BUCI HOTEL PARIS
22 RUE DE BUCI — PARIS 6
+33 1 55 42 74 74
INFO@BUCI-HOTEL.COM
WWW.BUCI-HOTEL.COM
BUCI
BOUTIQ
NE REPARTEZ PAS LES MAINS VIDES. RETROUVEZ À LA BOUTIQUE LES PRODUITS DE VOTRE CHAMBRE ET PROLONGEZ L'EXPÉRIENCE BUCI CHEZ VOUS. DÉCOUVREZ AUSSI NOTRE SÉLECTION D'OBJETS POUR RECRÉER L'AMBIANCE D'UN REFUGE INTIME.
Don't go home empty-handed. Find the products for your room in the store and extend the BUCI experience at home. Discover our selection of objects to recreate the atmosphere of an intimate refuge.
PEIGNOIR ADULTE
PEIGNOIR ENFANT
TAPIS DE BAIN EN FIBRE DE BAMBOU
PARURE DE LIT
BOUTEILLE EN VERRE
GOURDE
90€

BUCI

— GILBERT DURAND —
« Lait et miel sont douceur, délices de l'intimité retrouvée. »

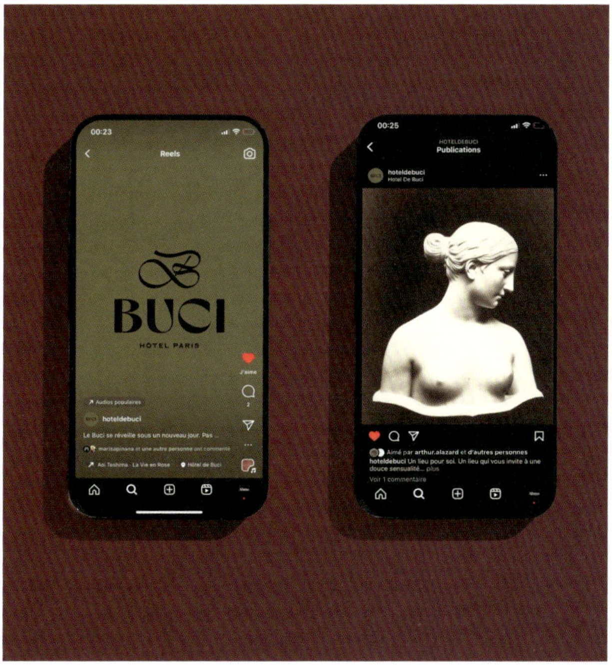
Reels
BUCI
HOTEL PARIS
hoteldebuci
Publications

NON,
MERCI
BIEN
PLEASE COME BACK LATER
BUCI

C15	M85	Y75	K5
R204	G68	B57	
C80	M25	Y80	K5
R28	G139	B86	
C85	M50	Y10	K0
R11	G111	B173	

Merluzo Fish & Chips

Merluzo is a fish & chips restaurant located in Barcelona with home delivery. The design of the identity is fixed in the origins of the type of business, in the fishermen, referring to the ancient Mediterranean boats. The design team sought the minimum expression, representing the boats with the minimum possible elements: the license plate and its characteristic colors.

Agency/
Murri Studio

Art Direction/
Maria Comella

Design/
Marc Blanes, Clara Faner

Copywriting/
Miqui Cerdà

Photography/
Pipin Alive

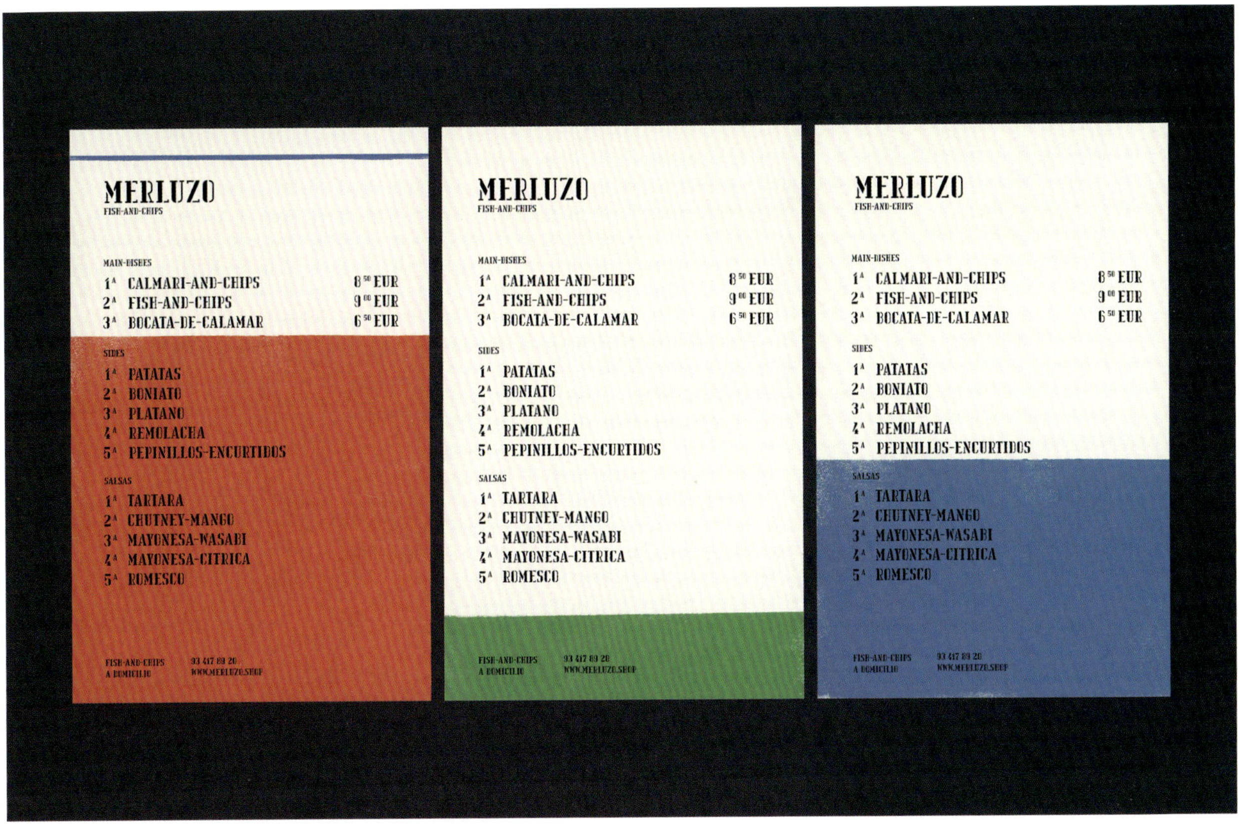
MERLUZO
FISH-AND-CHIPS
MAIN-DISHES
1ª CALMARI-AND-CHIPS 8^{50} EUR
2ª FISH-AND-CHIPS 9^{00} EUR
3ª BOCATA-DE-CALAMAR 6^{50} EUR
SIDES
1ª PATATAS
2ª BONIATO
3ª PLATANO
4ª REMOLACHA
5ª PEPINILLOS-ENCURTIDOS
SALSAS
1ª TARTARA
2ª CHUTNEY-MANGO
3ª MAYONESA-WASABI
4ª MAYONESA-CITRICA
5ª ROMESCO
FISH-AND-CHIPS A DOMICILIO
93 417 89 20
WWW.MERLUZO.SHOP
MERLUZO
FISH-AND-CHIPS
MAIN-DISHES
1ª CALMARI-AND-CHIPS 8^{50} EUR
2ª FISH-AND-CHIPS 9^{00} EUR
3ª BOCATA-DE-CALAMAR 6^{50} EUR
SIDES
1ª PATATAS
2ª BONIATO
3ª PLATANO
4ª REMOLACHA
5ª PEPINILLOS-ENCURTIDOS
SALSAS
1ª TARTARA
2ª CHUTNEY-MANGO
3ª MAYONESA-WASABI
4ª MAYONESA-CITRICA
5ª ROMESCO
FISH-AND-CHIPS A DOMICILIO
93 417 89 20
WWW.MERLUZO.SHOP
MERLUZO
FISH-AND-CHIPS
MAIN-DISHES
1ª CALMARI-AND-CHIPS 8^{50} EUR
2ª FISH-AND-CHIPS 9^{00} EUR
3ª BOCATA-DE-CALAMAR 6^{50} EUR
SIDES
1ª PATATAS
2ª BONIATO
3ª PLATANO
4ª REMOLACHA
5ª PEPINILLOS-ENCURTIDOS
SALSAS
1ª TARTARA
2ª CHUTNEY-MANGO
3ª MAYONESA-WASABI
4ª MAYONESA-CITRICA
5ª ROMESCO
FISH-AND-CHIPS A DOMICILIO
93 417 89 20
WWW.MERLUZO.SHOP

NOSOTROS NO LE TIRAMOS LA CAÑA A CUALQUIERA.

TIRAR PLÁSTICO AL MAR TIENE AÚN MÁS TELA QUE ESTA BOLSA.

C12 R231	M9 G227	Y20 B211	K0
C86 R39	M53 G92	Y33 B122	K19
C58 R106	M37 G114	Y82 B62	K26
C17 R198	M77 G81	Y81 B54	K6
C38 R150	M36 G136	Y51 B113	K20

Estúdio Degrau

Estúdio Degrau is an architecture and interior studio that seeks through its projects to elevate the space being worked on to a new level, where it becomes essential to pay attention to each step that will be reached so that this process makes the dreams of its customers. Its main objective is to translate personality, lightness, identity, color, and warmth into the designed space, relating clients' interests and the Brazilian essence, a characteristic belonging to the office's aesthetic vision.

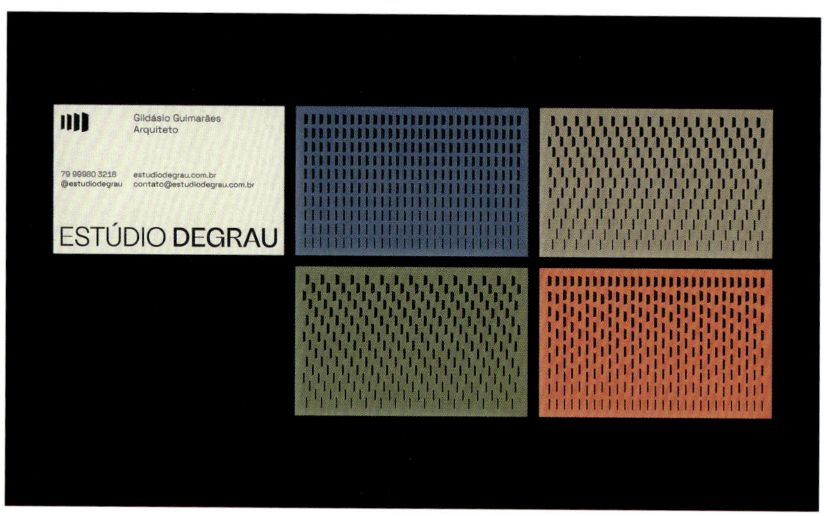

Agency/
Studio Xico Liborio

Client/
José Gildásio

CASES E
PROJETOS
2023
DEGRAU
ESTÚDIO DEGRAU

ESTÚDIO DEGRAU

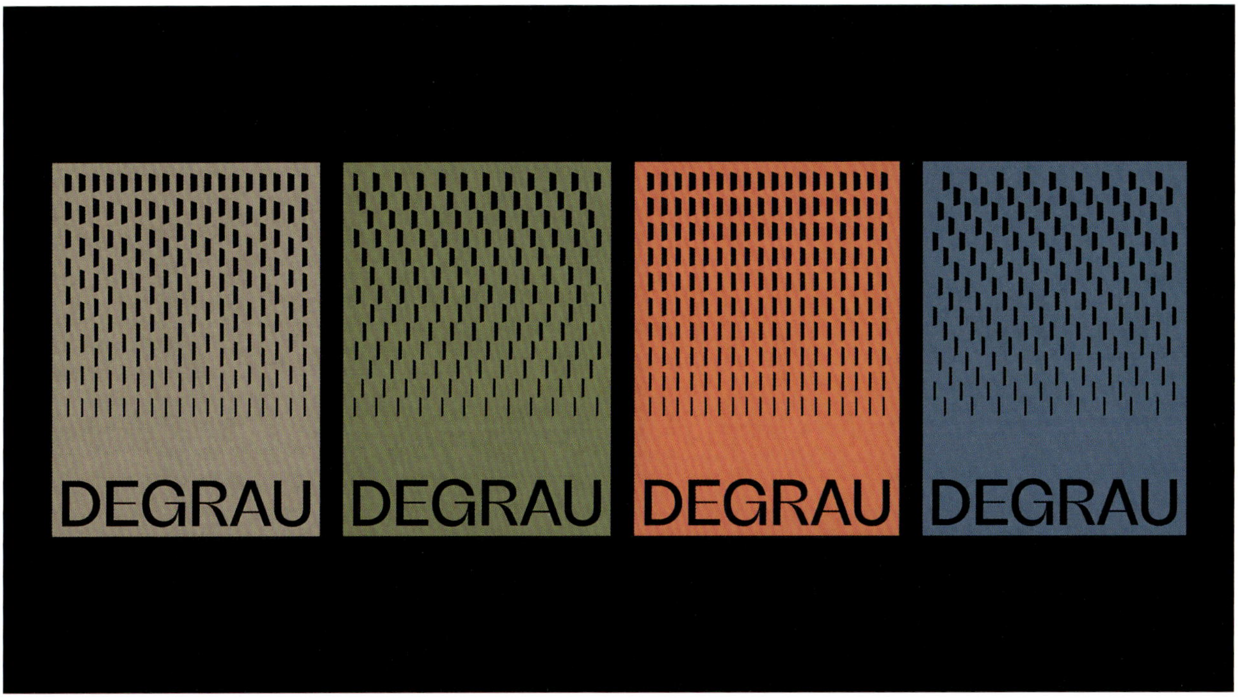
DEGRAU
DEGRAU
DEGRAU
DEGRAU

PROPOR AMBIENTES COM
CARACTERÍSTICAS ÚNICAS.
DEGRAU
VIVA A EXPERIÊNCIA
DE HABITAR UM
AMBIENTE QUE TE
ACOLHE E INSPIRA
TODOS OS DIAS.
ESTÚDIO DEGRAU

DEGRAU

Pantone P 127-7C				Pantone 3435 C			
C90	M0	Y48	K0	C89	M44	Y77	K52
R0	G162	B152		R17	G70	B52	
Pantone 7484 C				Pantone 7722 U			
C92	M38	Y76	K39	C95	M0	Y48	K55
R0	G87	B64		R0	G92	B87	
Pantone 328 C				Pantone 7735 C			
C100	M24	Y61	K17	C77	M42	Y76	K41
R0	G116	B104		R55	G87	B61	

Terra dell'acqua

It is a brand design strategy for the Province of Rieti, Italy. The territory is rich in water, due to the presence of lakes and rivers. The VI uses a generative system based on four parameters relating to water, to create eighty-one possible dynamic shapes. Also, the color palette varies according to the average water quality of the area, indicating six main levels, one color each. The levels go from "excellent" to "dangerous." The rest of the VI and prints use the main color of the brand, that is the one which indicates the excellent water quality state.

Design/
Matteo Simonetti

WHERE NATURE FLOWS

WHERE NATURE FLOWS
terra
dell'
acqua

terra
dell'
acqua
Mappa
Castel di
Tora

Nasce:
42°39'16.18"N
13°09'53"E
Sfocia:
42°33'10"N
12°42'52.62"E
terra
dell'
acqua
WHERE NATURE FLOWS
Fiume
Velino
Curiosità

C90 R36	M69 G85	Y64 B92	K0
C56 R122	M21 G170	Y35 B166	K0
C0 R12	M0 G11	Y0 B11	K98
C0 R237	M70 G108	Y100 B0	K0
C9 R237	M5 G238	Y17 B219	K0

Aurumbra

Aurumbra is a company based in South Africa that imports and distributes the best products from Brazil, focusing on premium cachaça (a distilled spirit). Through the VI, it was possible to transmit the brand's Brazilianness in an elegant and modern way with the construction of a unique typographic and color palette. Based on images from Brazil that represent the country, the color palette conveys sensations. Green comes from nature and the flag of Brazil, and beige is a color chosen to refer to sugar cane, cachaça, and earth. Orange represents the joy and energy of the Brazilian people.

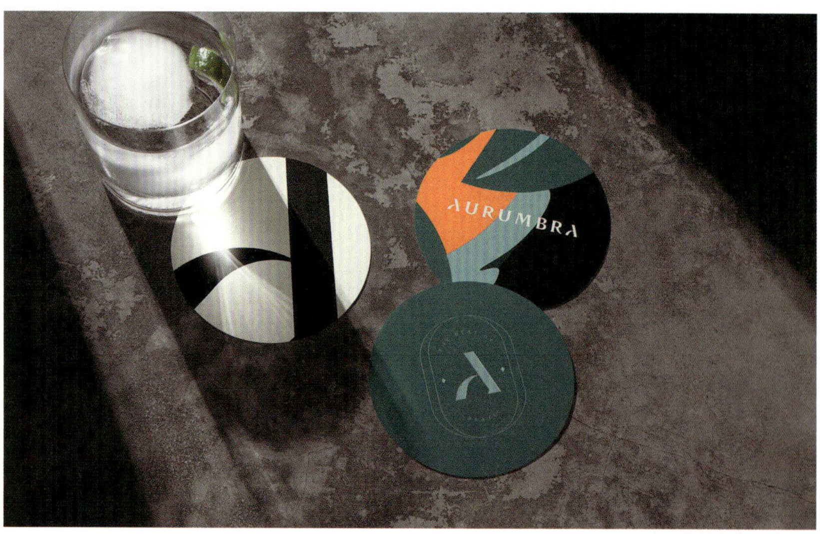

Agency/
Brakio Estratégia + Design

Design/
Lucas Barreira

The best of Brazil
AURUMBRA
The best of Brazil
The best of Brazil
AURUMBRA
AURUMBRA
Canabella
CACHAÇA
RUM
The best of Brazil

OAC #1121
PERMIT #120341077-01-SG
The best of Brazil
AURUMBRA
PERMIT# 120341086-01-SG
OAC #1121
PERMIT #120341095-01-SG
The best of Brazil
AURUMBRA
PERMIT #120341077-01-SG
PERMIT #120341095-01-SG

C0	M83	Y100	K0
R255	G80	B0	
C90	M40	Y68	K32
R0	G95	B82	

Sole Coffee

Sole, a coffee brand based in Da Lat, Vietnam, embodies the country's revered coffee culture. It goes beyond a simple beverage, creating an immersive experience. Vietnamese coffee lovers not only relish the taste but cherish the moments shared with loved ones in the captivating ambiance. The harmonious blend of coffee, space, people, and music culminates in extraordinary experiences. Sole was crafted to curate those exceptional moments. Vibrant orange represents the sun's energy, while refreshing green symbolizes Da Lat's lush flora. Combined with captivating illustrations, it delivers a truly unique and enchanting brand journey.

Agency/
ModiFox Creative Agency

Design/
Phat Tran (Visual)
Khang Huynh (Graphic)
Quang Hieu (Product)

Client/
Sole

Macchiato!
Macchiato!
NOT FOR SALE
Cappuccino!
Cappuccino!
Cappuccino!
Customer Gift Set

DOLCE MOCHA
100% ARABICA
WHOLE BEAN SPECIAL COFFEE
VIETNAM

COFFEE SHOP

a cup of coffee?
7.am and a hot cappuccino
have you ever see the sun?

7.am
and a hot
cappuccino!
Croissant lovers
Never Stop Eatingggg!
Wake Up My Sunshine
a coffee
cup!
timurisa?
Is that correct?
stay humble, stay cool
It's
latte
time!
Be The Sun To Shine
In a coffee shop
Why dont u
wake up
& enjoy life?

COFFEE SHOP
7.am and a hot cappuccino!
Address: District 3, HCM City

take a sit and have an americano!
have you ever love
THESUN!
I do.

OVERALL MURALS
COFFEE SHOP
7.am and a hot cappuccino!
Address: District 3, HCM City
VIETNAMESE COFFEE BRAND

Pantone 330 C
C89 M51 Y73 K59
R0 G57 B45

Pantone 2204 C
C26 M7 Y13 K0
R198 G220 B221

Pantone Bright Red C
C0 M91 Y100 K0
R232 G53 B13

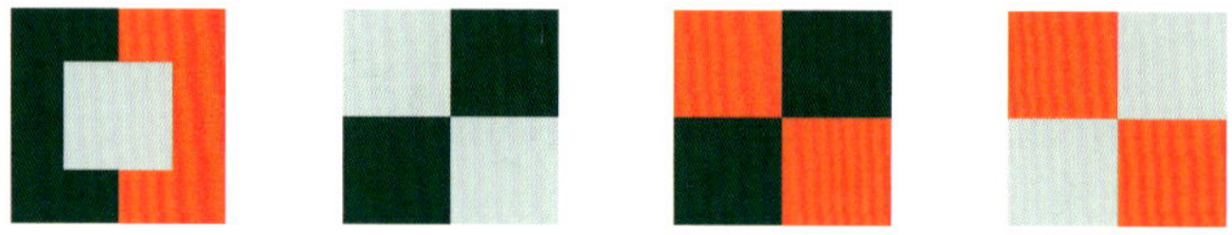

Hinterland

Agency/
Mano a Mano Club

Photography & Client/
Hinterland

The goal for Hinterland was to create a branding that embodies minimalism and modularity, resulting in a communication that leaves a lasting and impactful impression. Throughout the project, the design team used a modular design approach, allowing for flexibility and adaptability. It ensures that the space can be easily reconfigured to accommodate different needs and future growth, providing a versatile environment that can evolve with the changing requirements of Hinterland's clients.

HINTERL
01.1.0
HINTERLAND

HINTERLAND

ARCHITECTURE
HINTERLAND
STUDIO

ARCHITECTURE
ARCHITECTURE
H
A
S
STUDIO
HINTERLAND
HB
10 PENCILS
ARCHITECTURE STUDIO

C92 M14 Y67 K70
R2 G70 B56

C0 M85 Y95 K0
R231 G65 B27

C24 M26 Y30 K3
R200 G184 B173

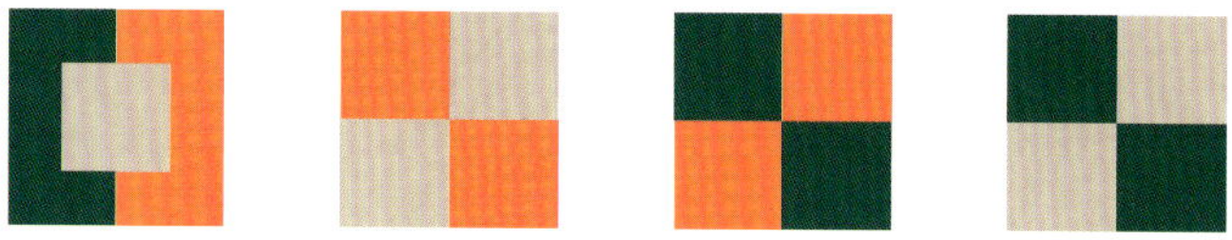

Okke

Okke is a sustainable and modular construction company. The designer created a strong, dynamic, and functional identity for it. The major colors used in the identity are green, orange, and nude.

Design/
Nil (Denilson Carvalho)

OKKE.

OKKE.

RODRIGO PETTERLE
OKKE.
OKKE.
Rodrigo Petterle
Sócio
CONSTRUÇÃO
& INOVAÇÃO
OKKE.

OKKE.

OK KE.
CONSTRUÇÃO
& INOVAÇÃO
OK
KE.
A construção do futuro, hoje.
OKKE.
okke.com.br

OK
KKE.
OKK
KE.
OKKE.

OKKE
okke.com.br
OK KE.
CONSTRUÇÃO
& INOVAÇÃO
STEEL FRAME
okke.com.br
Com o ideal de revolucionar a construção, oferecendo um sistema limpo, rápido, competitivo e com desempenho superior à alvenaria em todos os aspectos.
OKKE. CONSTRUÇÃO & INOVAÇÃO
OK
KKE.
OKK
KE.

OK
KE.
OKKE.
primesight|power

OKKE.

OK
KE.

C86 R34	M59 G82	Y72 B72	K25
C25 R202	M0 G229	Y25 B206	K0
C84 R16	M33 G131	Y87 B77	K0
C57 R114	M0 G192	Y55 B141	K0
C34 R183	M42 G150	Y80 B71	K0

AUSTERIA

AUSTERIA is a wine bar in Sidney, Ohio, that aims to become the place for learning about the local wine culture through unique experiences. More than a place, it is a state of mind where people can reconnect with themselves by enjoying the things they love and forgetting about the mundane. AUSTERIA wants to take people on a journey where every experience is memorable, elevates their spirit, and sharpens their senses. The exciting story will be told in sips from the palates of AUSTERIA's diners.

Agency/
ESTUDIO ALBINO

AUSTERIA

AUSTERIA
WINE BOUTIQUE
SAUVIGNON BLANC
AUSTERIA
WINE BOUTIQUE
A STATE OF MIND

●	C65 R86	M0 G184	Y65 B121	K0
●	C25 R198	M35 G173	Y0 B210	K0
●	C25 R200	M50 G140	Y90 B45	K0

AUTÓCTONXS FESTIVAL

This promotional work was created for the first-ever indigenous festival, an initiative by Teatro del Soho, conceived to showcase the talent of artists and residents from Malaga, Spain. It is a festival to highlight new languages, disciplines, and ways of experiencing performing arts. For the graphic design, a robust typography with distinctive features was used to enhance the concept of Málaga's identity, accompanied by different textures as a visual metaphor for the vibrant stage. The color palette is a reinterpretation of the colors of the flag of Málaga, projecting a festival that originates in this city, making the audience feel a sense of ownership.

Agency/
Tiquismiquis.club

Design Direction/
Alessandra Garcia, Dos Bengalas

Production/
Teatro del Soho CaixaBank, Málaga

Photography/
UveMTZ

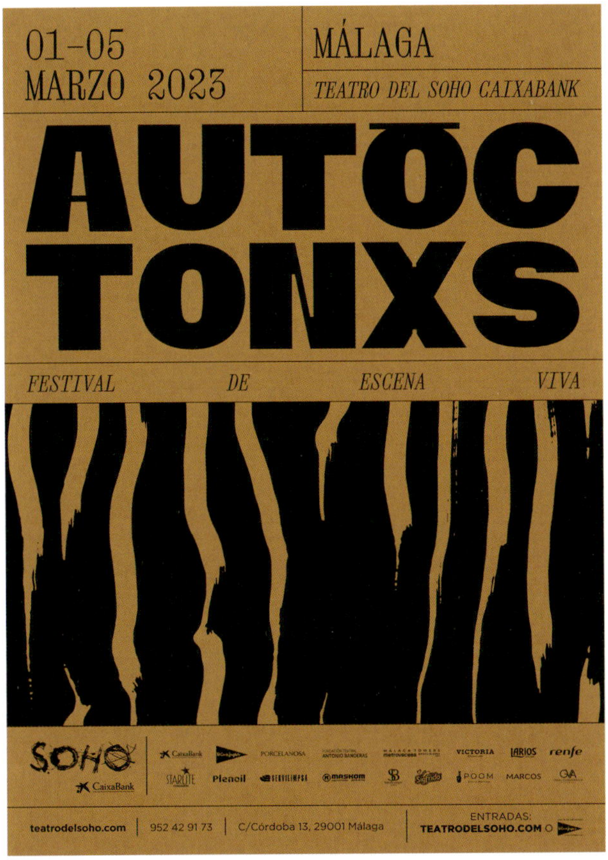
01-05
MARZO 2023
MÁLAGA
TEATRO DEL SOHO CAIXABANK
AUTOC
TONXS
FESTIVAL DE ESCENA VIVA
SOHO
CaixaBank
teatrodelsoho.com | 952 42 91 73 | C/Córdoba 13, 29001 Málaga
ENTRADAS:
TEATRODELSOHO.COM

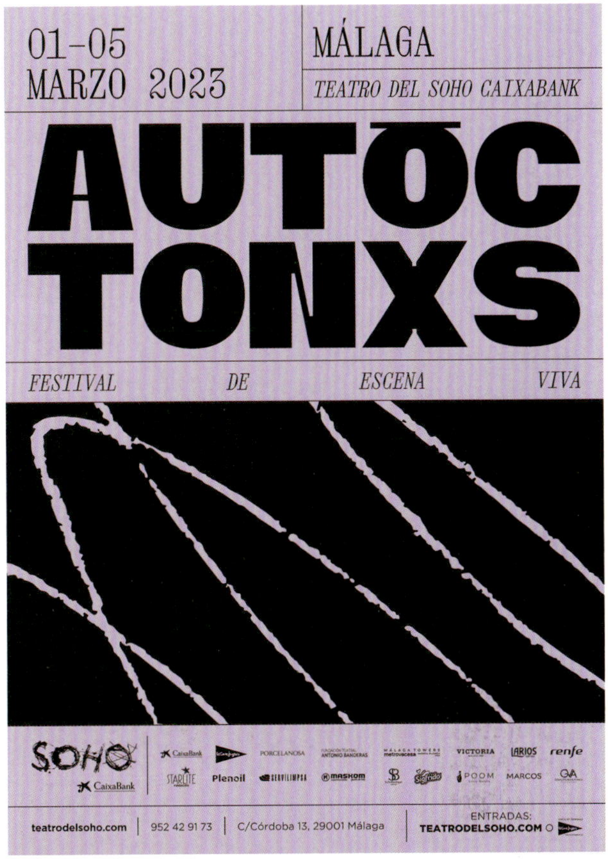
01-05
MARZO 2023
MÁLAGA
TEATRO DEL SOHO CAIXABANK
AUTOC
TONXS
FESTIVAL DE ESCENA VIVA
SOHO
CaixaBank
teatrodelsoho.com | 952 42 91 73 | C/Córdoba 13, 29001 Málaga
ENTRADAS:
TEATRODELSOHO.COM

autoctonxs_festival 2h
PROGRAMACIÓN
01-05 MARZO
Enviar mensaje
autoctonxs_festival 2h
STAFF
AUTOCTONXS
Enviar mensaje
autoctonxs_festival 2h
Enviar mensaje

Pantone 7761 U
C42 M13 Y64 K42
R112 G133 B79

Pantone 485 U
C5 M77 Y64 K0
R228 G93 B80

Pantone 2143 U
C69 M34 Y0 K0
R96 G142 B205

Pantone 128 U
C0 M21 Y70 K0
R253 G209 B91

Riikyu Packaging Design

Riikyu sees our pets as the human's best friends and closest family members. The designers want to interact more closely with their pets and equally live under the same roof. Their brand's main products are items people and pets can use together. They share their comfort and happiness with their little furry family members through these high-quality products.

Riikyu promotes the idea that all beings are equal. The designers don't just care about their own pets; they care about other animals and the sustainability of the entire planet. They hope to connect and make the world a better place through the brand. Therefore, they search for the most organic raw materials and the most environmentally friendly factories around the world to reduce pollution in manufacturing and protect the Earth. At the same time, they donate 1% of their company's annual profits to save endangered species.

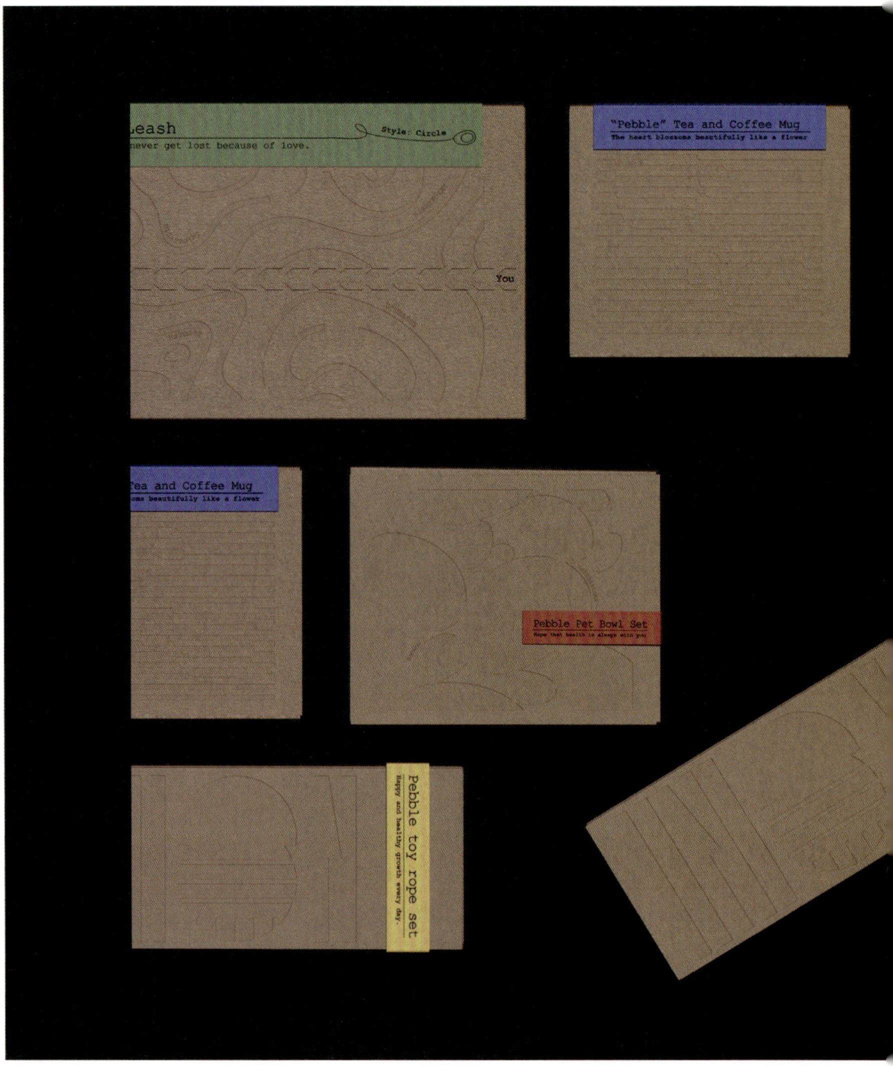

Design/
Koen Tan, Vicky Zhao

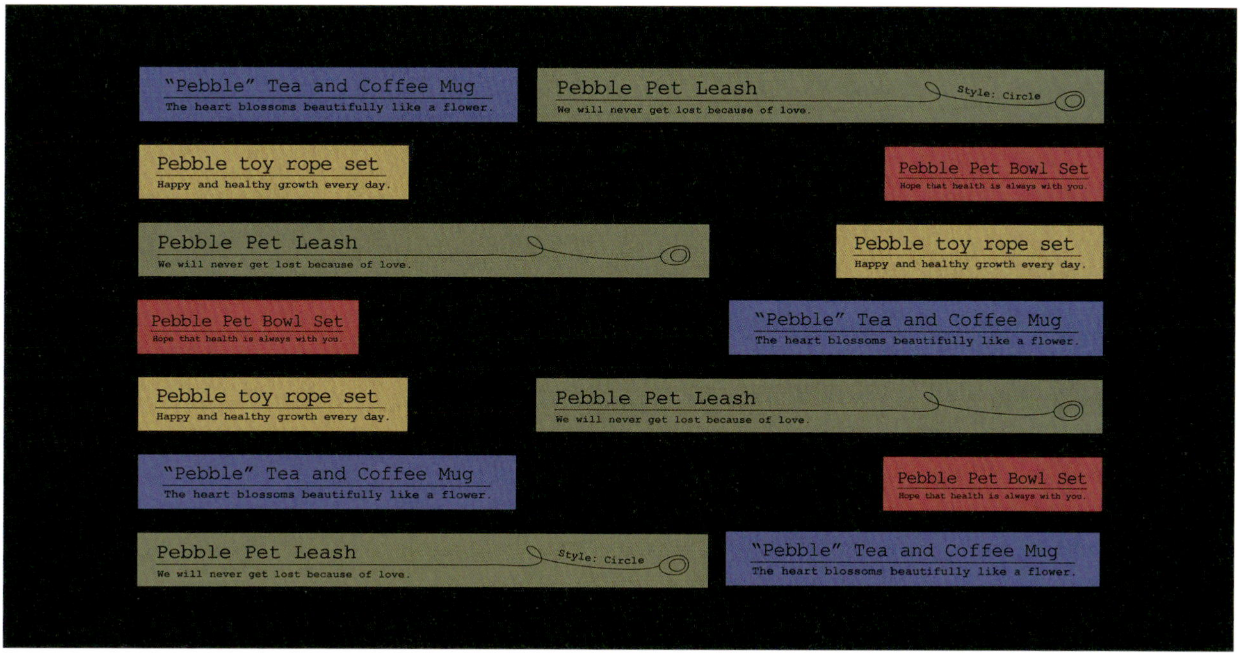
"Pebble" Tea and Coffee Mug
The heart blossoms beautifully like a flower.
Pebble Pet Leash
Style: Circle
We will never get lost because of love.
Pebble toy rope set
Happy and healthy growth every day.
Pebble Pet Bowl Set
Hope that health is always with you.

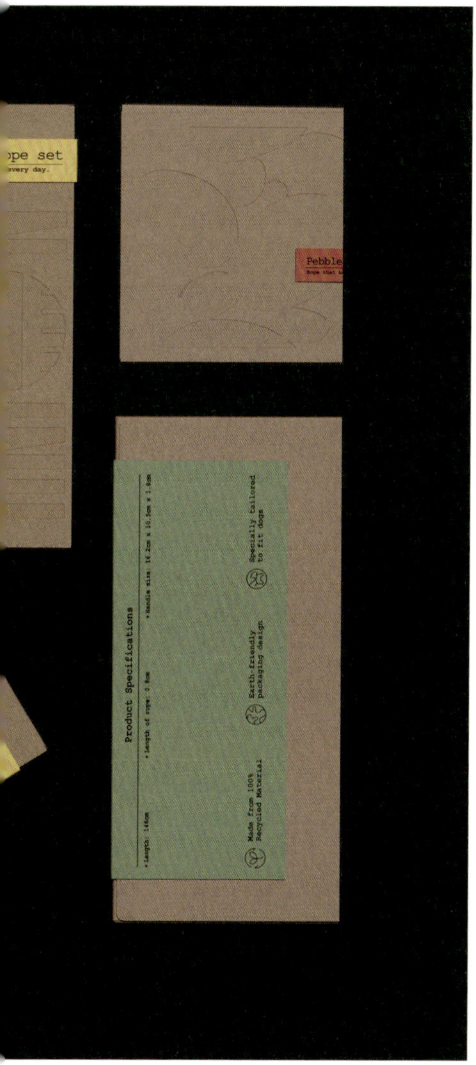
Product Specifications
Made from 100% Recycled Material
Earth-friendly packaging design
Specially tailored to fit dogs

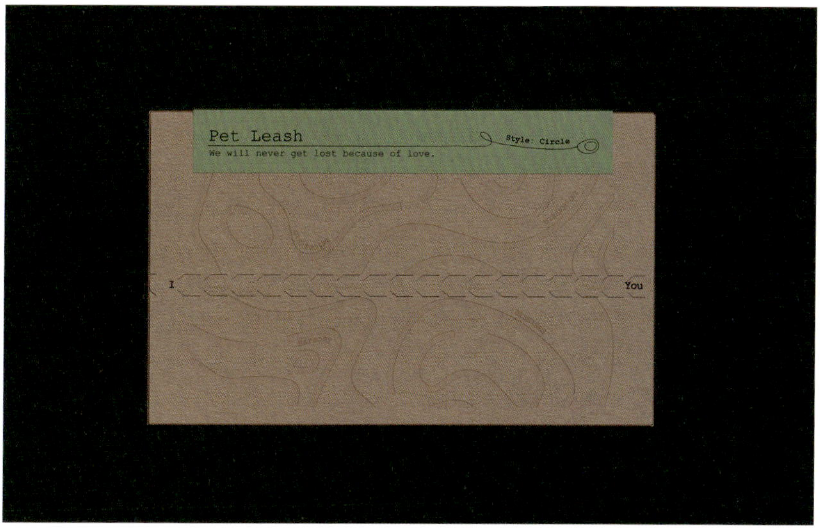
Pet Leash
Style: Circle
We will never get lost because of love.
I
You

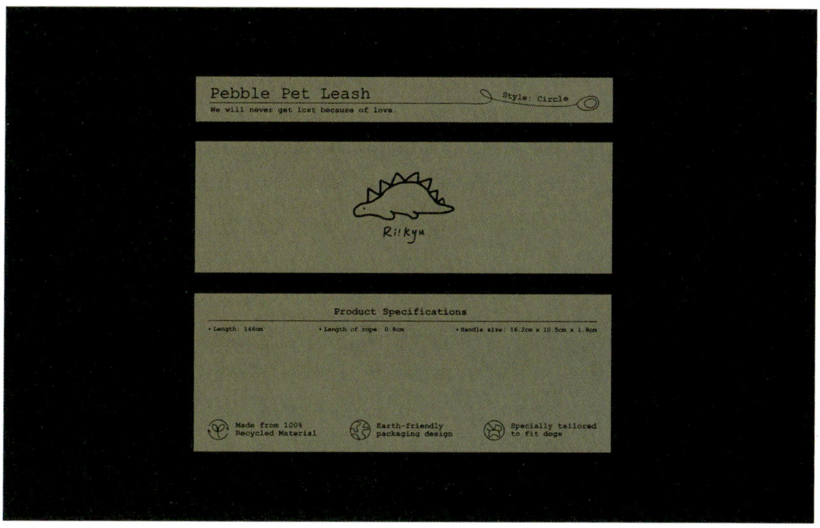
Pebble Pet Leash
Style: Circle
We will never get lost because of love.
Product Specifications
• Length: 146cm
• Length of rope: 0.8cm
• Handle size: 16.2cm x 10.5cm x 1.8cm
Made from 100% Recycled Material
Earth-friendly packaging design
Specially tailored to fit dogs

Pantone 2024 C				
	C0	M64	Y69	K0
	R248	G124	B86	
Pantone P 1085-5 C				
	C68	M48	Y21	K2
	R96	G122	B159	
Pantone 7549 U				
	C0	M31	Y89	K0
	R255	G184	B56	
Pantone 7721 C				
	C91	M44	Y58	K27
	R0	G94	B93	
Pantone 7513 U				
	C8	M29	Y22	K0
	R231	G186	B180	
Pantone 5445 C				
	C28	M13	Y12	K0
	R183	G201	B211	
Pantone Neutral Black				
	C71	M67	Y64	K73
	R35	G33	B34	

Brand Identity for Fitness Brand Reiform

Reiform is a Norwegian company delivering fitness equipment to work out from home. The brand was launched to help people keep fit during lockdown. The founders were looking for design solutions that matched traditional Scandinavian design traditions and mentality. Despite this, the ambiance of the whole project had to be light, energetic, and very simple, like orange juice. The designer decided to combine the classic principles of Swiss typography with modern color combination trends to modernize the traditional Scandinavian design and make it suitable for sports-related business.

Agency/
Spatio Studio

Art Direction & Design/
Daria Malovichko

Photography/
Unsplash

Client/
Reiform, Alex Rein

John Matthews
project manager, Reiform
Alex Rein
founder, Reiform
Gary Bryan
sales manager, Reiform

REiFORM
GET IN FIT
HOME

REIFORM

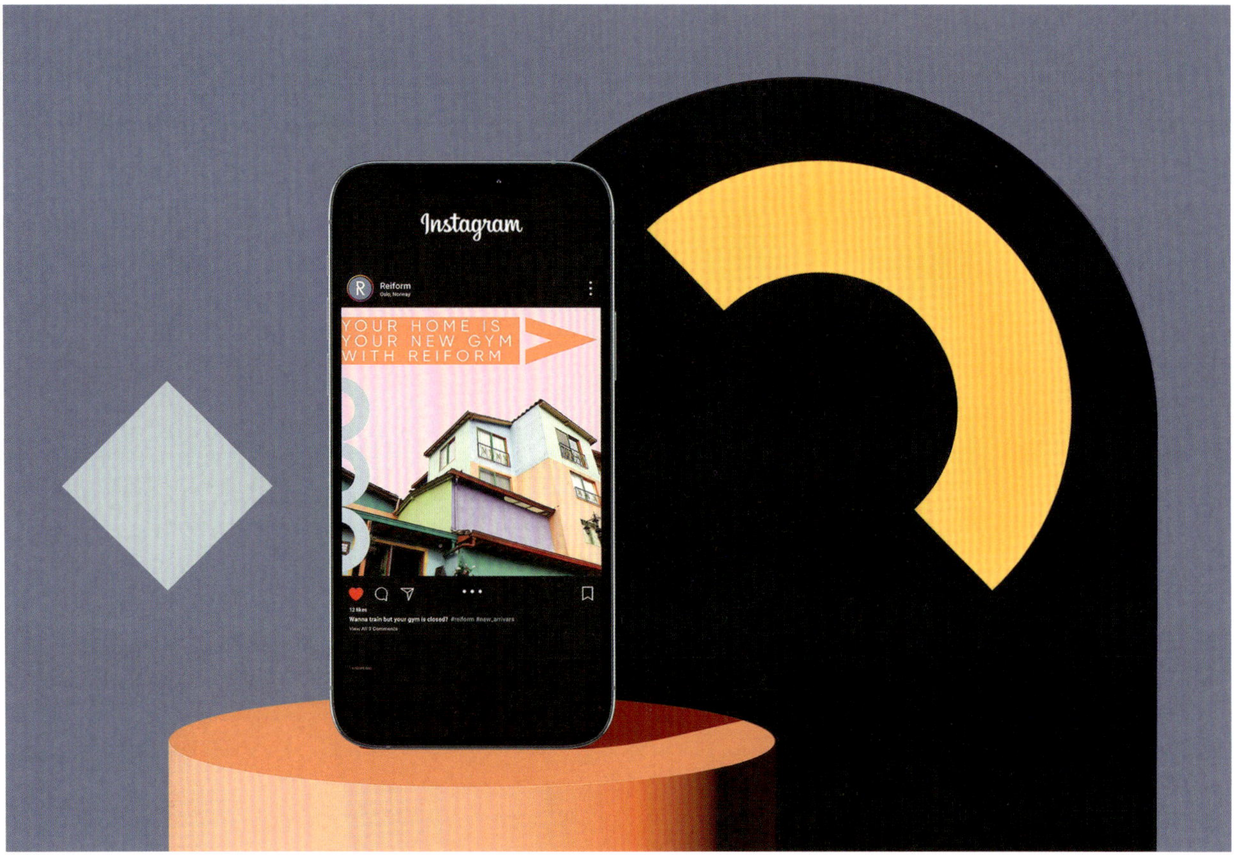
Instagram
Reiform
Oslo, Norway
YOUR HOME IS
YOUR NEW GYM
WITH REIFORM
12 likes
Wanna train but your gym is closed? #reiform #new_arrivals
View All 3 Comments

GET IN FIT HOME WITH
REiFORM

C	M	Y	K
C60	M78	Y5	K0
R125	G75	B150	
C3	M78	Y61	K0
R230	G89	B80	
C74	M7	Y50	K0
R30	G170	B147	
C2	M38	Y46	K0
R243	G179	B135	
C76	M38	Y19	K4
R55	G130	B171	
C82	M68	Y0	K0
R62	G85	B164	

WooHoop Rebranding

WooHoop is a leading company in the customized packaging sector. They called BRUTTO to do their rebranding. Since they work with global clients, including Coca-Cola, Siemens, Instagram, Disney, and many others. Their catalog is immense. Therefore, they asked BRUTTO to be able to divide their vastness of products into subcategories. Following their unmistakable style, BRUTTO decided that for each category a color and a geometric shape are used which, repeating themselves to form a pattern, give life to an almost infinite number of possible combinations. The shapes and colors are instead mixed for the web page and presentations, to represent the true essence of the company.

Agency/
BRUTTO

Client/
WooHoop

WOO HOOP.
Woohoop Packaging,
Broadwater House, Mundells,
Welwyn Garden City,
Hertfordshire, AL7 1EU
www.woohoop.com
WOO HOOP.
Business Card
85x55 mm
James Duncan
Managing Director
Direct 01707387741
Mobile 07887 805519
james@woohoop.com
www.woohoop.com
WP

WOO HOOP.

Bespoke packaging service
About Us
Contact
Printed Packaging
We are the best Packaging company in the world.
MacBook Pro

WOO HOOP.

C	M	Y	K	C	M	Y	K
C76 R44	M77 G36	Y84 B28	K59	C62 R88	M93 G30	Y68 B50	K40
C84 R36	M63 G62	Y100 B31	K44	C94 R39	M100 G34	Y53 B75	K22
C22 R198	M87 G66	Y86 B46	K0	C51 R131	M4 G197	Y34 B181	K0
C7 R234	M42 G165	Y83 B55	K0	C43 R162	M47 G138	Y63 B101	K0
C15 R223	M13 G218	Y24 B198	K0	C20 R211	M16 G211	Y15 B211	K0

Obra

Obra is a digital agency from Brazil, that focuses on delivering best-in-class digital transformation services through strategy, design, and technology. The main goal was to translate the mixture of the handmade, vernacular Brazilian imagery with a digitally inspired aspect.

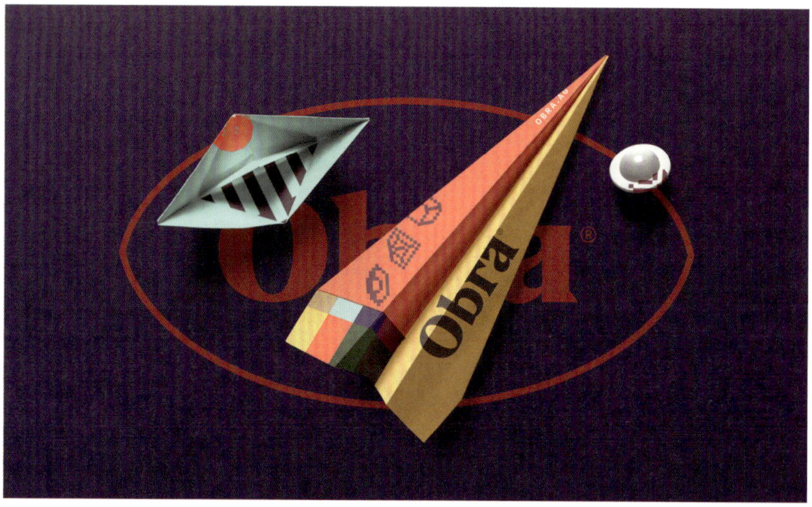

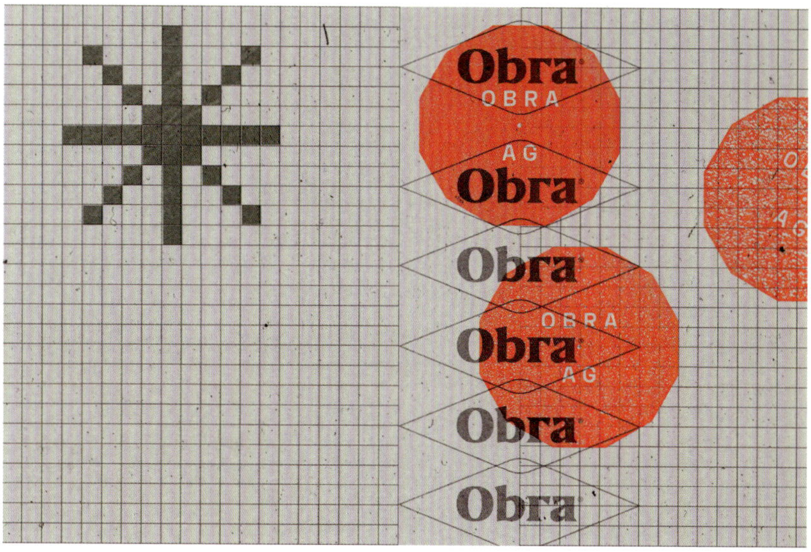

Design/
Nelson Balaban (Visual Identity)
Gustavo Gnatta (Iconography)

Obra
Obra

Obra
Obra
Obra
Laerte Jofre
Obra
Obra
OBRA
·
AG
Osmar Jr.
Obra
Obra

C100	M98	Y8	K0
R25	G20	B157	
C20	M96	Y10	K0
R215	G0	B134	

The Bar Affairr

The Bar Affairr is a travel bar in New Delhi, which celebrates through the most varied cocktails and drinks. And nothing fairer than elevating one's message with an artistic identity, which mixes the vibrant and elegant energy the brand wants to convey.

Agency/
Nord Brands

WE BRING THE
THE bar affair
PARTY TO YOU
WE BRING THE
PARTY TO YOU
WE BRING THE
PARTY TO YOU

THE bar affair
WE BRING THE PARTY TO YOU

COCK TAILS
THE bar affair
WE BRING THE PARTY TO YOU

THE bar affair
THE bar affair
PARTY TO YOU
WE BRING THE
THE bar affair
PARTY TO YOU
WE BRING THE
WE BRING THE PARTY TO YOU

- Pantone 2746 C
  C95 M91 Y0 K0
  R44 G47 B154
- Pantone 7504 C
  C48 M58 Y63 K1
  R153 G117 B95

The Module

The Module brand identity was built around creative programming, capable of generating dynamic animations and images, which the design team used to represent the progression of individual and transformative creative solutions. Individual columns and lines of movement and colors are stacked together to form a shared collective view. The primary color palette is blue and brown with the addition of white to create contrast. An infinite spectrum of possibilities was created with dynamic movement showing an adaptable and creative nature. All this adds up to a simple and robust layout system that not only allows a structured and rational presentation of the content but allows countless ways to see the creative world.

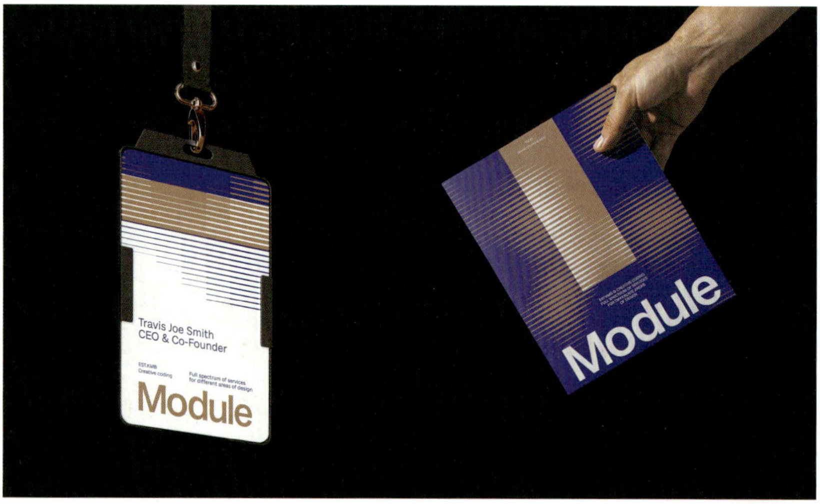

Agency/
Estúdio Kuumba

Design/
David Silva

Module
09/10

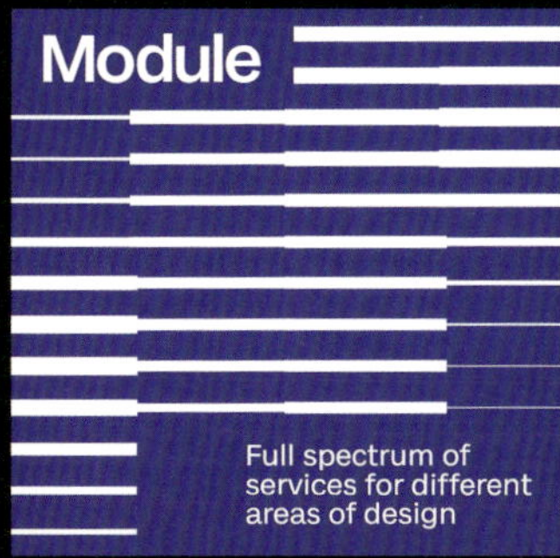
Module
Full spectrum of
services for different
areas of design

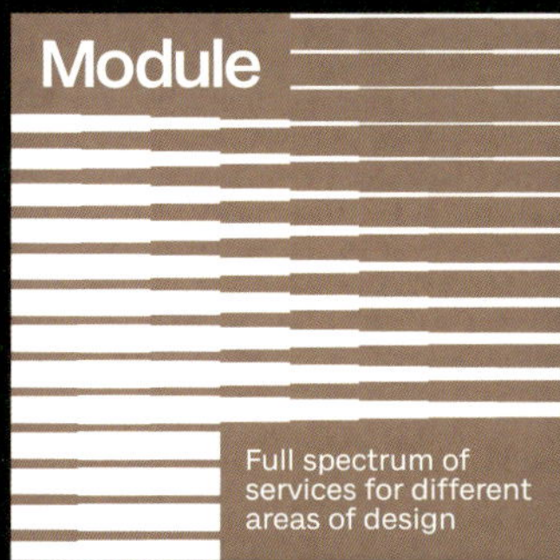
Module
Full spectrum of
services for different
areas of design

Module
EST.KMB
Creative coding
Full spectrum of
services for different
areas of design

Module

Module

Module

06/10
Module

Module
08/10

Module
01/10
Module
03/10
Full spectrum of
services for different
areas of design
04/10
Module
Module
09/10

Chapter 2

Pure and Natural

Through the matching of different hues with high value and low saturation, the cases mainly include sweet and pink, which are mainly warm colors, and fresh and clean, which are mainly cold colors in this chapter.

C0	M30	Y40	K0
R248	G196	B153	
C40	M20	Y0	K0
R163	G188	B226	
C10	M0	Y60	K0
R239	G237	B128	
C40	M68	Y91	K2
R172	G103	B48	

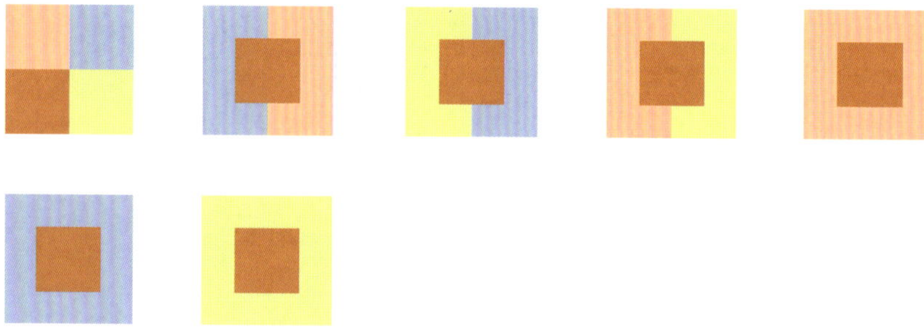

Villa Guadalupe

CULTO CREATIVE was tasked with creating a brand identity for Villa Guadalupe, a hotel and boutique located in the heart of Chapala, facing the largest lake in Mexico. They created a concept revolving around the nature and environment of that place. The selected colors are based on the blue color of the lake, the yellow of the sunrise, and a shade of salmon that reflects coziness. The logo was created with a custom typeface with simple geometric shapes that allude to the hotel's architecture. It has a relaxed personality that contrasts with the clean accommodations and solid colors that are part of the brand.

Agency/
CULTO CREATIVE

Art Direction/
Daniel Duran

Client/
Gerardo Pantoja

HOTEL + BOUTIQUE
VILLA
GUADALUPE

VILLA
GUADALUPE
HOTEL + BOUTIQUE

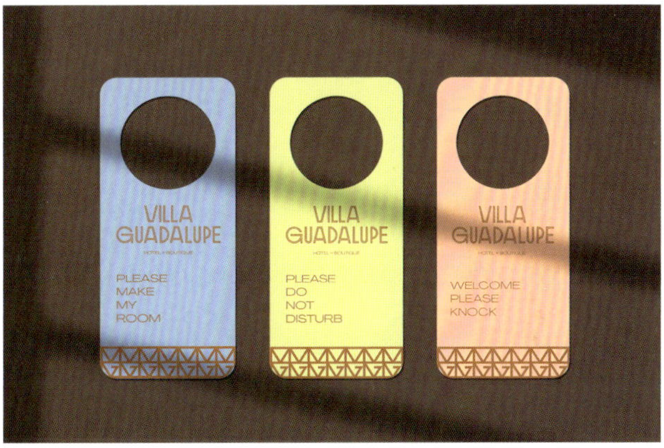
VILLA
GUADALUPE
PLEASE
MAKE
MY
ROOM
VILLA
GUADALUPE
PLEASE
DO
NOT
DISTURB
VILLA
GUADALUPE
WELCOME
PLEASE
KNOCK

VILLA
GUADALUPE
HOTEL + BOUTIQUE
VILLA GUADALUPE

C0 R255	M20 G216	Y28 B178	K0
C5 R245	M2 G245	Y10 B235	K0
C33 R158	M39 G131	Y76 B70	K22
C55 R111	M39 G114	Y66 B83	K29
C0 R255	M9 G255	Y86 B51	K0
C44 R87	M61 G60	Y74 B39	K69
C66 R87	M63 G60	Y63 B39	K78

La Roasterie

Art Direction/
STUDIO OUAM

Copywriting/
Millie Servant

Illustration/
Angélique Saubion

Client/
La Roasterie

La Roasterie is a roasting house with a half-chic, half-argot tone in Southern France. Specialty coffee is an art: a carefully selected product, roasted and prepared with precision, mastery, and technique. La Roasterie's identity highlights the preciousness of the product and the art of preparing coffee, a duality between research and experimentation, technique and precision. The elegant typography contrasts with experimental fluorescent colors that express the duality and break with conventional coffee codes.

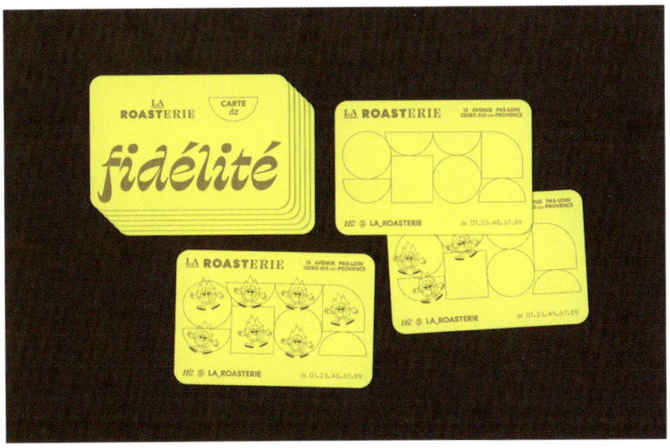
LA ROASTERIE
CARTE de
fidélité
LA ROASTERIE
13 AVENUE PAS-LOIN 13080 AIX-en-PROVENCE
LA_ROASTERIE
LA ROASTERIE
13 AVENUE PAS-LOIN 13080 AIX-en-PROVENCE
LA_ROASTERIE

RENCONTRE les BOISSONS CHAUDES de ta RÉGION
LA ROASTERIE

LA ROASTERIE
LA_ROASTERIE
MAISON de TORRÉFACTION
menu
How I Met Your Mouture → CAFÉ DU JOUR → 3€
Coffee therapy → SLOW COFFEE / CHEMEX → 3,50€
Poom Poom Shot → (RISTRETTO, ARABICA) → 3,50€
La vie en Black → ESPRESSO → simple 2€ ou double 3,50€
Ice, Ice, Coffee → COLD BREW → 3,50€
Le Grain Siffiera Deux Fois → DOUBLE ESPRESSO → 3,50€
Arabicadabra → BLUE MOUNTAIN , SL28, ARABICA → 3,50€
Bonjour Bourbon → BOURBON ROUGE, ARABICA → 3€
Chaud cacao → MOCHACCINO → 3€
The milky way → CAPPUCCINO → 3,50€
Soirée mousse → LATTE MACCHIATO → 3,50€
13 AVENUE PAS-LOIN 13080 AIX-en-PROVENCE
LA ROASTERIE

BONJOUR BOURBON
COFFEE THERAPY
HOW I MET your MOUTURE
LA ROASTERIE
MAISON de TORRÉFACTION

LA ROASTERIE
MAISON de TORRÉFACTION
POOM POOM SHOT
RISTRETTO ARABICA
LA_ROASTERIE
01.23.45.67.89
13 AVENUE PAS-LOIN
13080 AIX-en-PROVENCE

COFFEE THERAPY
LA ROASTERIE
MAISON de TORRÉFACTION

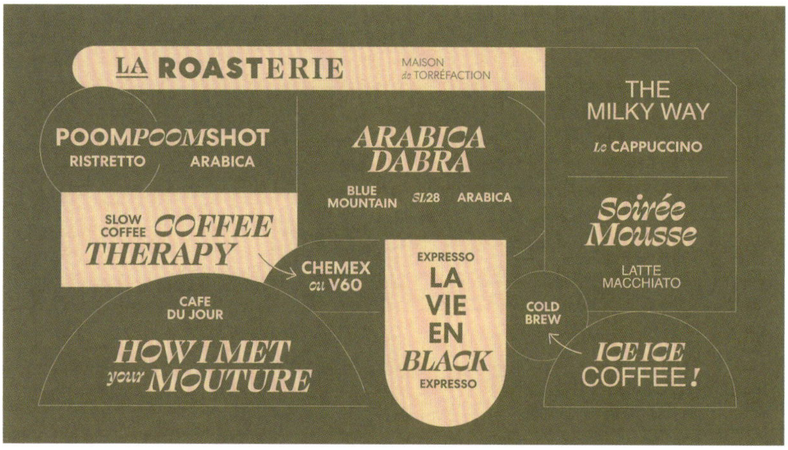
LA ROASTERIE
MAISON de TORRÉFACTION
POOMPOOMSHOT
RISTRETTO
ARABICA
ARABICA DABRA
BLUE MOUNTAIN
SL28
ARABICA
THE MILKY WAY
Le CAPPUCCINO
SLOW COFFEE
COFFEE THERAPY
CHEMEX ou V60
EXPRESSO
LA VIE EN BLACK
EXPRESSO
Soirée Mousse
LATTE MACCHIATO
CAFE DU JOUR
HOW I MET your MOUTURE
COLD BREW
ICE ICE COFFEE !

CHEMEX
ou
V60

LA ROASTERIE

LA ROASTERIE
Rade de
Haute
Mouture
13 AVENUE PAS-LOIN
13080 AIX-EN-PROVENCE

La Roasterie
Aix en Provence
CAFÉINOMANES
en
GUINGUETTE
CHAUD
& DOUX
COMME
VOUS
LE TEMPS
des CERISES
SL28
NATURE
CHEMEX
ou V60
BLUE
MOUNTAIN
RENCONTRE
les BOISSONS
CHAUDES
de ta RÉGION

C64	M40	Y71	K22
R93	G115	B79	
C40	M23	Y58	K1
R161	G171	B128	
C3	M2	Y16	K0
R246	G242	B216	
C30	M44	Y58	K4
R177	G140	B112	

REDOLENCE ROYALE

Located at the core of Pasig, Philippines, REDOLENCE ROYALE finds its muse in the diverse cultural heritage of the Philippines, seamlessly merging classic aromas with contemporary elegance. Every scent is thoughtfully crafted, combining premium elements to evoke memorable olfactory journeys. The logo design approach employs a minimalist style to uphold the product's luxurious appeal and ensure a sleek presentation, aligning with the client's aspiration for the brand identity to rival that of esteemed industry leaders.

Agency/
BEN STUDIO

Design/
Ben Macarilay

REDOLENCE
ROYALE
EAU DE PERFUME
100ML

REDOLENCE
ROYALE
MARIA SANTIAGO
Marketing Officer

REDOLENCE
ROYALE
EAU DE PERFUME
100ML
REDOLENCE
ROYALE
EAU DE PERFUME
100ML
REDOLENCE
ROYALE
EAU DE PERFUME
100ML
REDOLENCE
ROYALE
EAU DE PERFUME
100ML

www.redolenceroyale.com
REDOLENCE
ROYALE
OUTFRONT / PRIME
OUTFRONT / PRIME
M-1061

	C5 R240	M5 G235	Y11 B223	K0
●	C17 R220	M7 G211	Y100 B26	K0
●	C24 R193	M43 G147	Y59 B113	K2
●	C51 R119	M12 G186	Y8 B216	K0
●	C55 R119	M33 G137	Y69 B99	K10
●	C86 R12	M55 G47	Y71 B40	K66

Heeria Brand Identity

Heeria is a new sustainable jewelry brand, focusing on connecting people by embodying quality craftsmanship and materials in a conscious and considered way. Their goal is to provide a sense of conscious luxury with a low impact on the planet. These values drove the design team's approach to its brand identity. The clean yet dynamic visual identity incorporates geometric shapes inspired by various diamond forms and cuts. By merging "EE" from Heeria, the logomark forms a diamond viewed from below, symbolizing a shining jewel. The color palette is a reference to the colors found in nature to transmit authenticity.

Agency/
Humana Studio

Art Direction/
Ana Abreu

Design/
Tiago Narciso

Client/
Heeria

H✱RIA

Mother earth's
in your hands
Sustainable and
ethically sourced

H✱RIA
Mother earth's
in your hands
www.heeria.com

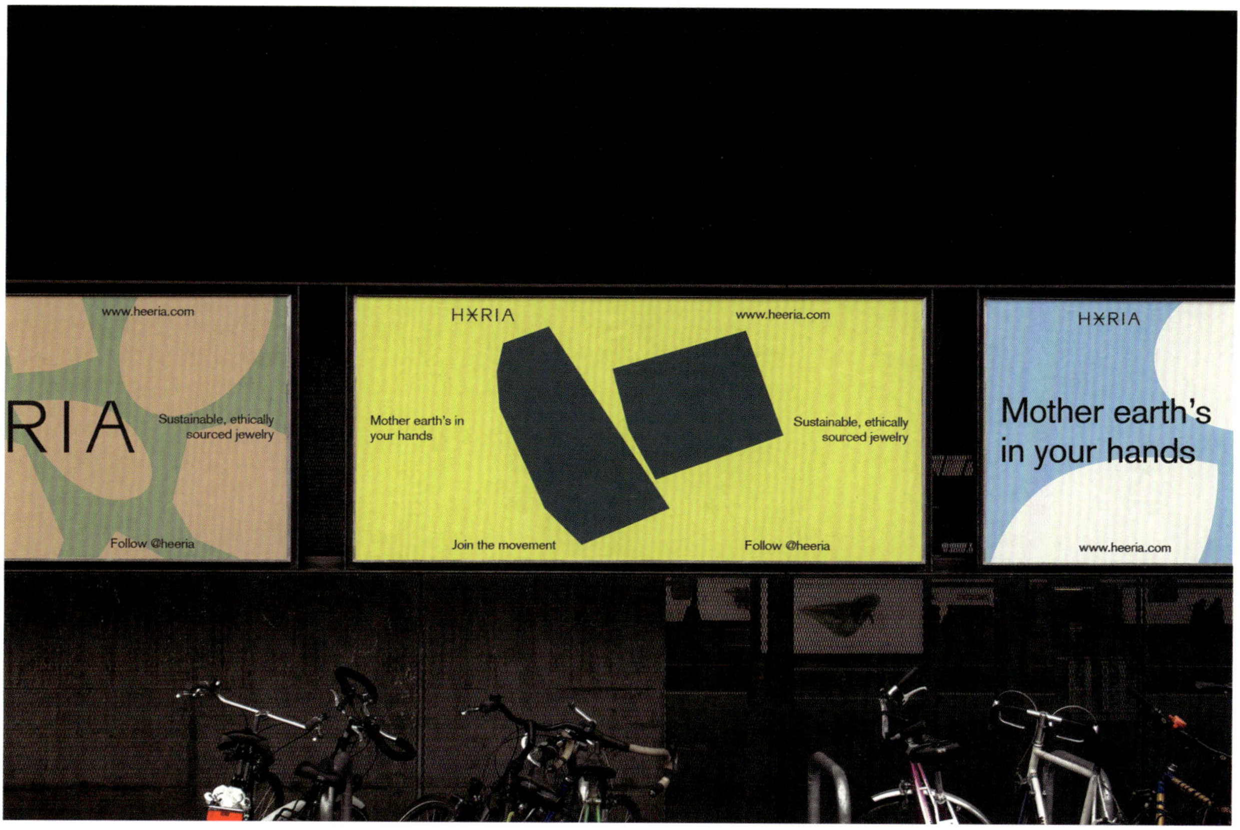
www.heeria.com
RIA
Sustainable, ethically
sourced jewelry
Follow @heeria
H✱RIA
www.heeria.com
Mother earth's in
your hands
Sustainable, ethically
sourced jewelry
Join the movement
Follow @heeria
H✱RIA
Mother earth's
in your hands
www.heeria.com

●	C75	M20	Y0	K0
	R0	G157	B218	
●	C0	M35	Y85	K0
	R248	G182	B45	
●	C65	M0	Y45	K0
	R79	G186	B161	

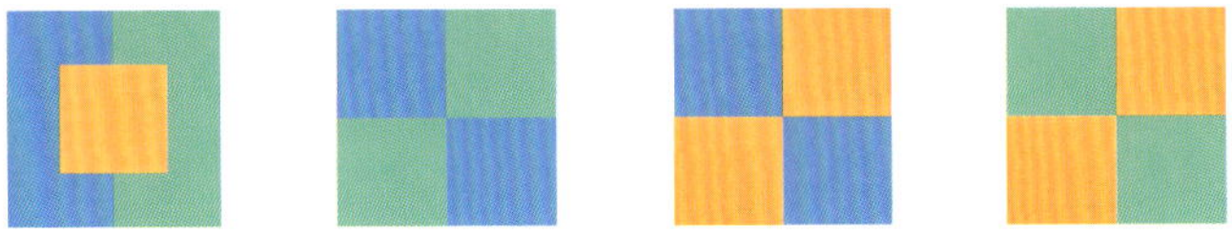

Lamma Mia

Lamma Mia is an island-scale art festival curated by the Art Promotion Office to enhance the connection between community, arts, and history, through the half-year event, to reintroduce the land to the public and also the locals. From the core concept of the identity system, the design team developed a module system that makes use of different shapes of mountains and waves to represent the idea of "islands speaking for themselves." They further extended the system to a tangible way-finding system for the visitors. They could experience a clear visual directional journey to help themselves dive into the art festival.

Agency/
for&st

Creative Direction, Art Direction & Design/
Ming Cheung

Client/
Art Promotion Office

Listen to
the sound of
land & sea
聽海與陸
之聲
南丫說：
Lamma Mia
公共藝術計劃
Public Art Project
Tuesday to Thursday
展覽地圖
Exhibition Map

Hear the
sound of
land & sea
南丫說：
Lamma
Mia
11.2021 ——
3.2022

公共藝術計劃
Public Art Project
南丫說:
Lamma
11.12.2021—
13.3.2022

看見風：旗旛
Visible Wind:
Burgees
03
南丫說:
Lamma Mia

南丫風采發電站
LAMMA WINDS (wind power station)
前往更多作品
To explore
more artworks
03
06
13
14
15
07
08
10
11
12

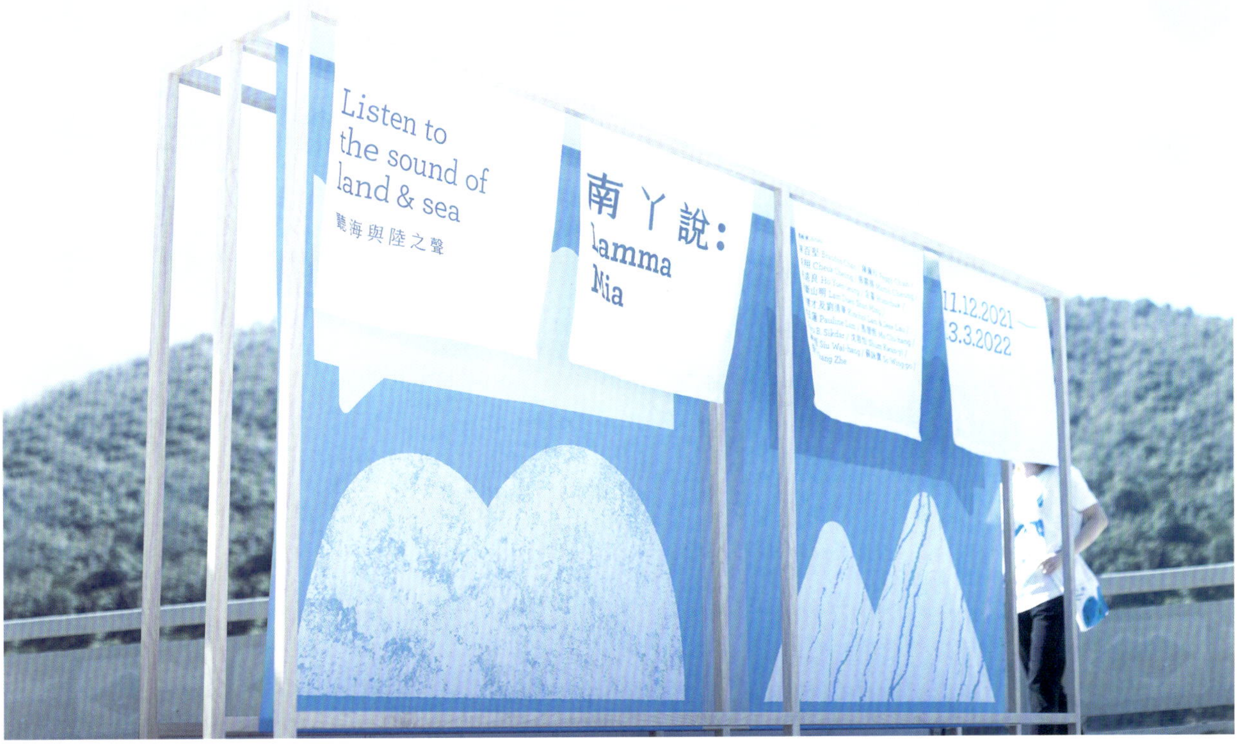
Listen to
the sound of
land & sea
聽海與陸之聲
南丫說：
Lamma
Mia
11.12.2021 —
13.3.2022

公共藝術計劃
Public Art Project
南丫說：
Lamma Mia
11.12.2021 — 13.3.2022

C20	M0	Y1	K0
R212	G242	B252	
C56	M27	Y46	K1
R128	G158	B140	
C87	M61	Y11	K0
R36	G97	B156	
C0	M23	Y11	K0
R250	G212	B212	
C2	M44	Y24	K0
R240	G168	B168	

La Pasteque

La Pasteque is a signature pastry shop created by Sandy Vinajera in Mérida, México. The brand takes inspiration from the classic French theater and bakeries from the 19th century. The logotypes, color palette, and editorial design reflect a delicate and romantic style that has been adapted to a more modern context. The isotype made by thick and seamless strokes gives the illusion of being written by meringue. This set of elements creates an environment that transports customers to another era.

Agency/
Puro Diseño

Design/
Cindy Montes de Oca, Cristina Gongora, Natalia Cejudo

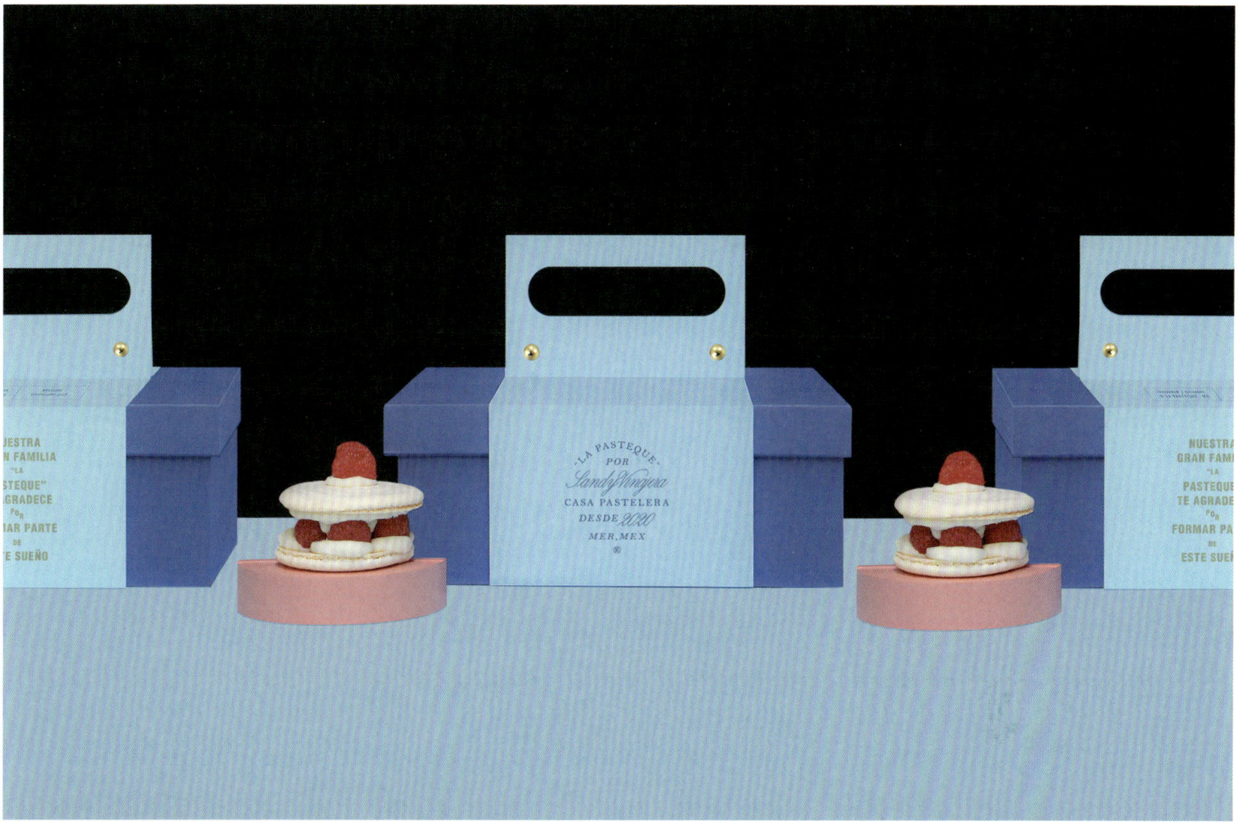
"LA PASTEQUE"
POR
CASA PASTELERA
DESDE 2020
MER,MEX
®

"LA PASTEQUE"
POR
CASA PASTELERA
DESDE 2020
MER,MEX
®
NUESTRA
GRAN FAMILIA
"LA
PASTEQUE"
TE AGRADECE
POR
FORMAR PARTE
DE
ESTE SUEÑO

●	C99	M93	Y3	K0
	R24	G44	B139	
●	C7	M7	Y27	K0
	R240	G234	B198	

LA BRIOCHE! Café and Bakery

Design/
Danara Khurgunova

Client/
LA BRIOCHE!

LA BRIOCHE! is a café emphasizing the concept of savoring every moment, even as mundane as coffee. The brand aims to create a movement of like-minded people with a direct and defiant approach. The distinctive characteristic reflects in the identity with the idea of disintegration: routine objects in an unexpected “dissolving” manner. The visuals resemble static noise, simulating the feeling of relishing: the idea of something so good that it melts on the customer’s tongue. To further develop the concept, the choice of a mellow blue shade, instead of classically hunger-inducing colors, calls for a slow pause.

O!
ENJOY BEING
LA BRIOCHE!
LA BRIOCHE!
ENJOY BEING

LA BRIOCHE!

LA BRIOCHE!

O!
LA BRIOCHE!
SLOW
DOWN
TO
WAKE
UP.

C	M	Y	K	R	G	B
C18	M6	Y45	K0	R225	G229	B162
C18	M10	Y76	K0	R230	G222	B82
C6	M18	Y28	K0	R244	G219	B188
C19	M63	Y97	K0	R216	G120	B18
C46	M73	Y98	K9	R152	G87	B39
C3	M13	Y0	K0	R249	G233	B243

C	M	Y	K	R	G	B
C2	M31	Y1	K0	R250	G201	B223
C29	M79	Y24	K0	R199	G84	B136
C56	M89	Y12	K0	R143	G57	B141
C9	M4	Y75	K0	R251	G240	B79
C19	M92	Y88	K0	R215	G51	B42
C39	M10	Y2	K0	R163	G204	B234

La Mia

La Mia is a Brazilian gelato brand that relies on the traditional Italian recipe, born to disrupt the ice cream shop model by offering high-quality yet affordable ice cream. The visual identity, characterized by a minimalistic typographically-driven system, presents a clean wordmark paired with a dynamic color palette, bold typography, endearing illustrations, and humorous verbal identity. The designers' approach addresses the challenges by creating a distinguishable, inviting, and lighthearted brand experience within the national market, spanning over 50 distinct packaging designs and various channels.

Agency/
Papanapa

Creative Direction/
Gustavo Garcia

Design/
Cássia Freire, Luana Cordeiro, Lucas Rodrigues

Project Management/
Lucas Rodrigues

Photography/
Livia Wu, Paulo Barros

La mia
TORTA DE LIMÃO
500 ML 350 G
SUNDAE DE MORANGO
DOCE DE LEITE

APPLE PIE
PISTACHE
FLOCOS
FRENCH VANILLA
BISCOITO BELGA
MORANGO AO LEITE
CHOCOLATE
TORTA DE LIMÃO
MILHO VERDE
COCO BRANCO
SUNDAE DE MORANGO
500 ML 350 G

GIANDUIA
TORTA DE LIMÃO
FRENCH VANILLA
GOIABADA
AÇAÍ
BISCOITO BELGA
MANGA
CHOCOLATE
PUDIM
FRAMBOESA
DOCE DE LEITE
BANANA

GELATO CONFORTO
La mia
A BASE ITALIANA E OS SABORES DO MUNDO

C0	M85	Y0	K0
R232	G65	B143	
C9	M5	Y91	K0
R242	G222	B21	
C63	M8	Y88	K0
R109	G172	B71	
C0	M64	Y100	K0
R237	G116	B2	
C8	M37	Y93	K0
R232	G168	B31	

Edénico

Agency/
Monograf Studio

Creative Direction/
Ramsés Lecourtois

Photography/
Liliana Barraza

Edénico is a distilled spirit that unites the European tradition of "Eau de Vie (Water of Life)" and the diversity of Mexican fruits. The brand takes inspiration from the story of Eden and its richness of fruits and vegetation. The symbol takes elements of the story and abstractly shows them.

A set of labels was designed to represent through bright colors and ethereal forms each one of the fruits that make up the Edénico collection. The packaging labels represent the main idea of distillation: to take the purest part of something and transform it while preserving its essence.

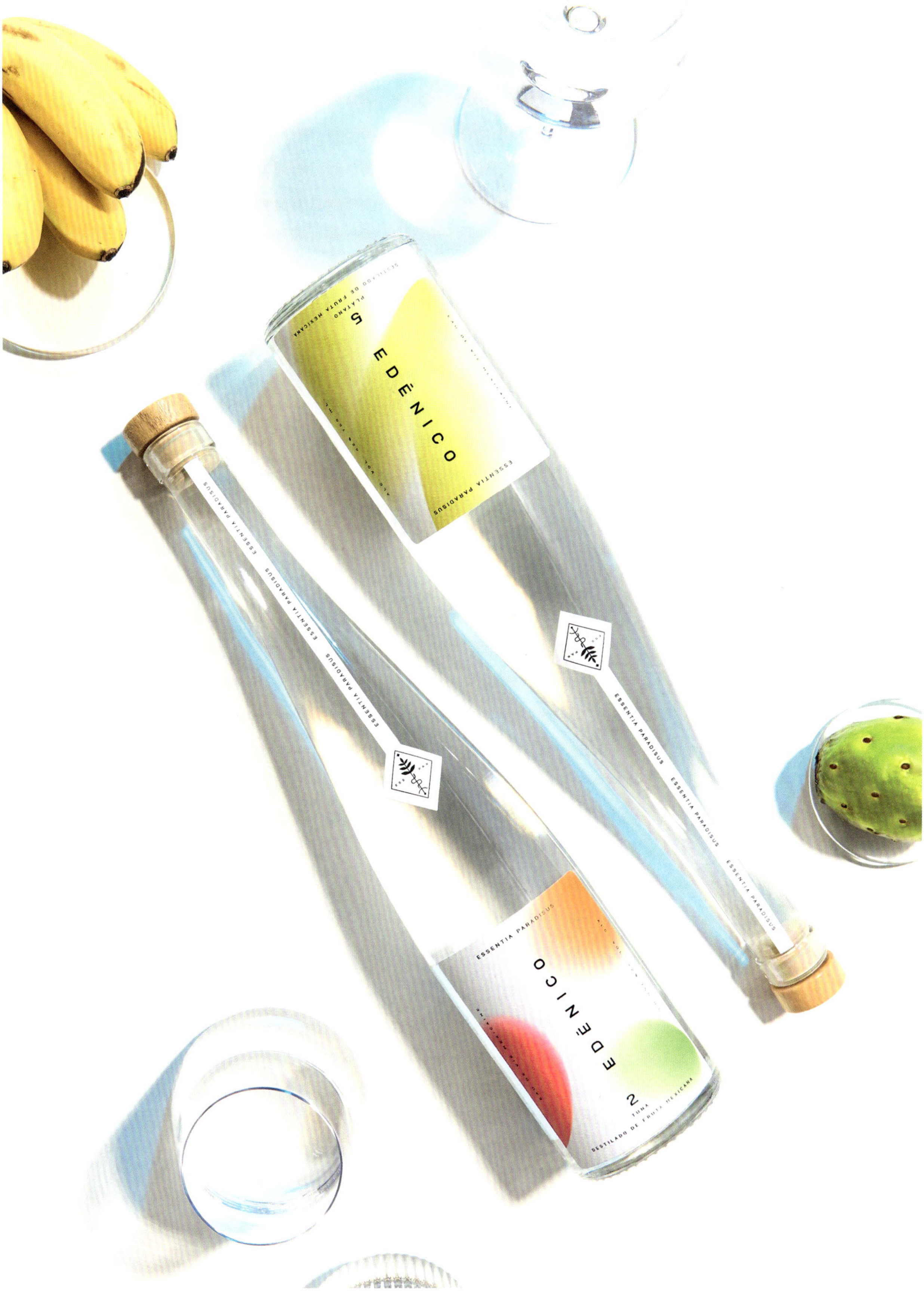
EDÉNICO
ESSENTIA PARADISUS
2
TUNA
DESTILADO DE FRUTA MEXICANA

C	M	Y	K	R	G	B
C0	M55	Y40	K0	R240	G144	B130
C83	M79	Y78	K62	R31	G31	B31
C6	M6	Y5	K0	R242	G240	B241
C45	M0	Y20	K0	R147	G210	B211
C30	M10	Y45	K0	R192	G208	B157
C40	M30	Y90	K0	R171	G165	B54
C80	M50	Y90	K20	R55	G97	B57
C90	M70	Y20	K0	R31	G82	B142
C50	M30	Y20	K0	R140	G163	B148
C5	M25	Y20	K0	R241	G205	B194
C10	M70	Y60	K0	R221	G107	B87
C40	M100	Y100	K0	R167	G33	B38

$moon^3$

The concept comes from the game of pokies played at the Mid-Autumn Festival in the southern Fujian province. The inner box forms the concept of a board game by turning the size of the dice numbers to match the poster, providing a new experience of a simple traditional folk game. The design assumes the dice are as square as the moon in the sky, providing the conjecture that the moon is not necessarily round, and uses the contrast between the foil stamping and the paper to provoke a collision of craftsmanship and materials to hook people's desire.

Agency/
BY-ENJOY DESIGN

金花
六杯红
遍地锦
黑六勃
秀才
进士
榜眼
四点红

C5	M20	Y90	K0
R245	G206	B19	
C40	M10	Y5	K0
R162	G203	B229	
C40	M75	Y100	K0
R169	G88	B36	
C25	M5	Y25	K0
R202	G222	B201	
C10	M10	Y10	K0
R234	G229	B227	
C20	M95	Y85	K0
R201	G42	B46	
C0	M35	Y5	K0
R246	G190	B208	

Colect Planner and Notebook

In 2023, LMD designed two products for the brand Colect: a notebook and a planner. Both prioritize functionality, organization, and creativity with an aesthetic that enhances any space.

The notebook set comprises six unique grid designs: triangle, square, dotted lines, ruled, and blank pages. Presented in a fabric-covered box, available in seven colors, they're versatile for drawing or writing, and individually portable.

The planner features 12-monthly notebooks, each with sections for monthly/weekly planning and notes. And an undated 2023/2024 calendar offers flexible organization.

Agency & Photography/
LMD

Art Direction & Concept/
Lucas Machado

Design/
Ângela Mayume,
Raquel Sales (Assistants)

Photo Editing & Website/
Camila Lissa

23

A5

23
COLECT
23
COLECT
23
COLECT
23

23
COLECT
23
COLECT
A5
COLECT
A5
COLECT

C	M	Y	K
C3 R248	M21 G208	Y68 B97	K0
C9 R202	M63 G110	Y59 B84	K1
C3 R246	M23 G208	Y36 B167	K0
C86 R43	M66 G87	Y0 B166	K0
C32 R184	M0 G223	Y18 B217	K0
C1 R219	M51 G137	Y66 B79	K0
C51 R137	M14 G182	Y50 B143	K0

Ótica Antunes

This rebranding is intended to be more graphic, light, fresh, and funny, appealing to a younger crowd. It was built from basic shapes with different symbolism: the triangle symbolizes sight and image perception, the circle represents the glasses shape, the broken arches stand for the eyes, and, at last, the square and rectangle represent the materials. Following this approach, the visual universe becomes more versatile, adaptative, and modular.

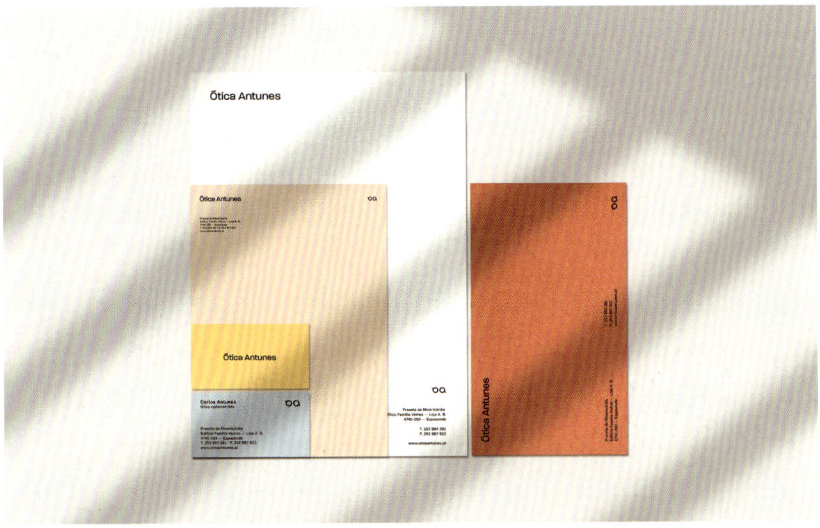

Agency/
Antecâmara Studio

Õtica
Antunes

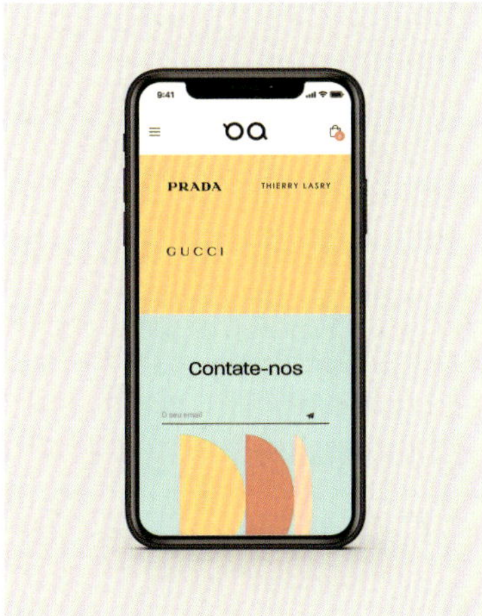
PRADA
THIERRY LASRY
GUCCI
Contate-nos

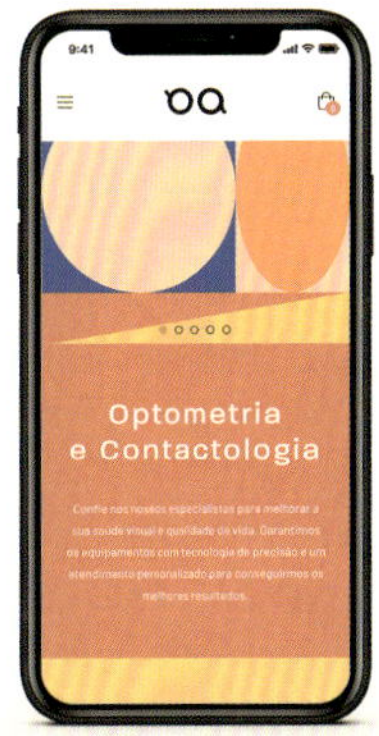
Optometria
e Contactologia

Õtica Antunes
Õtica Antunes
Õtica Antunes

BUILDHOLLYWOOD
Estamos mais perto.
www.oticaantunes.pt
Estamos mais perto.
www.oticaantunes.pt
Õtica
Antunes
Õtica
Antunes

C40	M10	Y0	K0
R161	G203	B237	
C20	M30	Y0	K0
R209	G186	B218	
C0	M15	Y20	K0
R252	G227	B205	
C30	M0	Y30	K0
R190	G223	B194	

podo Makeup Sponge Brand Packaging Design

The podo makeup sponge advocates the use of natural sponges, using the natural super-elastic sponge to gently pat the skin to create a natural and compliant makeup. The designers disassembled the English font of podo, and the circles in the text were expanded and contracted rhythmically, echoing the high elasticity of the product interestingly. For the packaging, the designers emphasized the natural and comfortable feeling, using blurred edges and gradients to express comfort. The extended parts of the makeup sponge pattern on the front and back are treated in pure white, emphasizing the product concept—the part patted by the podo will be traceless on the skin.

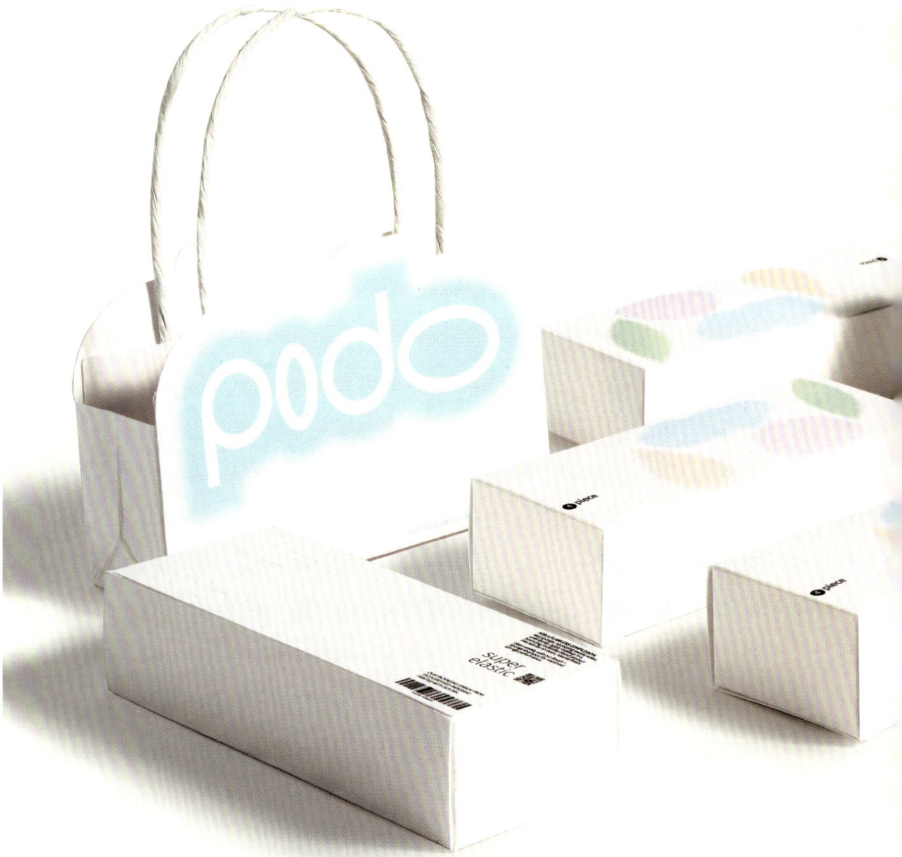

Agency/
XXD DESIGN

Art Direction & Design/
Xu Yuqing, Xiao Qiyuan

Client/
PODOPODO Co., Ltd

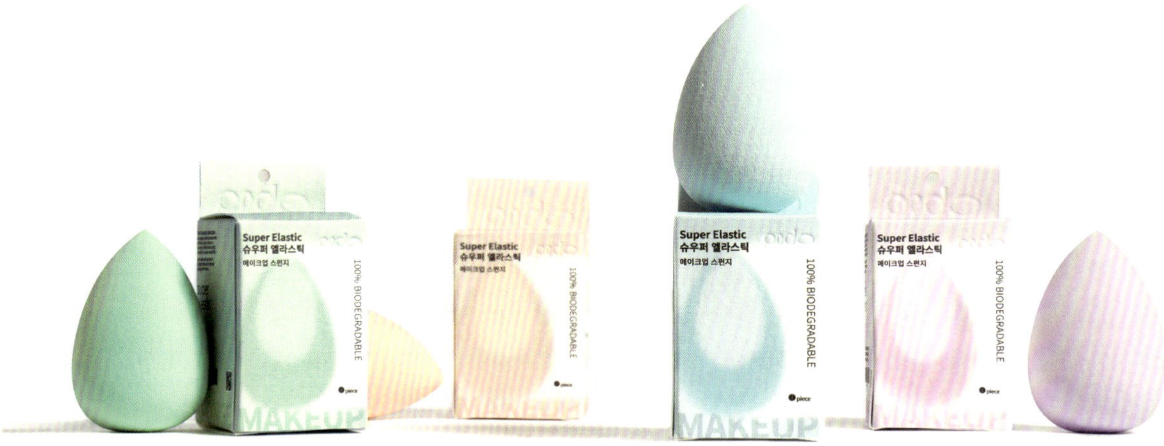
Super Elastic
슈우퍼 엘라스틱
메이크업 스펀지
100% BIODEGRADABLE
MAKEUP

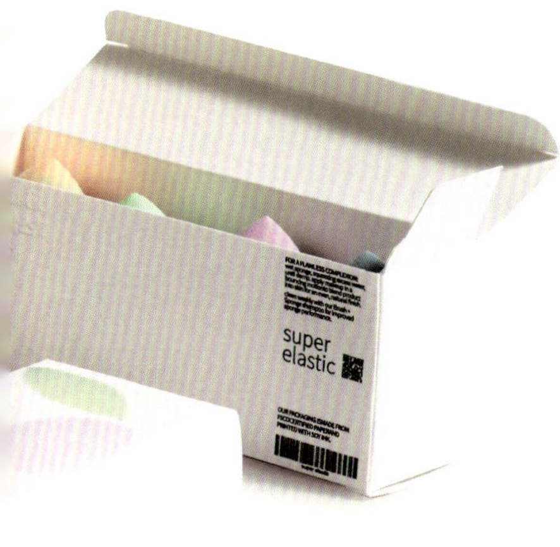
super
elastic

podo

podo

C32	M26	Y0	K0
R183	G184	B220	
C48	M0	Y50	K0
R143	G203	B151	
C0	M24	Y63	K0
R251	G205	B108	

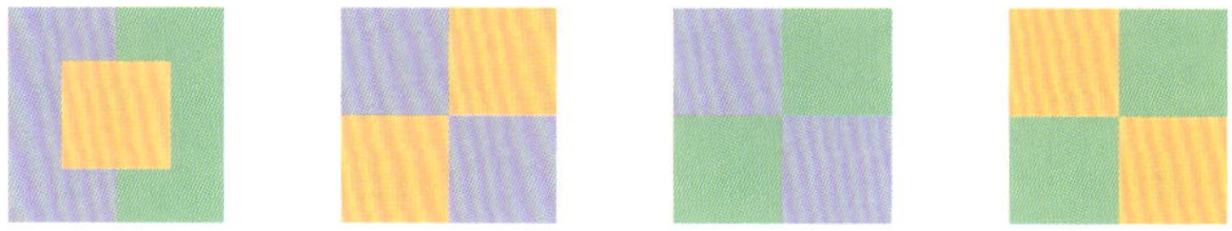

Bánkitó Festival 22

Every year, Bánkitó focuses on an important topic, which defines its programs, messages, and entire image. The designer always looks for a current and exciting topic that best summarizes the processes that affect people's daily lives. In 2023, the theme of Bánkitó is "agriculture." The main symbol of the identity is fertility and a small grain of wheat.

Design/
Réka Neszmélyi

ARTIST
SZÍNHÁZ
CREW
ALL ACCESS STAFF
PRESS PHOTO
ARTIST
ÉSZAKI SZÍNPAD
STAFF
CREW
ALL ACCESS STAFF
CREW
PRESS PHOTO
ARTIST

SÁTOR
SÁTOR
SÁTOR
SÁTOR
KÖZREMŰKÖDŐ
LÁTOGATÓ

●	C70 R64	M8 G161	Y67 B108	K10
●	C42 R161	M44 G146	Y0 B197	K0
●	C12 R218	M24 G188	Y60 B110	K8
●	C3 R250	M4 G246	Y11 B232	K0
●	C0 R0	M0 G0	Y0 B0	K100

Asóno Festival

ASÓNO is a unique open-air festival, focusing on music and nature. You will gain a new understanding of the world around you and yourself through emotional, intellectual, and physical participation.

Design/
Dima Nislin

ПОГРУЗИТЕСЬ В МУЗЫКУ,
ВПЛЕТЁННУЮ В ПРИРОДНЫЙ
ЛАНДШАФТ АРХЫЗА
МУЗЫКА
& ПРИРОДА
АРХЫЗА
5/6/7.
08.
ОТ СОФИЙСКОГО
ВОДОПАДА,
ЧЕРЕЗ ХРАМ X ВЕКА
И ОЗЕРО ЛЮБВИ,
ДО ВЕРШИНЫ ГОРЫ
ПАСТУХОВА —
В СОПРОВОЖДЕНИИ
ОРКЕСТРА ASÓNO.
2023
ASONO_FEST.COM
asóno

asóno
asóno
asóno

asóno
asóno
asóno

5/6/7.
08.
2023
asóno
МУЗЫКА
& ПРИРОДА
АРХЫЗА

asóno

C50	M45	Y80	K0
R150	G133	B76	
C0	M25	Y10	K0
R250	G209	B214	
C50	M20	Y30	K0
R142	G177	B178	
C85	M80	Y70	K50
R48	G44	B48	

TAT: Taller Alvarado Teles

ESTUDIO ALBINO developed this branding package for TAT, a Mexican architecture firm. The brand identity is focused on accentuating the craftsmanship behind the firm's work. Modules and angles placed together emulate spaces and structures. They represent the crossing point between people and the environment. The color palette reflects a search for versatility in different environments that coexist in harmony. The contrasts produced by light and shadow in spaces, warm and cold, pale and dim, make viewers feel like they are in a place that is in tune. Integrating sensitivity and balance, the mixing textures aim to protect the essence of the authentic.

Agency/
ESTUDIO ALBINO

TALLER
ALVARADO
TELES

TALLER
ALVARADO
TELES
TALLER
ALVARADO
TELES

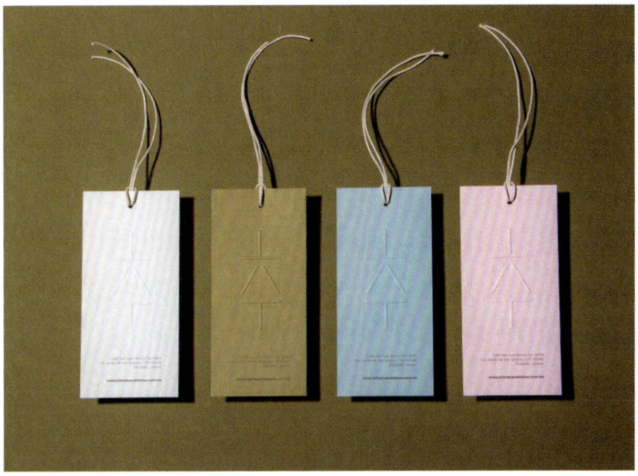

TALLER
ALVARADO
TELES
TALLER
ALVARADO
TELES
TALLER
ALVARADO
TELES

C1	M39	Y89	K0
R246	G174	B30	
C69	M35	Y11	K0
R82	G142	B189	
C37	M48	Y51	K0
R175	G140	B119	
C9	M41	Y24	K0
R229	G171	B170	

LC Coffee

Reborn in the process of grinding, slowly brewing unique flavor over time, the brand uses the letters "L" and "C" to build up a visual communication from top to bottom, forming a unique brand framework and logic.

Agency/
B&W Graphic Lab

LANCHONG
懒虫
NET WEIGHT 12 oz (340g)
A SLOW GUIDE TO LIFE
COFFEE
BEVERAGES
LANCHONG
ESPRESSO · SPECIAL · OTHER DRINK
BEVERAGES
ESPRESSO COFFEE
ESPRESSO 25
AMERICANO 27
CAPPUCCINO 30
MOCHA COFFEE 36
FLAVORED LATTE 35
SPECIAL COFFEE
MATCHA LATTE 38
CHA LATTE 35
COLD BREW 35
PLUM COLD BREW 38
OTHER DRINK
HOT CHOCOLATE 32
FRESH JUICE 29
TEA 30
LANCHONG
DAILY FREASH
FRENCH
DESSERTS
THANK YOU FOR YOUR CHOICE
LANCHONG
LANCHONG
LANCHONG
LANCHONG
乐
碰
A SLOW GUIDE TO LIFE
100% HAND MADE
DAILY FREASH
LANCHONG
DAILY FREASH
FRENCH
LANCHONG

C	M	Y	K
C75 R67	M45 G123	Y10 B179	K0
C15 R222	M30 G186	Y50 B133	K0
C15 R213	M70 G105	Y70 B72	K0
C50 R133	M70 G84	Y40 B107	K0
C0 R244	M45 G164	Y70 B82	K0
C65 R96	M15 G167	Y70 B106	K0

Beanstory

Beanstory, a subscription-based service for consumers to get beans directly, was born with a clear intent to reconnect people to what they eat, where their food comes from, and the profound impact their everyday choices have. With a selection of nine bean varieties consciously sourced from select organic farms around the US, the packaging needed to be bold and considered yet flexible enough to allow for future products. The design team designed a typeface inspired by the shape of a bean and the letter "B" that is ownable and recognizable, giving room for constant play.

Agency/
Blok Design

Photography/
Blok Design,
Danika Zandboer

beanstory
Organic Garbanzo Beans
beanstory
Organic Peruano Beans
16OZ / 454G
beanstory
Organic Rio Zape Beans
NET WT.
16OZ / 454G
beanstory
Organic Black Beans
16OZ / 454G

beanstory
Organic Silver Cloud Cannellini Beans
NET WT.
16OZ / 454G
beanstory
Organic Black Beans
16OZ / 454G
UNEARTHING BEAUTY
BEANSTORY CO.

C9 M71 Y69 K0
R232 G118 B84

C10 M31 Y74 K0
R241 G190 B91

C88 M66 Y74 K33
R33 G68 B58

C7 M9 Y16 K0
R242 G236 B223

PPGMAT

PPGMAT (Post Graduate Program in Mathematics Teaching) from the Federal University of Technology – Paraná invited the design team to redesign the department's logo and visual identity. The designers' goal was to develop an aesthetic that projected a welcoming and humane environment. The team chose recurring shapes that can create a variety of forms and compositions.

Agency/
Leste

Art Direction/
Felipe Augusto

Design/
Gustavo Andre (Logo)

Production/
Marina Bigardi

ppgmat
PROGRAMA DE
PÓS-GRADUAÇÃO
EM ENSINO
DE MATEMÁTICA

ppgmat

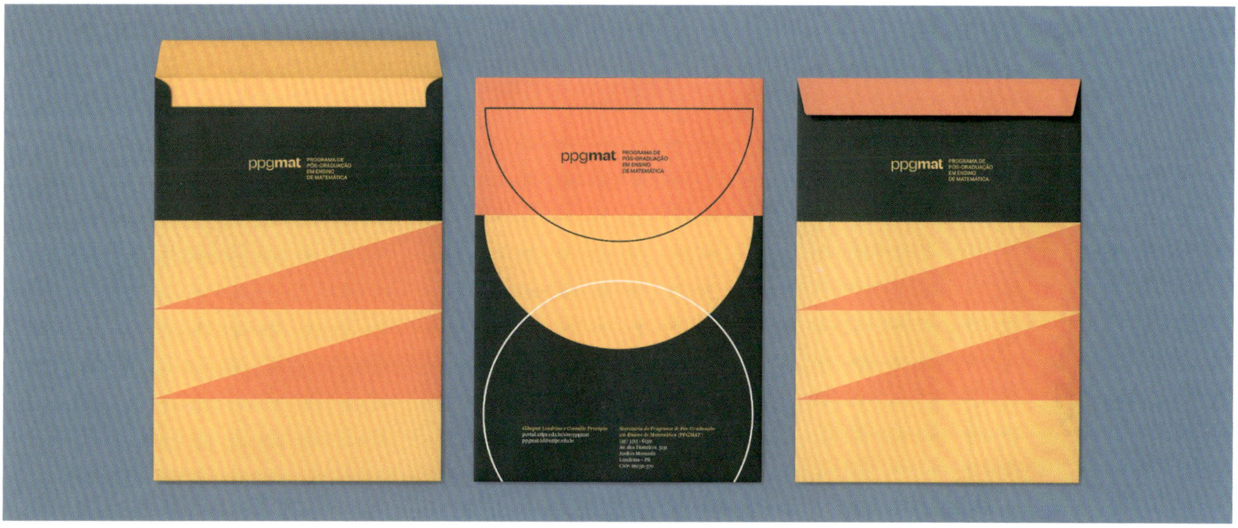
ppgmat

ppgmat
PROGRAMA DE
PÓS-GRADUAÇÃO
EM ENSINO
DE MATEMÁTICA
APRESENTAÇÃO
SOBRE O
PROGRAMA

C68 R79	M30 G127	Y60 B101	K20
C0 R244	M40 G179	Y10 B194	K0
C10 R235	M10 G227	Y28 B193	K0
C10 R42	M10 G33	Y10 B31	K95

Hotel Palacio de Arozteguia

This brand identity for the Palacio de Arozteguia hotel located in the Baztan Valley of northern Spain reflects the region's history and natural beauty. The hotel emerges as a singular project, committed to architectural heritage and local development. This redesign includes the incorporation of the hotel's old coat of arms, as well as the development of a visual identity inspired by natural elements and characteristic colors of that area, such as green, pink, and tones of local stones.

Agency/
Acc comunicación

Art Direction & Graphic Design/
Diego Bellorin

Illustration/
Diego Besné

drink txakoli
A
est 1366
drink txakoli

PALACIO de AROZTEGUIA BAZTAN
CURIO
Janiina Ojanen
Directora de Marketing
y comunicaciones
Lekaroz, Baztán, Navarra
+34 953 467 891
janiina@arozteguia.es
www.palaciodearozteguia.es
PALACIO de AROZTEGUIA BAZTAN
CURIO
Lekaroz, Baztán, Navarra
+34 953 467 891
www.palaciodearozteguia.es

ENTORNO NATURAL
est 1366
Thanks to be here!
PALACIO de AROZTEGUIA BAZTAN
Nº 13
PALACIO de AROZTEGUIA BAZTAN
Nº 08
PALACIO de AROZTEGUIA BAZTAN
Nº 02
PALACIO de AROZTEGUIA BAZTAN
CURIO
Reservation
Date
Time
Name
Email
Room
PALACIO de AROZTEGUIA BAZTAN

AROZTEGUIA
POSTCARD FROM BAZTAN
PALACIO de AROZTEGUIA BAZTAN
"the Navarran Switzerland", an almost magical place that shelters an infinity of towns and hamlets with an extensive history

Chili Paloma healthy cocktail
Cocktails
Tres Brujas
Aviation
Breakfast Martini
Clover Club
Corpse Reviver No Blue
Cuba Libre
Mint Julep

●	C87 R0	M31 G116	Y74 B84	K19
●	C0 R243	M44 G170	Y12 B186	K0
	C7 R241	M5 G241	Y6 B239	K0
●	C15 R228	M0 G233	Y60 B128	K0

Thai Wok Rebranding

Thai Wok contains original herbs, fresh vegetables, unique recipes, and high-quality ingredients without GMOs and glutamate. In the rebranding, as in the former, nature is the basis. The new design aims to emphasize the freshness of the ingredients further, bring the brand closer to nature, and indicate kinship with Thai culture and Asian cuisine in general.

Design/
Nastia Butkevich

Photography/
Pexels, Adobe Stock

Thai Wok
Thai Wok
Thai Wok
Thai Wok
Thai Wok
Thai Wok

Thai Wok
thaiwok.pl
Thai Wok
thaiwok.pl
Thai Wok
thaiwok.pl
Thai Wok
thaiwok.pl

Thai Wok
Thai Wok
Thai Wok
thaiwok.pl
Thai Wok

Thai Wok
thaiwok.pl
Thai Wok
thaiwok.pl
Thai Wok
thaiwok.pl
Thai Wok

C0	M80	Y10	K0
R232	G82	B142	
C25	M19	Y19	K0
R200	G201	B200	
C68	M4	Y83	K0
R79	G176	B86	
C88	M91	Y28	K0
R61	G52	B117	

Blanc Festival n.10

Born in 2009, Blanc Festival is one of the most important graphic design festivals in our country. The winning combination of a familiar approach with a high-level lineup has made of Blanc a must-go event for designers from Catalonia and Spain.

We were commissioned to design the visual identity and the opening credits for its 10th edition.

The identity is based on the fact that all inks (design) tend to white (blanc, in Catalan) with the effect of time (10th anniversary).

Agency/
Forma

Blanc Festiva
n.10 del 18 al
20 d'octubre
al Casino
de l'Aliança
del Poblenou,
Barcelona
blancfestival.com
#blancfest
Alex Trochut, Bruce Mau, Bisi Williams, Patrick Thomas,
Mario Eskenazi, Jordi Duró, Naranjo-Etxeberria, Noe Blanco,
Onionlab, Esiete, Ana Mirats Studio, Javier Royo, Marc Català
+ Tilman Solé + Pancho Tolchinsky, Alexandra Zsigmond,
Núria Vila, The Bold Studio, Eide Estudio, Ana Illueca,
Verónica Fumanal, Monstruo Espagueti i Luis Armero.
Blanc Festival
n.10 del 18 al
20 d'octubre
del Poblenou,
Barcelona

Blanc
Festival
n.10

Blanc
Festival
n.10

Alex

Gràcies!!!

Amics del Blanc
Núria Vila
The Bold Studio
Ana Llueca
Eide Estudio

Blanc
Festival
n.10

C35	M15	Y95	K0
R192	G199	B15	
C62	M75	Y0	K0
R152	G75	B214	
C8	M11	Y15	K0
R238	G229	B217	

Taaveti laulud

Taaveti laulud means "Psalms of David." The design team made the poster design for Kammerkoor Voces Tallinn's performance of the cycle "Psalms of David" under the direction of Pärt Uusberg.

Agency/
Frank Wo

UUSBERG
Taaveti
laulud
VOCES TALLINN
L 01.10 kl 18
Tartu Jaani kirikus
Kammerkoor VOCES TALLINN
Dirigent PÄRT UUSBERG
Esiettekanne
KREEK
Tallinn

UUSBERG
KREEK

TAAVETI LAULUD
L 01.10 kl 18
Tartu Jaani kirikus
Kammerkoor VOCES TALLINN
Dirigent PÄRT UUSBERG
Esiettekanne
UUSBERG
KREEK

C0	M53	Y80	K0
R242	G146	B57	
C10	M49	Y0	K0
R224	G155	B194	
C44	M48	Y0	K0
R157	G137	B191	
C53	M0	Y13	K0
R119	G202	B222	
C89	M66	Y0	K0
R26	G86	B166	
C84	M95	Y0	K0
R73	G39	B139	
C44	M0	Y100	K0
R160	G201	B18	

Speak Up Conference

Speak Up Conference is the most popular Youth Christian Conference in Belarus. It's an annual weekend event where young Christians can gather for worship and fellowship.

The designer has created a bold and multicolor visual identity for the conference. The use of bright colors is one of the most impressive aspects of the identity. The colors are used in a way that is both playful and sophisticated. They help to create a sense of energy and positive impressions. The lettering piece "Speak Up" is a beautiful and creative example of how typography can be used to create a visually appealing and meaningful design.

Design/
Alina Gonchar

speakup.conference
Минск
speakup.conference
Минск
speakup.conference
Минск

C0	M84	Y82	K0
R233	G74	B46	
C42	M0	Y6	K0
R154	G214	B236	
C95	M89	Y24	K13
R32	G49	B114	
C25	M45	Y93	K16
R180	G134	B31	

FESTEME

Agency/
Tiquismiquis.club

Production/
Vicente Luque

Production Team/
Andrea Pérez, Antonio Rodríguez

Digital Marketing/
Sábado

Photography/
India Gitana

FESTEME, a Spanish musical theater festival, presents as a unique initiative that celebrates and encourages the creation of original productions within the theatrical-musical genre. It's a national reference that had its first edition in Córdoba from October 13 to 16, 2022. It is a cultural and creative explosion that served as an intersection and platform for professional artists of theater, music, dance, literature, design, etc. More than a festival, it's a collective, collaborative, and multidisciplinary creation movement for artistic promotion and innovation. The design team has worked on elements, such as the pentagram, and concepts like the movement that they captured graphically through the use of asymmetric horizontal lines that interfere and add dynamism to the identity. In addition, the typographic presence is important. The use of Galgo and Cabinet Grotesk provides the composition with closeness and personality to the event, making it recognizable.

CORDOBA
Festeme

Festeme
Festeme

1er Festival de Teatro
Musical Español
13–16 OCT 2022
Córdoba
Festeme

Pantone 7463 C
C100 M53 Y0 K72
R0 G43 B73

Pantone 2174 C
C90 M44 Y0 K0
R0 G118 B206

Pantone 545 C
C20 M0 Y0 K0
R198 G218 B231

Pantone 165 C
C0 M68 Y96 K0
R255 G103 B32

Rodrigo Marchondes

Dr. Rodrigo Marcondes, a famous physiotherapist and former scientist, focuses on translating academic knowledge into a humanized clinical practice guided by scientific evidence. Through an ethical and dynamic approach he aims to enhance sports functions with minimal pain. Inspired by his academic journey, the brand emphasizes personalized care, symbolized by cells and DNA. The core value centers on evidence-based practices depicted graphically.
The symbol harmonizes cell, DNA, data, and movement, epitomizing personalized, scientifically grounded physiotherapy for aspiring athletes. The color palette, featuring shades of blue for seriousness and calm, alongside vibrant orange for movement and modernity, complements the brand's essence.

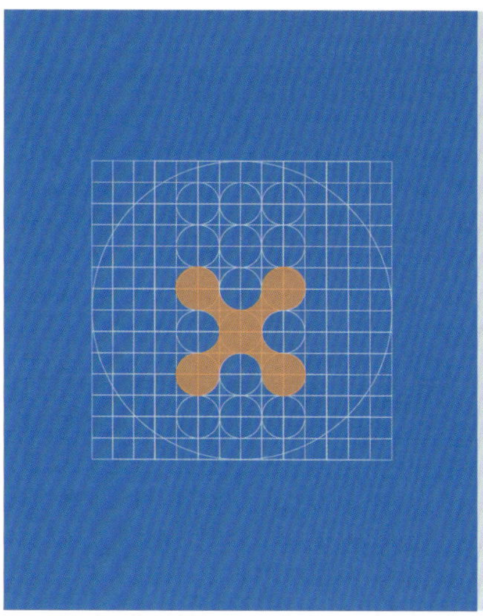

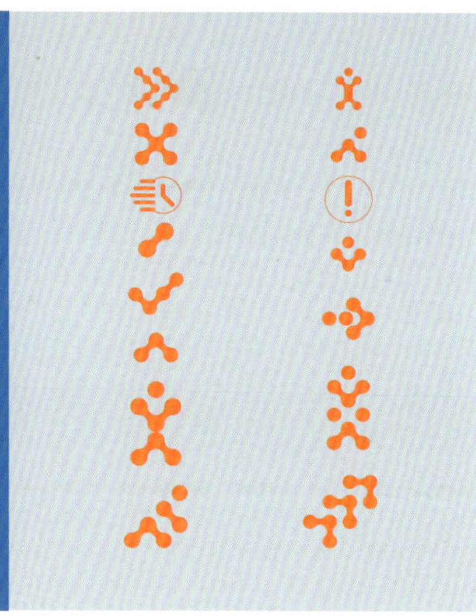

Design/
Eduardo Nolasco

Rodrigo Marcondes
Fisioterapeuta, PhD
(11) 9.9898-1223
(11) 3445- 0948
rodrigomarcondes@fisio.com.br
Rua Delphino Alves Gregório, 755
Vila Mogilar, Mogi das Cruzes

Rodrigo Marcondes
Rodrigo Marcondes

Rodrigo Marcondes
Fisioterapeuta, PhD.

Rodrigo Marcondes
Ciclismo
Rodrigo Marcondes
Corrida
Rodrigo Marcondes
Musculação
Rodrigo Marcondes
Natação

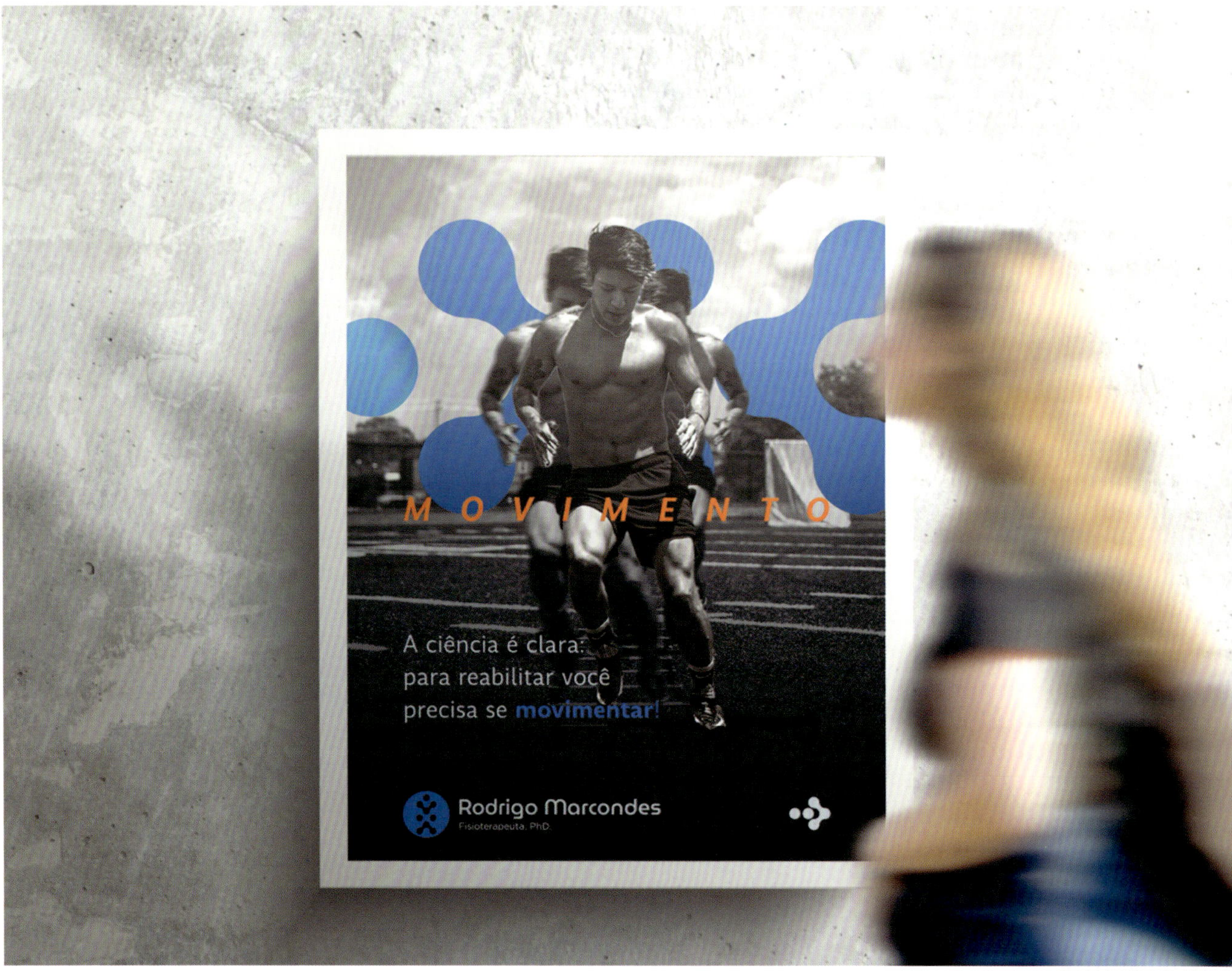
MOVIMENTO
A ciência é clara:
para reabilitar você
precisa se movimentar!
Rodrigo Marcondes
Fisioterapeuta, PhD.

A fisioterapia baseada em
EVIDÊNCIAS
Rodrigo Marcondes
Seu tratamento
para dor começa
no primeiro passo.
Rodrigo Marcondes
Nós cuidamos
de você com
MO
VI
MEN
TO
Rodrigo
Marcondes
Cuidamos de você
para que você
cuide melhor de você.
Movimente-se
todo dia
Rodrigo
Marcondes
A melhora
vem do
movimento.
Rodrigo Marcondes
Movimento é
cura.
Rodrigo Marcondes

A ciência é clara,
MO
VI
MEN
TE
SE
Rodrigo Marcondes
Ciência &
Ciclismo &
Corrida &
Natação &
Ventosa
Rodrigo Marcondes
Nós cuidamos
de você com
mO
Vi
MeN
tO

C1	M98	Y98	K0
R235	G32	B36	
C32	M0	Y33	K0
R173	G217	B186	
C62	M8	Y0	K0
R70	G185	B234	
C61	M47	Y41	K10
R108	G117	B125	
C34	M71	Y76	K29
R134	G75	B57	

Anthony Clark

Anthony Clark is a freelance photographer based in the UK who specializes in portrait photography. He mainly shoots black and white photos with deep focus on people's facial expressions, especially on the emotions and experiences evoked by his subjects' eyes.

The color palette took inspiration from the colors that usually appear in the camera setting and menu. These colors also resemble with the RGB colors which people are usually familiar with. The designer also combined this idea with the human eye colors as well, where the eyes are usually the main emotional capture in most of his client's works.

Design & Art Direction/
Liam Nguyen

Client/
Anthony Clark

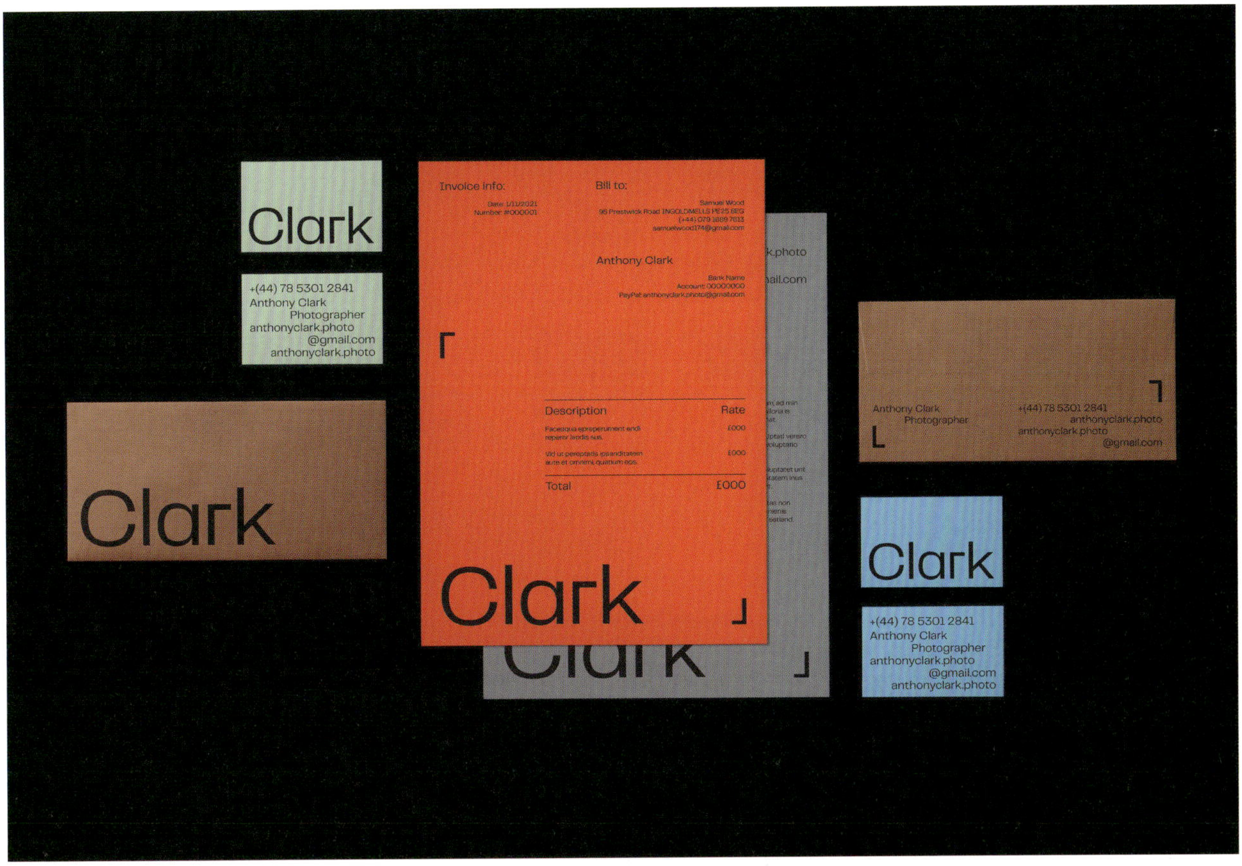
Clark
+(44) 78 5301 2841
Anthony Clark
Photographer
anthonyclark.photo
@gmail.com
anthonyclark.photo
Invoice info:
Bill to:
Anthony Clark
Description
Rate
Total
£000
Clark
Clark
Anthony Clark
Photographer
+(44) 78 5301 2841
anthonyclark.photo
anthonyclark.photo
@gmail.com
Clark
+(44) 78 5301 2841
Anthony Clark
Photographer
anthonyclark.photo
@gmail.com
anthonyclark.photo

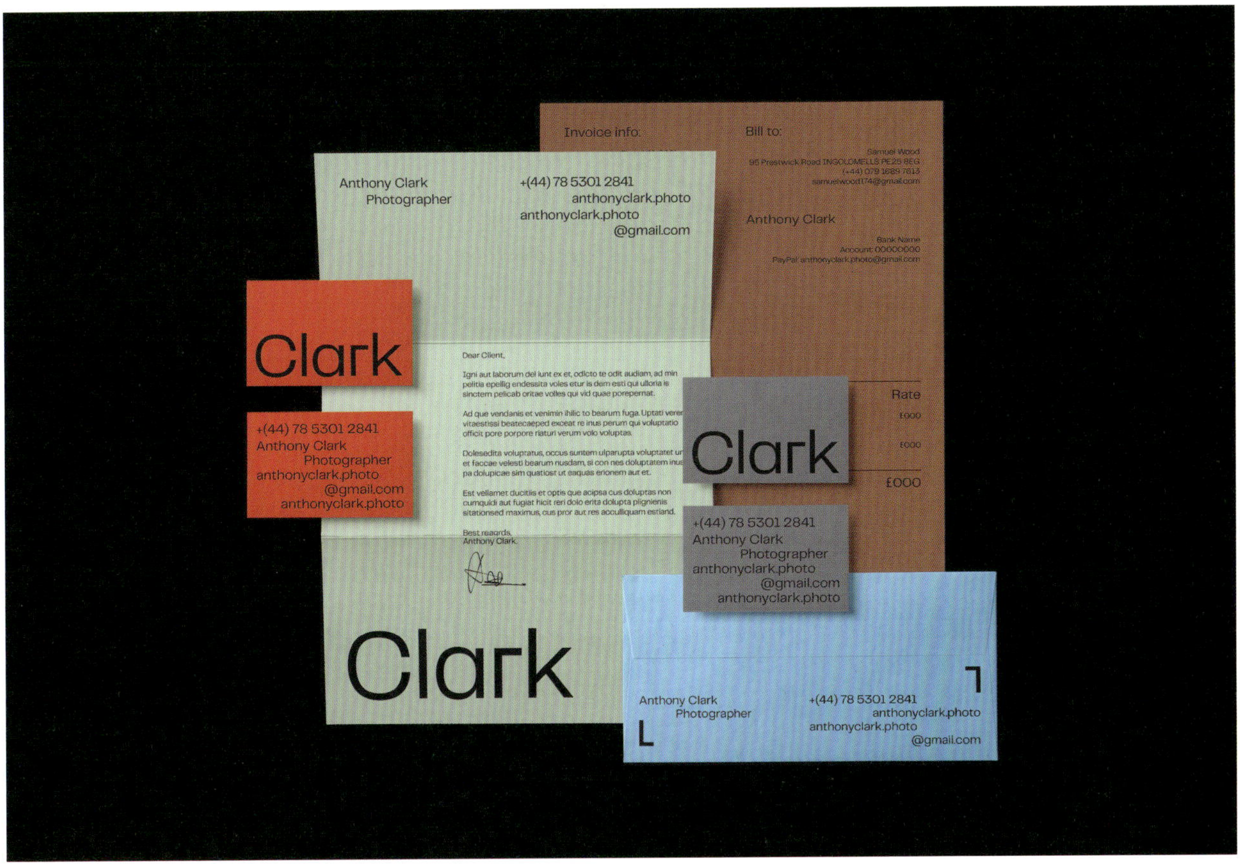
Invoice info:
Bill to:
Anthony Clark
Photographer
+(44) 78 5301 2841
anthonyclark.photo
anthonyclark.photo
@gmail.com
Anthony Clark
Clark
+(44) 78 5301 2841
Anthony Clark
Photographer
anthonyclark.photo
@gmail.com
anthonyclark.photo
Dear Client,
Rate
£000
Clark
+(44) 78 5301 2841
Anthony Clark
Photographer
anthonyclark.photo
@gmail.com
anthonyclark.photo
Clark
Anthony Clark
Photographer
+(44) 78 5301 2841
anthonyclark.photo
anthonyclark.photo
@gmail.com

C3	M45	Y81	K0
R239	G156	B62	
C18	M83	Y84	K7
R192	G67	B47	
C88	M31	Y77	K22
R2	G109	B76	
C0	M47	Y27	K0
R245	G164	B163	
C79	M70	Y62	K89
R17	G17	B17	

sesoni

The design team took charge of the naming, visual identity, and photography for sesoni, a local business of sustainable urban gardening and bioclimatic architecture based in Valencia, Spain. “Sesoni” is the pronunciation of “Seasons” in Bulgarian, the native country of Lily Deneva, the soul of this beautiful project. The design team wanted to create a brand that mixed the disciplines of architecture and gardening, and express the idea of transformation that happens through the seasons of a year. The flexible visual language mixes straight, organic lines, and colors.

Agency & Photography/
errorerror.studio

sesoni
JARDINERÍA URBANA SOSTENIBLE & ARQUITECTURA BIOCLIMÁTICA. LILY DENEVA. ARQUITECTA & TÉCNICA PAISAJISMO.
[T] 620 004 430
[M] LILY@SESONI.COM
[C] VALENCIA
[W] SESONI.COM
[IG] @_SESONI

talleres
abril · junio
JARDINERÍA [URBANA] SOSTENIBLE
24 ABR PLANTAS DE POCO RIEGO Y [BAJO MANTENIMIENTO]
7 MAY CUIDADOS PARA CERRAR E INICIAR CICLOS [VEGETALES]
21 MAY HUERTO URBANO. PREVENCIÓN Y [ACTUACIÓN]
18 JUN CÓMO RODEARTE DE PLANTAS [EN CASA]
12€ /TALLER
[10:30H – 12:30H] HORARIO
LLAMA Y RESERVA TU PLAZA [620 004 430]
TURIA, 60 LILY@SESONI.COM @_SESONI
talleres
ene · mar
JARDINERÍA [URBANA] SOSTENIBLE
19 ENE ELECCIÓN DE PLANTAS PARA [ESPACIOS] DOMÉSTICOS
26 FEB PREPARA TUS PLANTAS PARA LA [PRIMAVERA]
12 MAR INICIA TU [HUERTO URBANO]
12€
[10:30H – 12:30H] HORARIO
LLAMA Y RESERVA TU PLAZA [620 004 430]
TURIA, 60 LILY@SESONI.COM @_SESONI
talleres
abril · junio
JARDINERÍA [URBANA] SOSTENIBLE
24 ABR PLANTAS DE POCO RIEGO Y [BAJO MANTENIMIENTO]
7 MAY CUIDADOS PARA CERRAR E INICIAR CICLOS [VEGETALES]
21 MAY HUERTO URBANO. PREVENCIÓN Y [ACTUACIÓN]
18 JUN CÓMO RODEARTE DE PLANTAS [EN CASA]
12€
[10:30H – 12:30H] HORARIO
LLAMA Y RESERVA TU PLAZA [620 004 430]
TURIA, 60 LILY@SESONI.COM @_SESONI

sesoni
sesoni
sesoni

taller
ELECCIÓN DE PLANTAS PARA [ESPACIOS] DOMÉSTICOS
19FEB
10:30H – 12:30H
C/ TURIA, 60
[NIVEL] PRINCIPIANTE
10€
10€
taller
C/ TURIA, 60
[NIVEL] PRINCIPIANTE
INICIA TU [HUERTO URBANO]
12MAR
10:30H – 12:30H
PREPARA TUS PLANTAS PARA LA [PRIMAVERA]
26FEB
10:30H – 12:30H
C/ TURIA, 60
[NIVEL] PRINCIPIANTE
10€
taller

C4	M93	Y96	K0
R240	G40	B20	
C82	M34	Y100	K0
R35	G135	B55	
C73	M74	Y88	K54
R55	G45	B30	

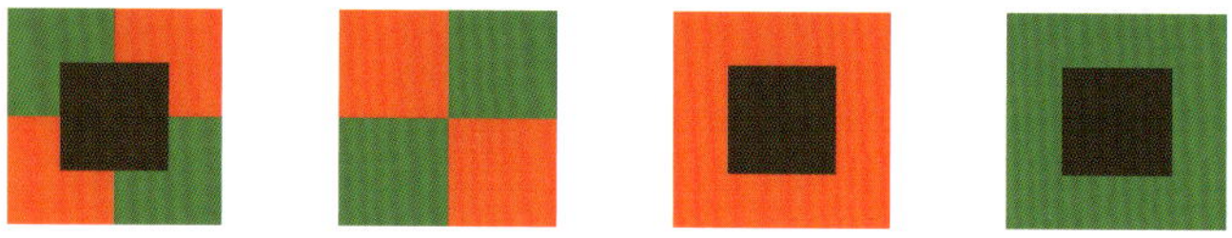

Diàlegs de Sant Jordi 2023

Agency/
Forma

Organized by Biblioteques de Barcelona, Diàlegs de Sant Jordi is an event consisting of three days of conversations and talks between writers from all over the world based on similarities in their latest works. We were commissioned to design the campaign for the 2023 edition.

Diàlegs de
Sant Jordi '23
del 19 al 22
d'abril
Biblioteques
de Barcelona

Pl. Universitat
Diàlegs de
Sant Jordi '23
del 19 al 22
d'abril
Biblioteques
de Barcelona

Diàlegs de
Sant Jordi '23
del 19 al 22
d'abril
Biblioteques
de Barcelona
barcelona.cat/biblioteques
19 d'abril
Gabriela Adamesteanu
Juan Gómez Bárcena
20 d'abril
21 d'abril

C	M	Y	K
C91 R0	M79 G0	Y62 B0	K97
C61 R115	M29 G157	Y56 B126	K0
C56 R138	M59 G116	Y7 B178	K0
C21 R214	M84 G70	Y13 B144	K0
C9 R235	M72 G104	Y78 B56	K0
C2 R255	M3 G249	Y17 B223	K0

Personal Branding

Design/
Vanessa Rudger

This visual identity project developed for the designer's own studio combines sturdy, enigmatic forms with a simple restricted color palette.

WHERE
HAVE
MY WINGS
GONE?
VANE
SSA
graphic designer

B-E-Y-O-N-D
YOU
DESIGN
S
E
E

take a time to think about
DESIGN BEYOND
YOU SEE

C	M	Y	K
C22 R189	M0 G204	Y99 B51	K0
C82 R36	M66 G92	Y0 B224	K0
C1 R231	M81 G75	Y89 B37	K0
C16 R241	M51 G199	Y0 B232	K0
C38 R135	M44 G114	Y52 B96	K30
C80 R0	M9 G161	Y60 B128	K0
C55 R132	M55 G118	Y0 B181	K0
C25 R200	M18 G202	Y18 B202	K0
C0 R231	M96 G31	Y84 B41	K0

Winifred Cultural Center

Agency/
Parco Studio

Design/
Loredana Bontempi, Emanuele Bonetti

Winifred is an innovative cultural center, a project of the Municipality of Crema (Italy), which has recovered a beautiful space in the historic complex of Sant'Agostino—a disused library now ready to host culture again. The goal is to create a cultural innovation laboratory open to the whole town.

The identity of the cultural center is colorful, with a unique and recognizable palette that brings energy and familiarity with a range of colors from warm to cold, from saturated to delicate grey.

For the logo, the designers designed the "W" and the space signs, to

guide the user through the doors of this historic building into a new reality, a new space dedicated to the future.

The typography plays an essential role because it identifies this cultural presence right from the entrance, and is declined in numerous variations following the material that needs to be presented, from publications to prints and digital events.

Also, photography is the protagonist of Winifred's work—using art images and enriching the more informal pictures for workshops.

← Winifred
Caffetteria →
Winifred →

In questo laboratorio intensivo si sperimenteranno diversi linguaggi espressivi dove l'azione performativa indaga e lascia emergere le proprie urgenze, i propri stati emotivi e le proprie dinamiche interne per dare forma, movimento e voce a quelle parti di noi spesso inascoltate.
Sono fuori di me
Arti performative per adulti
Workshop con
Elisa Tagliati
10/06, ore 15–18

Il corso si svolgerà in presenza e ha l'obiettivo di fornire una formazione di base sui temi della scrittura, produzione fino alla distribuzione per un podcast.
Il workshop prevede un numero massimo di 12 partecipanti e le iscrizioni saranno registrate in ordine di arrivo.
Premere REC
Ideare, progettare e realizzare un podcast
Workshop con
Mariachiara Montera
27/05, ore 9–17

Quali sono le competenze richieste, le sfide da affrontare, le opportunità da cogliere e i percorsi da seguire?
Proviamo a dare alcune risposte a queste e altre domande con i professionisti invitati e con alcuni workshop che proporremo durante l'Open Day. I partecipanti avranno la possibilità di muoversi
Target
Obiettivo
Bonus finale
Aperitivo per tutti
Open Day
Professioni di oggi verso il futuro
21/05, ore 15:30

Winifred
Centro d'innovazione culturale
Crema
Art as Political Activism
Vida Americana: mexican muralists remake american art.
L'esposizione è la più grande retrospettiva dedicata al lavoro e all'attivismo di Claudia Andujar, che ha trascorso oltre cinquant'anni a fotografare e proteggere gli Yanomami, uno dei più grandi gruppi indigeni del Brasile oggi minacciato dai cercatori d'oro illegali e dai rischi di contagio.
23/09 — 25/01/2021
winifred

Centro d'innovazione culturale
Crema
André Cepeda
Ballad of Today
23/09 — 25/01/2021
winifred
His project seems like a long walk through a city, at first hesitant, then accelerating. In bright daylight, at dusk, in the dark, in the gloom of the night, along many different cross paths, that lead up to the alluring yet simultaneously repellent glare of the business district and down the dark suction of the sewers. André Cepeda seems to follow the dogs, the strays, the paths of the night owls and the unemployed through the channels of a confusing organism. Silently, with few direct contacts, but with a heightened state of attention, with a perception that seems to unite smell, touch and sight into one big all-embracing sense.
The city André Cepeda immerses himself in is Lisbon. Two years ago he moved with his family to Lisbon from Porto, after early years in the Netherlands and his youth in Coimbra, with sojourns in Belgium. He wanders, creeps into his new city, digs himself into it, pushes himself off, searches, questions and combs through it — less in a descriptive way, less in the form of an overview, more as if he wanted to pierce the body of the city with his camera, punch holes into it, rub against it, sharpen his senses and his thinking in its complexity.

Centro d'innovazione culturale
Crema
Vida Americana: Mexican Muralists Remake American Art.
Art as Political Activism
23/09 — 25/01/2021
His project seems like a long walk through a city, at first hesitant, then accelerating. In bright daylight, at dusk, in the dark, in the gloom of the night, along many different cross paths, that lead up to the alluring yet simultaneously repellent glare of the business district and down the dark suction of the sewers. André Cepeda seems to follow the dogs, the strays, the paths of the night owls and the unemployed through the channels of a confusing organism. Silently, with few direct contacts, but with a heightened state of attention, with a perception that seems to unite smell, touch and sight into one big all-embracing sense.
The city André Cepeda immerses himself in is Lisbon. Two years ago he moved with his family to Lisbon from Porto, after early years in the Netherlands and his youth in Coimbra, with sojourns in Belgium. He wanders, creeps into his new city, digs himself into it, pushes himself off, searches, questions and combs through it — less in a descriptive way, less in the form of an overview, more as if he wanted to pierce the body of the city with his camera, punch holes into it, rub against it, sharpen his senses and his thinking in its complexity.
winifred

Winifred
Centro d'innovazione culturale
Crema
winifred
André Cepeda
Ballad of Today
L'esposizione è la più grande retrospettiva dedicata al lavoro e all'attivismo di Claudia Andujar, che ha trascorso oltre cinquant'anni a fotografare e proteggere gli Yanomami, uno dei più grandi gruppi indigeni del Brasile oggi minacciato dai cercatori d'oro illegali e dai rischi di contagio.
23/09 — 25/01/2021

Pantone	C	M	Y	K
Pantone Orange 021 C	C0	M80	Y100	K0
	R255	G95	B25	
Pantone Yellow C	C0	M5	Y100	K0
	R255	G225	B0	
Pantone 3385 C	C60	M0	Y40	K0
	R0	G215	B170	
Pantone 2282 C	C30	M0	Y60	K0
	R190	G235	B150	
Pantone 2129 C	C70	M40	Y0	K0
	R110	G135	B255	
Pantone 291 C	C40	M0	Y0	K0
	R140	G220	B255	
Pantone 2582 C	C40	M70	Y0	K0
	R210	G50	B255	
Pantone 2375 C	C5	M50	Y0	K0
	R255	G130	B255	
Pantone 2755 C	C100	M5	Y0	K85
	R15	G20	B65	

Guri

Guri is a musical education and sociocultural inclusion program run by the Government of the State of São Paulo (Brazil) and the State Department of Culture and Creative Economy. Since its foundation in 1995, it has served more than one million young people, promoting human development through music and culture.

Agency/
Papanapa

Creative Direction/
Gustavo Garcia

Design/
Cássia Freire, Gustavo Kone, Lucas Rodrigues, Luana Cordeiro

Motion Design/
Gustavo Kone

Project Management/
Lucas Rodrigues

Client/
Guri

CORAL DO GURI
Polo Ourinhos
4 de junho
Domingo, às 17h
Teatro Municipal Miguel Cury, em Ourinhos/SP
Sob regência de Vinícius Guedes

GURI

Polo Itaquá
Regente
GURI
Polo São Paulo
GURI
PROFESSOR
Polo Sorocaba
PROFESSOR
GURI

GURI

música e cultura
GURI
inspirando vidas
A formação do Guri é assim.
Valorizamos o protagonismo de cada aluno e aluna, sempre pensando na sua relação com o todo: o coro, a orquestra, o público e a sociedade.
Santa Marcelina
GURI
Secretaria da Cultura e Economia Criativa
SP SÃO PAULO GOVERNO DO ESTADO

GURi
ecoar HISTORIAS
Saiba mais em:
guri.org.br
Matrículas abertas
a partir do dia
19 de janeiro.

sinfonica
Banda sinfonica
Sob regência de
Devanildo Balmant

artepub
DO GURI
percussão
Sob regência de
Devanildo Balmant
3 DE JUNHO
Sábado, às 20h
Auditório da Banda e Orquestra
Municipal de Bauru/SP
SÃO PAULO

Boarding
Sinfonica
Banda
JCDecaux
SÃO PAULO

artepub
Guri
de CORDAS
do GURI
artepub
Polo Ourinhos
4 de Junho
Confira a programação:
Conhecendo
instrumento
SÃO PAULO

C	M	Y	K
C0 R255	M10 G227	Y80 B63	K0
C20 R214	M20 G194	Y90 B0	K0
C40 R170	M40 G148	Y95 B41	K0
C50 R135	M25 G170	Y0 B217	K0
C0 R232	M80 G84	Y38 B109	K0
C80 R0	M35 G136	Y35 B164	K0
C44 R148	M0 G211	Y9 B230	K0

C	M	Y	K
C100 R29	M30 G179	Y0 B211	K0
C6 R222	M95 G37	Y95 B27	K0
C0 R234	M70 G109	Y0 B164	K0
C0 R253	M18 G212	Y85 B42	K0
C65 R54	M0 G189	Y0 B239	K0
C100 R0	M30 G128	Y0 B203	K0
C90 R0	M0 G161	Y70 B114	K0

Korea Public Design Awards 2023

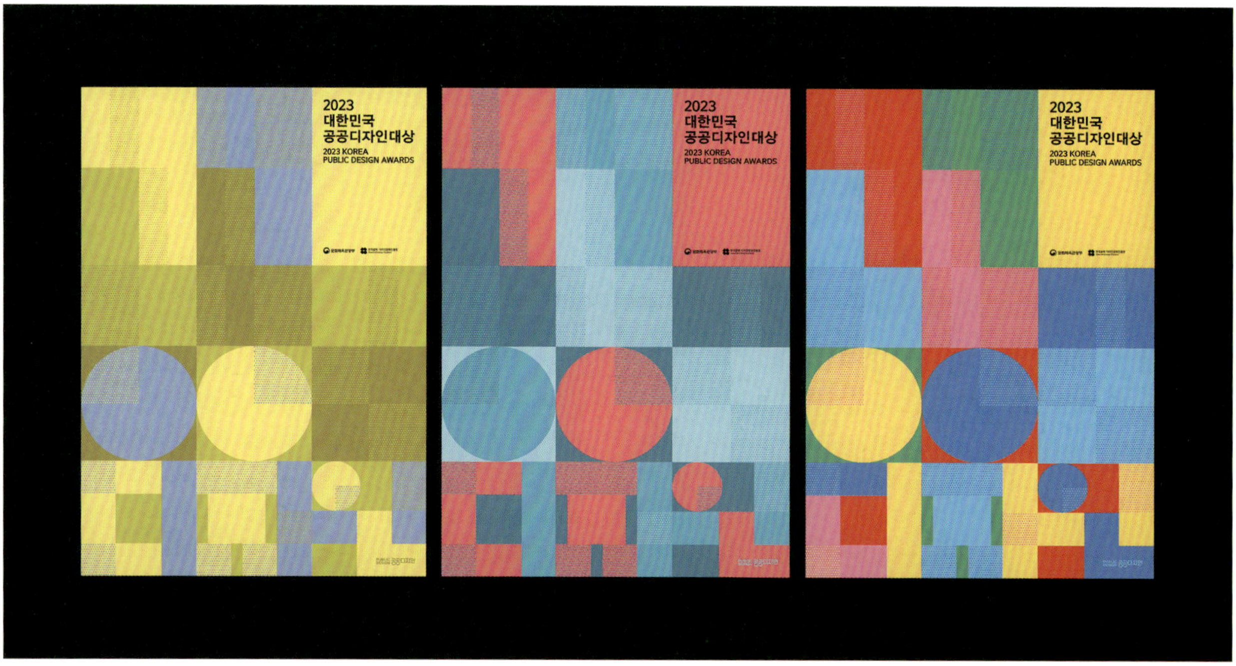

Agency/
MAUM STUDIO

Creative Direction/
Dalwoo Lee

Art Direction/
Yoonji Lee

Design/
Jeawon Chung (Graphic)
Hyeonsoo Joe (Motion/Editorial)

Project Management/
Minjeong Woo, Yujin Choi (KCDF)

MAUM STUDIO designed and created posters and graphic productions for the contest, as well as field productions, trophies, and casebooks needed for the awards ceremony held in October 2023.

The visual motif is public design coming together to create a better tomorrow. Using the colors that humans can see, such as those with normal color vision and those with color vision impairment, as a motif, representative colors are set in the palette and applied to graphics. Patterns (textures) that help people with color vision impairment to recognize shapes are applied to graphics.

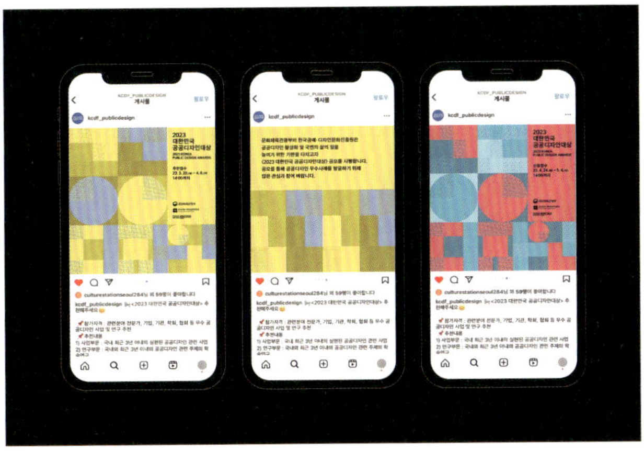

디자인
DESIGN
2023
대한민국
공공디자인대상
디자인하우스 M+ 에서
더 많은 인사이트를
발견하세요!
KOREA DESIGN
AWARD 2022

공공디자인 종합정보시스템
사업소개
사업안내
공공디자인 인증발급
지식정보
알림소식
같이 만들고 함께 나누는
공공디자인
2023
대한민국
공공디자인대상
2023 KOREA
PUBLIC DESIGN AWARDS
추천접수
23. 3. 20.(월) - 4. 6.(목) 14:00까지
신청접수
23. 4. 24.(월) - 5. 4.(목) 14:00까지
최근소식
반려견 공원에 스며 있는 디자이너의 생각
동대구역 광장, 공공디자인으로 '재탄생'
같이의 가치 국내외 반려동물 친화 공간 사례

대한민국
공공디자인
대상
2023
대한민국
공공디자인대상
시상식
Korea Public Design
Awards 2023
공공디자인
국민아이디어
공모전

C	M	Y	K
C80 R40	M32 G92	Y52 B77	K54
C0 R255	M5 G205	Y100 B0	K0
C50 R117	M40 G120	Y34 B123	K17
C0 R239	M100 G51	Y89 B64	K0
C100 R0	M69 G71	Y0 B187	K0
C81 R95	M99 G36	Y0 B159	K0
C84 R0	M0 G198	Y74 B94	K0
C92 R0	M0 G166	Y12 B200	K0
C63 R110	M53 G124	Y6 B160	K8
C0 R254	M67 G80	Y100 B0	K0
C1 R181	M97 G37	Y31 B85	K18

MYLIGHT

Agency/
LMD

Art Direction & Concept/
Lucas Machado

Design/
Ângela Mayume (Assistant)
Studio Rodolfo Brizola (3D)

LMD's approach integrated the essence of the company's name "MYLIGHT" with its educational offerings, resulting in a symbol reminiscent of both rays of light and the pages of an open book. For the book covers, the design team derived patterns from the symbol's design, incorporating horizontal, vertical, and angled lines. These patterns not only enhance visual appeal but establish a cohesive aesthetic across the collection. To streamline book organization within the packaging, the designers introduced vertical text on the covers. This addition serves as a navigational aid, akin to the functionality of a book spine, facilitating easy identification and retrieval of specific titles.

ENGLISH
01
LEVEL 1
VOCABULARY

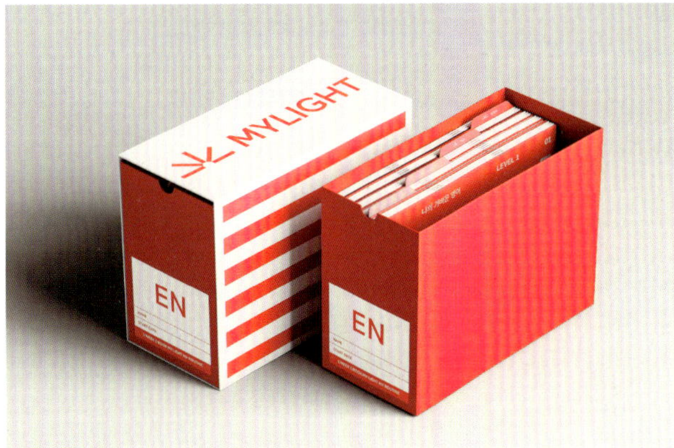
MYLIGHT
EN
EN

MYLIGHT
AR
CN
DE
EN
FR
ID
IT
JP
RU
SP
TR

MYLIGHT

Pantone	C	M	Y	K
Pantone 877 C	C10	M6	Y7	K21
Pantone 802 C	C51	M0	Y85	K0
Pantone 2736 C	C97	M95	Y0	K0
Pantone 185 C	C0	M93	Y79	K0
Pantone 803 C	C0	M3	Y97	K0
Pantone 801 C	C85	M0	Y8	K0
Pantone 806 C	C0	M72	Y0	K0

TEAM KOREA GOODS

MAUM STUDIO planned, designed, and produced goods to promote and commemorate the Korean Sport & Olympic Committee. The color of the stadium, which is characterized by the seven sports of the Korea Sports Council, is the motif of the overall design, which is comprised of postcards, stickers, pouches, towels, and bowls. The design team aims to create bright, appealing products with attractive graphics.

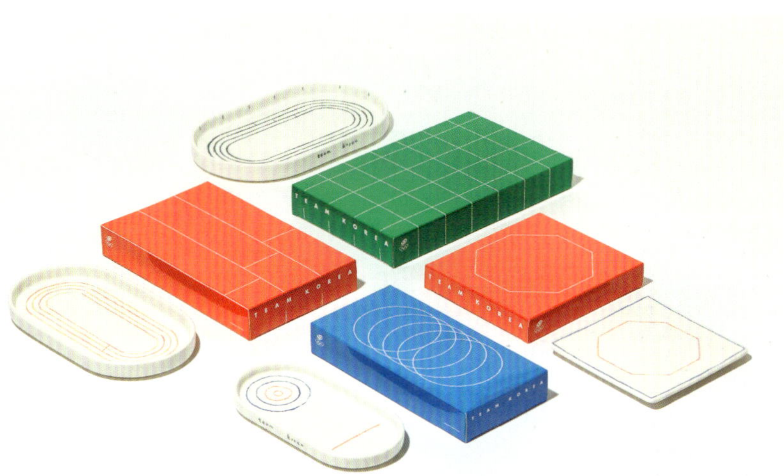

Agency/
MAUM STUDIO

Creative Direction/
Dalwoo Lee

Art Direction/
Yoonji Lee

Design/
Jaewon Chung (Graphic)

Photography/
Juyeon Lee

FENCING
SWIMMING
CURLING
ATHLETICS
SHOOTING

TEAM KOREA
TEAM KOREA

C	M	Y	K
C17 R210	M55 G138	Y0 B185	K0
C76 R94	M12 G164	Y100 B40	K0
C24 R209	M18 G209	Y17 B211	K0
C82 R33	M77 G33	Y79 B31	K60
C84 R68	M54 G116	Y0 B224	K0

FAD FORUM

Bakoom Studio took charge of the art direction and communication design for FAD Forum 2022 which organized conferences and workshops where the main topic was artificial intelligence applied to the professional practice of art, design, and architecture. The graphic identity must be flexible enough to be used in different formats.

Agency/
Bakoom Studio

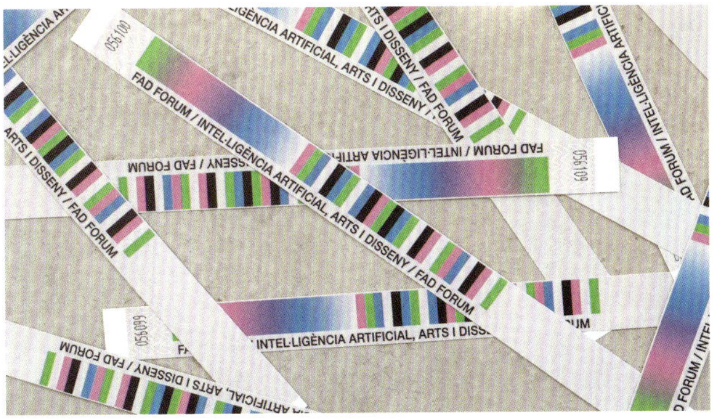

FAD FORUM / INTEL·LIGÈNCIA ARTIFICIAL
056100
056099

OSCAR HORMIGOS
> COLECCIÓN SOLO & ONKAOS
DIRECTOR CREATIVO
FAD FORUM / INTEL·LIGÈNCIA ARTIFICIAL, ARTS I DISSENY / FAD FORUM / INTELIGENCIA ARTIFICIAL, ARTES Y DISEÑO

FAD FORUM
SHAJAY BOOSHAN
ZAHA HADID ARCHITECTS
Enviar mensajes
Enviar mensajes
fad_barcelona
FAD FORUM
17.06
2022

C49	M0	Y74	K0
R134	G248	B116	
C90	M40	Y67	K44
R6	G80	B68	
C27	M56	Y0	K0
R229	G130	B232	
C69	M96	Y22	K11
R105	G41	B107	
C11	M3	Y5	K0
R233	G240	B242	

Robolab

Robolab is a robotics brand focusing on the development of children and adolescents through robotics and thus also encouraging sports. The brand's main objective is to provide an educational culture of robotics to develop children and teenagers and provide knowledge to practice the sport.

Agency/
Studio Xico Liborio

Client/
Thyago Neves

ROBOLAB
ROBOLAB
Oportunidades ilimitadas de aprendizado e crescimento.
ROBOLAB

ROBOLAB

ROBOLAB
ROBOLAB
ROBOLAB
Aprender, adaptar e superar.
Oportunidades ilimitadas de aprendizado e crescimento.
ROBOLAB
ROBOLAB
ROBOLAB
ROBOLAB
Somos uma equipe, apoiando uns aos outros em nossa jornada.
Construimos pontes entre a curiosidade e a descoberta.
ROBOLAB

ROBOLAB
ESPORTE
PARA
MENTE
ROBOLAB

ROBOLAB
Somos uma equipe,
apoiando uns aos
outros em nossa
jornada.

ESPORTE
PARA
MENTE
ROBOLAB
Construímos
pontes entre a
curiosidade e
a descoberta.

ROBOLAB
ROBOLAB
Inspiramos a
próxima geração
de inovadores.

Chapter 3

Bold and Bright

The combination of different hues with high value and high saturation creates a vibrant atmosphere in this chapter.

●	C49 R132	M0 G206	Y11 B226	K0
●	C0 R255	M2 G241	Y79 B67	K0
●	C56 R123	M0 G191	Y87 B73	K0
●	C40 R166	M51 G134	Y0 B188	K0

Amics Imaginaris

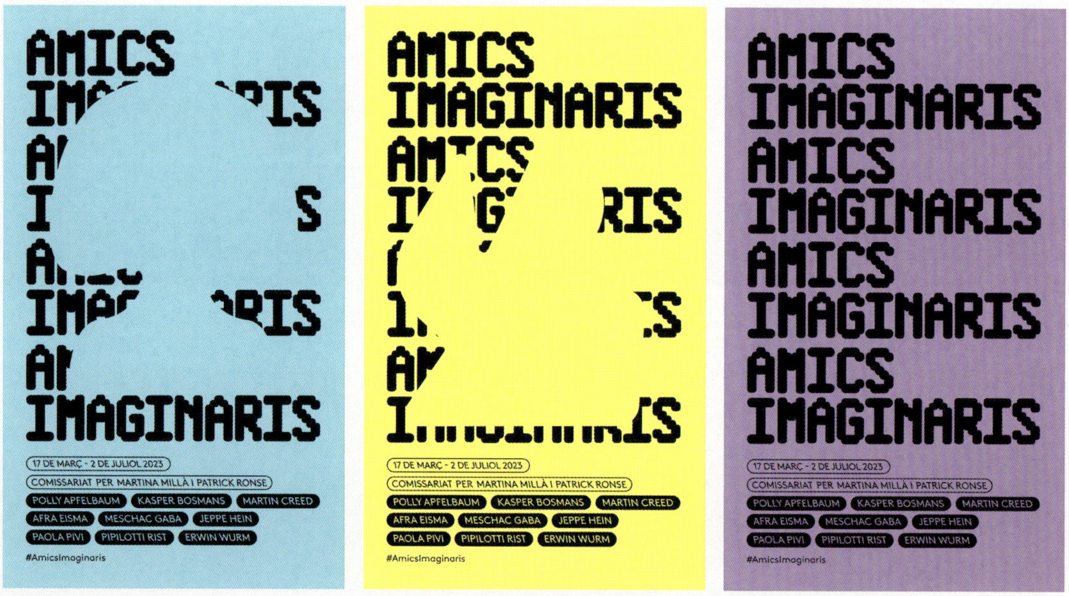

Agency/
Toormix

Photography/
JovalArderiu Studio

Client/
Fundació Joan Miró

Amics Imaginaris (Imaginary Friends) is the first exhibition at the Fundació Joan Miró in Barcelona that presents a selection of works and installations by nine contemporary artists. The concept on which the designers articulate the design is the imaginary space that is created between the artistic piece and the spectator, that space that people compliment, that friend that only someone can see and that only someone can imagine. The communication generates hollow spaces within the composition to make the idea explicit. The participation of the spectator is the key to completing the proposal. The designers created a specific typeface called New Mercat for the project.

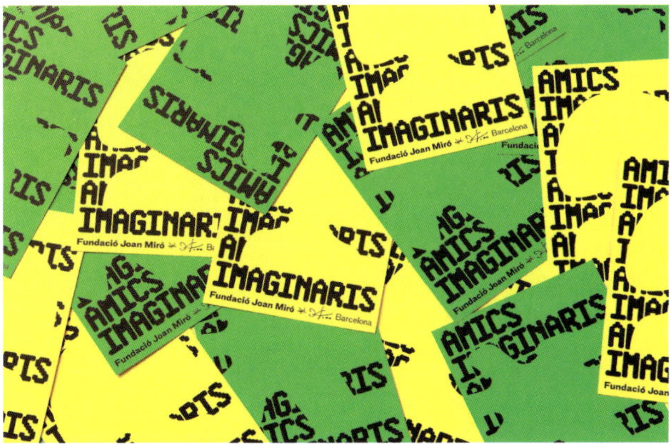
AMICS IMAGINARIS
Fundació Joan Miró Barcelona

HAVE FUN!
L'ART TAMBÉ ÉS DIVERTIT
Fundació Joan Miró Barcelona

IMAGINARY FRIENDS
AMICS IMAGINARIS

ESPAI PER A LA IMAGINACIÓ
Fundació Joan Miró Barcelona
HAVE FUN! L'ART TAMBÉ ÉS DIVERTIT
ESPAI PER A LA IMAGINACIÓ
AMICS IMAGINARIS

C	M	Y	K
C61 R78	M0 G217	Y46 B171	K0
C0 R251	M58 G132	Y80 B56	K0
C81 R20	M69 G22	Y61 B23	K85
C6 R242	M5 G240	Y6 B240	K0
C0 R255	M21 G204	Y84 B51	K0
C72 R48	M0 G181	Y60 B133	K0

Sepsi Tabakó Festival

Agency/
Bloomberry Agency

Design/
Gósuly Timea (Logo), Fekete Balázs, Péntek Réka, Szőke Timea, Vajas Aliz

Collaboration/
Diversity Advertising

Held in the historical tobacco factory of Sfântu-Gheorghe, Romania, the Sepsi Tabakó Festival celebrates local culture and history, creating a bridge between the past and the present. The challenge was to design a brand image that encapsulated the spirit of the festival and its unique setting. The designers drew inspiration from the festival's rich heritage and the dynamism of its musical performances, leading them to the use of spirals and vivid colors. The spiral, a symbol of growth and evolution, was a nod to the festival's transformative power in reviving the old tobacco factory. The vibrant color palette was chosen to mirror the festival's energy and diversity. The result was a distinctive brand image that paid homage to the festival's historical roots while capturing its contemporary relevance and vibrancy.

TRAFIK
ARTIST
TECH
PRESS
SEPSI TABAKÓ FESTIVAL
VENDOR
SEPSI TABAKÓ FESTIVAL
VOLUNTEER
SEPSI TABAKÓ FESTIVAL
SPEAKER

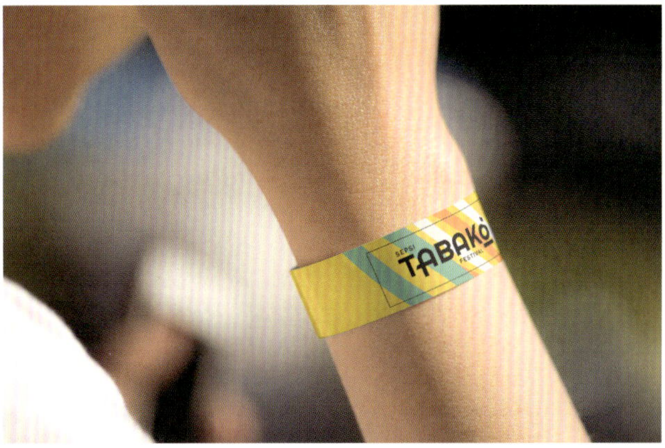
SEPSI TABAKÓ FESTIVAL

SEPSI TABAKÓ FESTIVAL

SEPSI TABAKÓ FESTIVAL
PUNNANY MASSIF CARSON COMA
MARGARET ISLAND ANNA & THE BARBIES
FOLLOW THE FLOW IRIE MAFFIA
SZEMPÖL HŐSÖK SAIID DZSÚDLÓ
BYEALEX ÉS A SLEPP AZAHRIAH
ALEE BSW BRAINS BETON.HOFI
KONYHA RICSÁRDGIR 3AD
HOUSE OF PIONEERS ÁLLJUNK MEG!
DREAMFLOW A CSAJOD
SEPSI TABAKÓ FESTIVAL
MARGARET ISLAND
SEPSI TABAKÓ FESTIVAL
SEPSI TABAKÓ FESTIVAL
CARSON COMA
SEPSISZENTGYÖRGY 2022 SZEPTEMBER 1-3.
SFÂNTU GHEORGHE 2022 1-3. SEPTEMBRIE

C	M	Y	K	R	G	B
C78	M10	Y71	K0	R43	G166	B117
C3	M0	Y94	K0	R253	G238	B27
C31	M0	Y13	K0	R173	G222	B224
C3	M89	Y69	K0	R231	G66	B77
C39	M58	Y71	K22	R136	G98	B75
C0	M30	Y25	K0	R250	G190	B175
C0	M75	Y71	K0	R242	G103	B79
C38	M0	Y4	K0	R151	G217	B237
C66	M44	Y0	K0	R88	G131	B195

Teixeta Music Festival

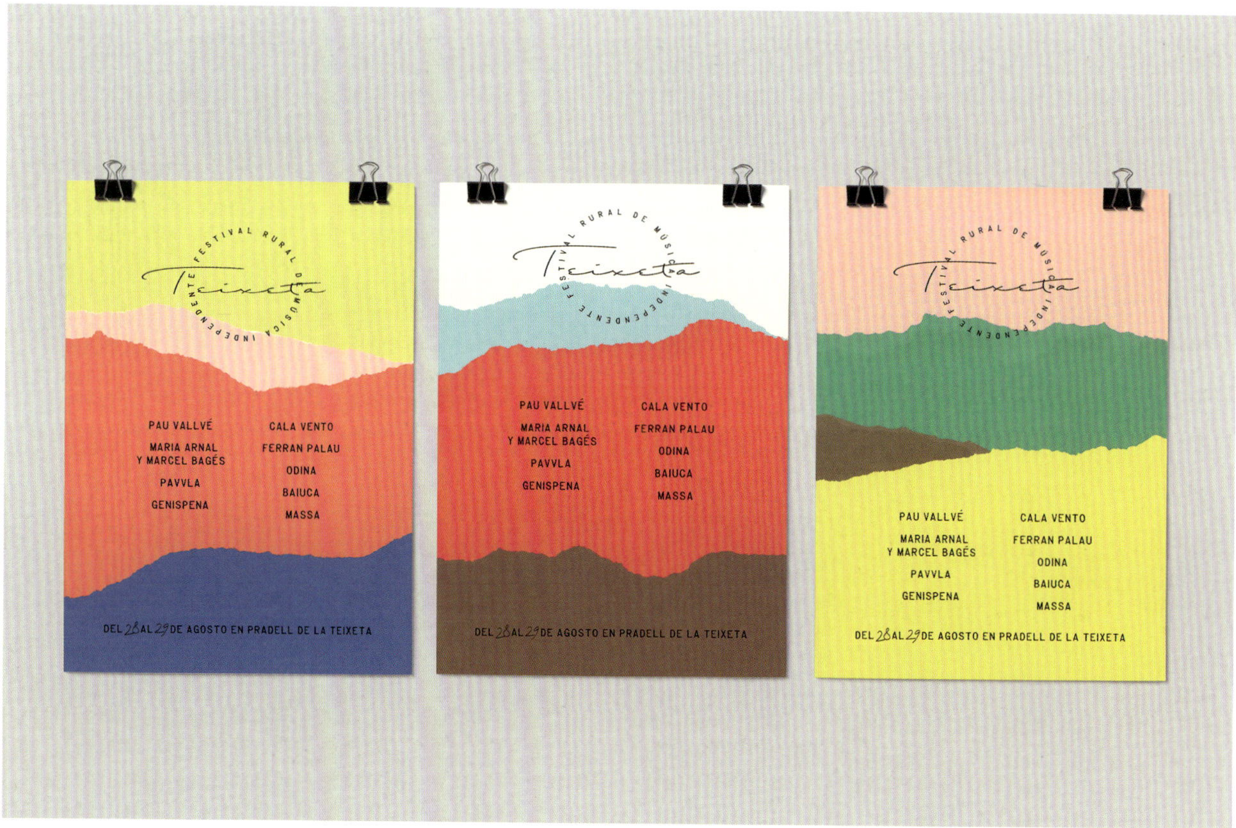

Art Direction & Design/
Victor Mazariegos

Concept/
Victor Mazariegos, Carolina Monreal

This attractive visual identity created for a Rural Music Festival in the village of Pradell de la Teixeta (Catalonia, Spain) utilizes sensuous colors and simple forms to attract concert-goers.

STAFF
PRENSA
ARTISTA

MASSA
PAVVLA
MARIA ARN
MARCEL B
BAIUCA
AU VALLVE

C39 R162	M0 G217	Y4 B241	K0
C15 R210	M93 G48	Y100 B25	K0
C7 R226	M75 G96	B88 B38	K0
C11 R230	M20 G212	Y0 B231	K0
C67 R88	M5 G175	Y98 B54	K0
C3 R245	M32 G187	Y81 B60	K0

Wine - Good Twin

Good Twin is an alcohol-free wine made from organic grapes, available in three varieties: Spanish Red, Spanish White, and Spanish Rosé.

The design team was tasked with creating the visual identity and packaging, which features bold colors and typography to infuse energy into this delightful and guilt-free beverage. Double thumbs up for a delicious taste without the hangover!

Agency/
Forth+Back

3D Visualization/
Sample Studio

Client/
Winc

ALCOHOL REMOVED WINE
Good Twin
SPANISH ROSÉ
MADE WITH ORGANIC GRAPES
ALCOHOL REMOVED WINE
Good Twin
SPANISH RED WINE
MADE WITH ORGANIC GRAPES
ALCOHOL REMOVED WINE
Good Twin
SPANISH WHITE WINE
MADE WITH ORGANIC GRAPES

Twin
SPANISH WHITE WINE
MADE WITH ORGANIC GRAPES

ALCOHOL REMOVED WINE
Twin
SPANISH ROSÉ
MADE WITH ORGANIC GRAPES

Good
Twin
SPANISH RED WINE
MADE WITH ORGANIC GRAPES

Twin

C94	M75	Y0	K0
R40	G74	B154	
C12	M2	Y0	K0
R231	G242	B253	
C0	M44	Y100	K0
R245	G158	B0	
C9	M9	Y21	K0
R237	G229	B209	
C0	M93	Y100	K0
R229	G42	B18	
C80	M43	Y0	K0
R44	G125	B193	
C29	M7	Y15	K0
R193	G216	B218	
C0	M11	Y6	K0
R253	G235	B235	

Armónico Bakery

Armónico Bakery is a project conceptually based on the idea of balance, seeking harmony between delicacy and health. The brand uses organic forms to explore the concept of balance. All the graphic compositions try to have a balance between form and space. The color palette is soft with pastel tones. And some strong tones create contrast.

Art Direction & Graphic Design/
Aragon Estudio

Illustration/
Brenda Cardona

C0	M48	Y0	K0
R255	G166	B209	
C0	M62	Y59	K0
R255	G132	B94	
C35	M0	Y6	K0
R171	G235	B255	
C35	M40	Y0	K0
R195	G161	B255	

MOZOO

Agency/
Brand Brothers

Creative Direction/
Johan Debit

Mozoo is a social content factory founded in 2010 and employs over 60 people. As an expert digital agency, Mozoo helps innovative companies adapt to an increasingly complex and fast-paced technological environment creatively and effectively. Their motto: "Creating at the speed of change" by imagining brand stories anchored in their time around the disciplines of brand content, social media, and video production on Web3. Mozoo set a challenge for Brand Brothers—redefining the visual identity of one of Paris' most energetic creative agencies.

Brand Brothers worked with the agency on this major narrative and graphic overhaul, based on an agile, lively identity proposition. Wishing to

position it as a purely creative structure, the designers first strengthened and simplified the typographic logo around 100% custom lettering, robust, massive, and contemporary, to establish the name in the panorama of Parisian agencies. Introduced in four neon shades, black and white, and two accompanying typefaces (Parafina, Feliciano Type and Diatype, Dinamo), the new visual system is made up of generative waves whose shape is infinitely adaptable. As a dynamic graphic illustration of Mozoo's signature, the waves cohabit with the agency's productions and messages. The designers developed the comprehensive graphic standards that synthesize the entire new visual language, which is used in multiple vectors, both print and digital.

CREATING AT THE SPEED OF CHANGE
WEAREMOZOO @ WEAREMOZOO @ WEAREMOZOO
MOZOO
CREATING AT THE SPEED OF CHANGE
WEAREMOZOO @ WEAREMOZOO @ WEAREMOZOO

MOZOO
NICOLAS BILLIÈRES
DIRECTEUR MARKETING
37 BOULEVARD DES CAPUCINES 75002 PARIS
NICOLAS MOZOO.COM
MOZOO.COM
@ WEAREMOZOO

MOZOO
MENU
BRAND CONTENT TIKTOK PRODUCTION VIDEO AMPLIFICATION
TOUS NOS PROJETS
CONTACT
@ WEAREMOZOO
CREATING AT THE SPEED OF CHANGE
Agence créative digitale, fondée en 2010 et située au cœur de Paris.
Nous aidons les entreprises innovantes à s'adapter de façon créative et efficace à l'évolution toujours plus complexe des technologies, des comportements et des usages.

CREATING AT THE SPEED OF CHANGE
MOZOO.COM
@ WEAREMOZOO
MOZOO

MOZOO
CREATING AT THE SPEED OF CHANGE
BRAND CONTENT
TIKTOK
AMPLIFICATION
@ WEAREMOZOO

CREATING
AT THE SPEED
OF CHANGE
MOZOO

MOZOO
CREATING AT THE
SPEED OF CHANGE

CREATING
AT THE SPEED
OF CHANGE
MOZOO
@
WE
ARE
MO
ZOO
MOZOO
CREATING
AT THE SPEED
OF CHANGE
MOZOO

C0	M70	Y0	K0
R237	G110	B167	
C0	M83	Y96	K0
R232	G70	B26	
C0	M98	Y81	K0
R228	G19	B45	
C81	M0	Y93	K0
R0	G165	B70	
C44	M31	Y0	K0
R155	G168	B214	
C6	M6	Y9	K0
R242	G239	B234	

Sexto 'Nplugged

This identity proposal for the 18th edition of Sexto 'Nplugged, an alternative music festival centered around intimacy and sound experimentation, seeks to capture the essence of the event's unique atmosphere.

The limited color scheme conveys a sense of sophistication and minimalism, while the boldness of the palette injects energy and excitement, mirroring the daring spirit that defines the festival.

Design/
Lorenzo Tre

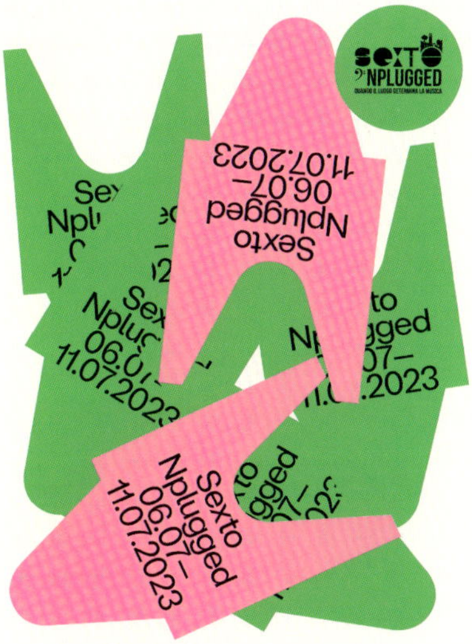
Sexto Nplugged 06.07– 11.07.2023

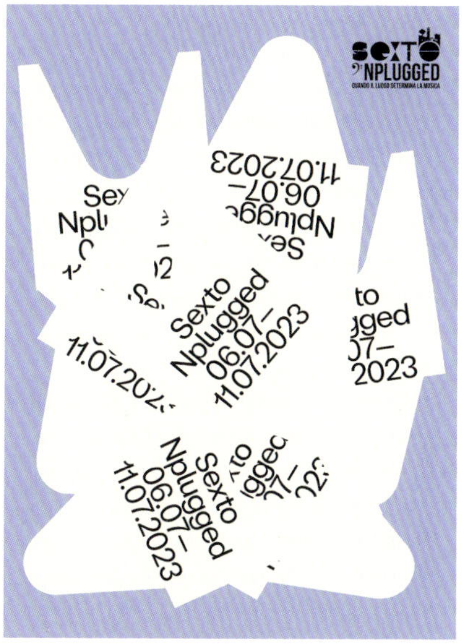
Sexto Nplugged 06.07– 11.07.2023

Sexto Nplugged 06.07– 11.07.2023

Programma Festival
XVIII edizione
Sexto Nplugged 2023
06—11 Lug, 2023
Sesto al Reghena
06.07.2023
Hania Rani
07.07.2023
King Hannah
09.07.2023
Ben Howard
11.07.2023
Dry Cleaning
Piazza Castello Sesto al Reghena

Programma Festival
XVIII edizione
Sexto Nplugged 2023
06—11 Lug, 2023
Sesto al Reghena
06.07.2023
Hania Rani
07.07.2023
King Hannah
09.07.2023
Ben Howard
11.07.2023
Dry Cleaning
Piazza Castello Sesto al Reghena

Programma Festival
XVIII edizione
Sexto Nplugged 2023
06—11 Lug, 2023
Sesto al Reghena
06.07.2023
Hania Rani
07.07.2023
King Hannah
09.07.2023
Ben Howard
11.07.2023
Dry Cleaning
Piazza Castello Sesto al Reghena

Programma Festival
XVIII edizione
Sexto Nplugged 2023
06—11 Lug, 2023
Sesto al Reghena
06.07.2023
Hania Rani
07.07.2023
King Hannah
09.07.2023
Ben Howard
11.07.2023
Dry Cleaning
Piazza Castello Sesto al Reghena

Programma Festival
XVIII edizione
Sexto Nplugged 2023
06—11 Lug, 2023
Sesto al Reghena
06.07.2023
Hania Rani
07.07.2023
King Hannah
09.07.2023
Ben Howard
11.07.2023
Dry Cleaning
Piazza Castello Sesto al Reghena

Programma Festival
XVIII edizione
Sexto Nplugged 2023
06—11 Lug, 2023
Sesto al Reghena
06.07.2023
Hania Rani
07.07.2023
King Hannah
09.07.2023
Ben Howard
11.07.2023
Dry Cleaning
Piazza Castello Sesto al Reghena

C6 R253	M0 G237	Y89 B0	K0
C0 R255	M85 G56	Y94 B0	K0
C0 R255	M37 G187	Y12 B197	K0
C20 R215	M2 G232	Y17 B221	K0
C74 R29	M65 G29	Y63 B27	K81

TAC! Urban Architecture Festival

TAC! is an annual festival organized by Spain's Ministry of Transport, Mobility, and Urban Agenda in collaboration with the Arquia Foundation, which promotes innovation and experimentation in architecture through the construction of a temporary pavilion in different cities throughout Spain. The festival unites contemporary architecture, young practice, and reflection on the urban and social through meetings and cultural activities around the pavilion that will dialogue with citizens. To provide this new brand with its visual universe, the design team explored the architecture beyond buildings, interpreting the construction of space in its most essential sense. They defined a dynamic grid that forms structures delimiting the space and defining which elements are outside and which are inside. The visual identity can adapt to all types of formats, content, and proposals, integrating an institutional dimension with a contemporary cultural event.

Agency/
The Woork

Convocatoria
Abierta para
el Diseño del
Pabellón
TAC!

MIEMBRO → 03 DE 07
Marta
Torrejón
14 SEP/
13 NOV
Nueva
Convocatoria
2023
TAC!
SEGUNDO
PREMIO
T!
GRANADA
TAC! Festival
de Arquitectura
14 OCT / 14 NOV

TAC!
Festival de
Arquitectura
Urbana

#TAC!FESTIVAL
TAC!
Festival de
Arquitectura
Urbana

C	M	Y	K	R	G	B
C75	M5	Y99	K0	R46	G167	B58
C71	M5	Y0	K0	R0	G178	B234
C0	M70	Y0	K0	R235	G110	B65
C15	M100	Y100	K0	R209	G17	B27
C0	M1	Y11	K0	R255	G251	B234
C0	M11	Y91	K0	R255	G255	B0
C0	M68	Y98	K0	R237	G112	B0
C85	M38	Y0	K0	R0	G127	B198
C0	M51	Y10	K0	R241	G154	B179
C48	M45	Y0	K0	R146	G140	B195
C0	M0	Y100	K0	R255	G241	B0

Mittelfest

Mittelfest is a multidisciplinary international festival that celebrates the finest live entertainment from Central Europe. For its 32nd edition, the festival embraces the theme "Inevitable," brought to life through a minimalist, type-driven design and a restricted color palette. The visual identity, lead by the domino motif, explores the theme's with striking simplicity and thoughtful symbolism.

Agency/
DM+B&Associati

Design/
Lorenzo Tre

M/TTEL
FEST
—/N
EV/
TA
B/LE

M/TTEL
FEST
—/N
EV/
TA
B/LE

M/TTEL
FEST
CIVIDALE
DEL FRIULI
—/N
EV/
TEATRO
DANZA
MUSICA
CIRCO
TA
21–30
07.2023
B/LE

M/TTEL
FEST
—/N
EV/
TA
B/LE

M/TTEL
FEST
—/N
EV/
TA
B/LE

M/TTEL
FEST
—/N
EV/
TA
B/LE

M/TTEL
YOUNG
—/N
CIVIDALE
DEL FRIULI
EV/
TA
TEATRO
DANZA
MUSICA
CIRCO
18–21
05.2023
B/LE

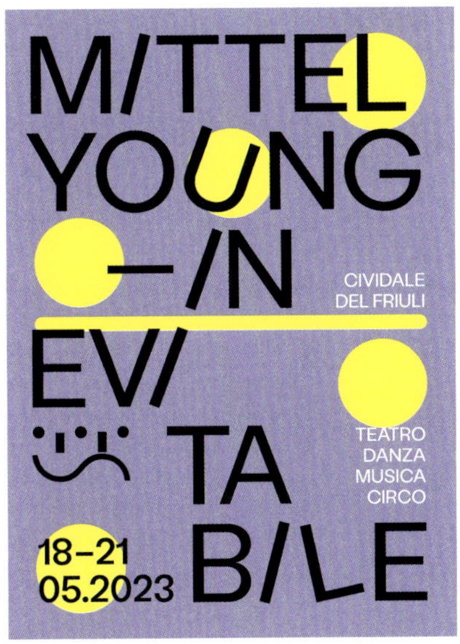
M/TTEL
YOUNG
—/N
CIVIDALE
DEL FRIULI
EV/
TA
TEATRO
DANZA
MUSICA
CIRCO
18–21
05.2023
B/LE

Pantone	C	M	Y	K	R	G	B
Pantone 2655 C	C53	M55	Y0	K0	R151	G109	B232
Pantone Black C	C0	M0	Y0	K100	R0	G0	B0
Pantone 283 C	C40	M8	Y0	K0	R105	G163	B219
Pantone 714 C	C0	M62	Y97	K0	R244	G166	B84
Pantone 3255 C	C85	M0	Y38	K0	R51	G214	B161
Pantone 101 C	C0	M0	Y70	K0	R255	G242	B94
Pantone 4545 C	C3	M5	Y25	K5	R123	G201	B160
Pantone 230 C	C2	M62	Y0	K0	R224	G133	B168

Oiils

Essential oils have transcended centuries and miles as companions for everyday life. Oiils celebrates daily rituals that make people want to be conscious of where they stand, allowing them to live here and now; to connect with their senses, spaces, and conscious state. Its branding system speaks on these different moments where these practices become essential for the self in a friendly and approachable way by incorporating an unexpected color scheme and funky illustrations to the mix.

Agency/
Monumento Co.

Tu esencia
es tu hogar.
BIENVENIDO
La sabiduría de lo 100% puro y natural formulada para tu bienestar.
Oiils
más info: Oiils.com

Oiils (W.L.)
Wellness for Life.

oiils.com
Natural
MENTA
Aceite
esencial
100% Puro
Oiils (W.L.)

C0	M25	Y25	K0
R249	G208	B186	
C80	M60	Y0	K0
R61	G98	B173	
C10	M10	Y60	K0
R237	G222	B123	
C80	M10	Y70	K0
R0	G160	B110	

dada

dada is an exclusive children's toys and accessories store located in Chapala Jalisco, Mexico. The store offers a selection of unique, avant-garde, and original items for children.

The definition of dada is an informal term for father, derived from baby talk. The brand is inspired by basic geometric figures (circles, squares, and triangles). The logo has a fun and memorable appearance. The color palette seeks to reflect the personality of a child using primary colors and pastels.

Agency/
CULTO CREATIVE

Art Direction/
Daniel Duran

Client/
Elaine Duran

dada.mx
Emiliano Zapata, 185
Guadalajara, Jalisco
T. 33 106 2013
Lunes a Viernes
10am – 7pm
dada.mx
dada.mx
Emiliano Zapata, 185
Guadalajara, Jalisco
T. 33 106 2013

dada.mx
dada.mx

Catálogo Mensual
Mayo 2020
dada.mx

dada.mx
Emiliano Zapata, 185
Guadalajara, Jalisco
T. 33 106 2013
Lunes a Viernes
10am – 7pm
dada.mx
dada.mx
Emiliano Zapata, 185
Guadalajara, Jalisco
T. 33 106 2013
Lunes a Viernes
10am – 7pm
Emiliano Zapata, 185
Guadalajara, Jalisco
T. 33 106 2013
Lunes a Viernes
10am – 7pm
dada.mx

C80	M50	Y0	K0
R0	G120	B239	
C4	M50	Y0	K0
R245	G147	B207	
C5	M13	Y96	K0
R245	G212	B30	
C0	M80	Y100	K0
R255	G90	B17	
C83	M18	Y88	K4
R32	G146	B84	
C9	M6	Y7	K0
R229	G229	B229	

Look Around Festival 2022

Creative Direction/
Irina Hamdohova

Art Direction & Design/
Tanya Devaeva

Technical Design/
Alena Kolbeneva

Look Around Festival 2022 was held in Yerevan, Armenia. It was a science festival, which brought together more than five thousand people at the site. The designers created the corporate identity, environmental design, navigation, screen design, prints, and advertising media.

LOOK AROUND
ԳԻՏՈՒԹՅԱՆ ՓԱՌԱՏՈՆ
ՍՊԱՍՎԱԾ ԲԱՑՕԹՅԱ ՄԻՋՈՑԱՌՈՒՄ ԸՆԿԵՐՆԵՐԻ ԵՎ ԱՄԲՈՂՋ ԸՆՏԱՆԻՔԻ ՀԱՄԱՐ

LOOK AROUND
ԳԻՏՈՒԹՅԱՆ ՓԱՌԱՏՈՆ
2022 թ. հոկտեմբերի 15
Անցկացման վայրը՝ Հայաստանի ազգային պոլիտեխնիկական համալսարան

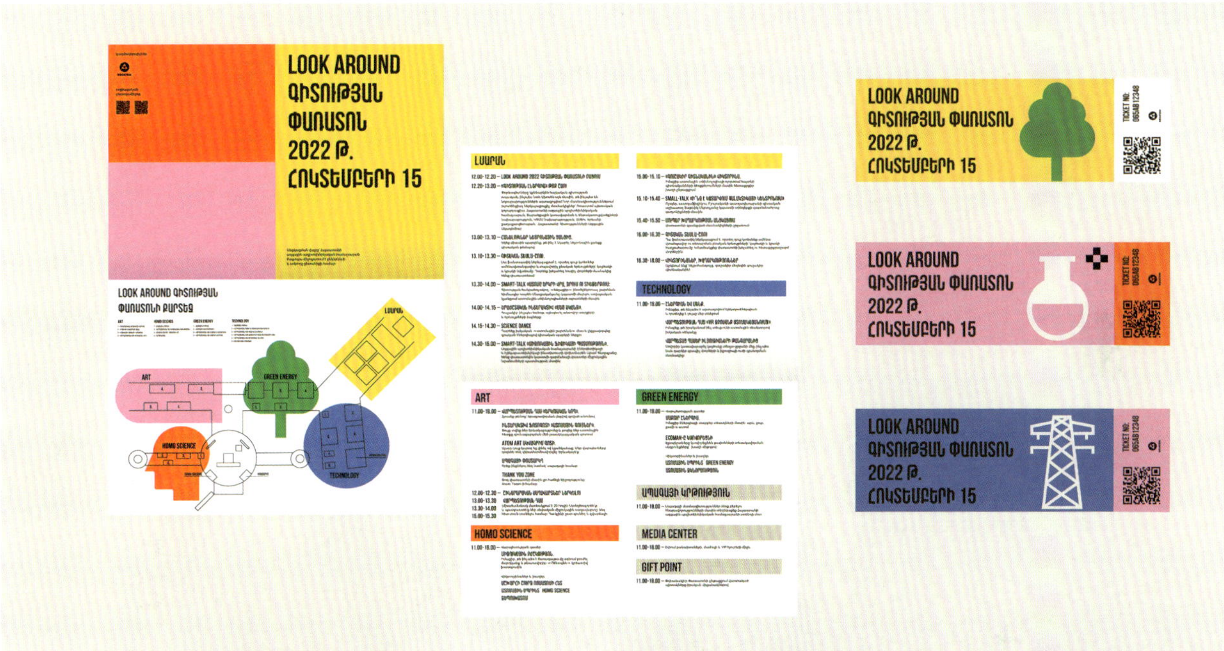
LOOK AROUND
ԳԻՏՈՒԹՅԱՆ
ՓԱՌԱՏՈՆ
2022 Թ.
ՀՈԿՏԵՄԲԵՐԻ 15
LOOK AROUND ԳԻՏՈՒԹՅԱՆ
ՓԱՌԱՏՈՆԻ ՔԱՐՏԵԶ
ART
GREEN ENERGY
HOMO SCIENCE
TECHNOLOGY
ԼՍԱՐԱՆ
ԱՊԱԳԱՅԻ ԿՐԹՈՒԹՅՈՒՆ
MEDIA CENTER
GIFT POINT
LOOK AROUND
ԳԻՏՈՒԹՅԱՆ ՓԱՌԱՏՈՆ
2022 Թ.
ՀՈԿՏԵՄԲԵՐԻ 15

LOOK AROUND
ԳԻՏՈՒԹՅԱՆ
ՓԱՌԱՏՈՆ
2022 Թ.
ՀՈԿՏԵՄԲԵՐԻ 15

C85	M0	Y85	K0
R0	G176	B86	
C70	M20	Y0	K0
R48	G151	B248	
C0	M75	Y0	K0
R235	G96	B169	
C100	M35	Y0	K0
R0	G111	B234	
C0	M5	Y80	K0
R255	G231	B67	

GOODS IS GOOD

MAUM STUDIO designed the key visual for GOODS IS GOOD, which will be held for the first time in 2024. "Goods" include various fields such as images, stories, and videos.

"What kind of goods can you find at this event?", "What creators can we see?"—The facial expression of a curious visitor expresses the appearance of an event that is going viral.

Agency/
MAUM STUDIO

Design/
Yoonji Lee (Key Visual, Graphic)
Jaewon Chung (Assist)
Hyeonsoo Joe (Assist)

Client/
OCMAKERS

GOODS
IS
GOOD

GOODS IS GOOD
GOODS IS GOOD

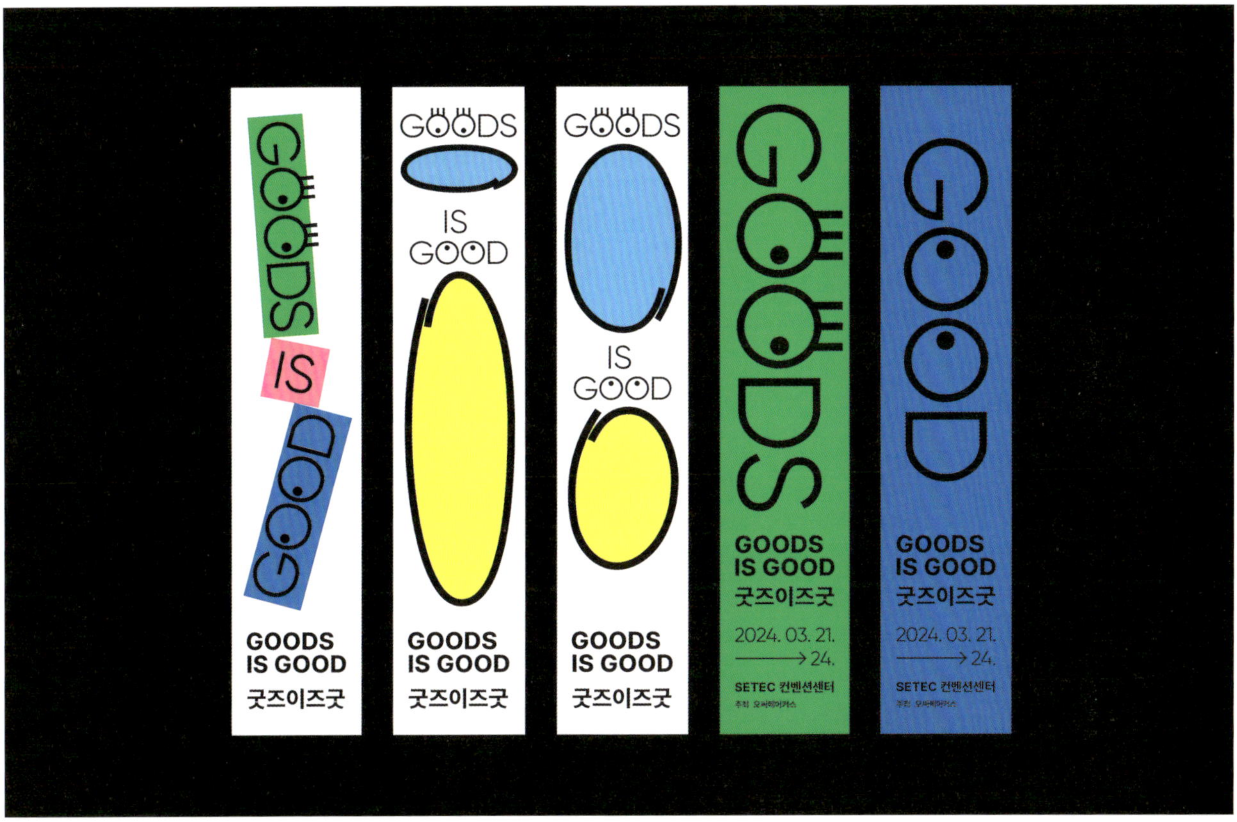
GOODS IS GOOD
GOODS
IS GOOD
굿즈이즈굿
GOODS
IS
GOOD
GOODS
IS GOOD
굿즈이즈굿
GOODS
IS
GOOD
GOODS
IS GOOD
굿즈이즈굿
GOODS
GOODS
IS GOOD
굿즈이즈굿
2024. 03. 21.
→ 24.
SETEC 컨벤션센터
GOOD
GOODS
IS GOOD
굿즈이즈굿
2024. 03. 21.
→ 24.
SETEC 컨벤션센터

GOODS
IS
GOOD
GOODS IS GOOD
서일페가 3월,
새로이 굿즈굿으로
찾아옵니다.
GOODS IS GOOD
굿즈이즈굿
관람예약
OPEN

C57 M0 Y100 K0
R128 G186 B39

C78 M0 Y100 K0
R39 G167 B55

C88 M20 Y88 K0
R0 G140 B77

C64 M0 Y60 K0
R96 G184 B133

C46 M0 Y28 K0
R149 G208 B197

C42 M8 Y0 K0
R157 G205 B240

C77 M46 Y0 K0
R64 G123 B190

C93 M65 Y0 K0
R21 G88 B165

C72 M65 Y0 K0
R96 G97 B169

C51 M52 Y0 K0
R144 G129 B187

C80 M79 Y0 K0
R84 G71 B151

C52 M65 Y0 K0
R144 G105 B171

C38 M42 Y0 K0
R171 G154 B202

C20 M40 Y0 K0
R208 G169 B208

C16 M52 Y33 K0
R215 G144 B148

C0 M91 Y91 K0
R230 G48 B33

C25 M100 Y100 K0
R189 G29 B29

C0 M60 Y90 K0
R240 G126 B38

C0 M50 Y80 K0
R243 G149 B63

C0 M20 Y90 K0
R255 G205 B28

C0 M7 Y100 K0
R255 G226 B0

C33 M0 Y82 K0
R192 G21 B75

C3 M4 Y9 K0
R249 G245 B237

Syra Coffee

Syra is one of Barcelona's biggest specialty coffee companies. The new identity aims to modernize the brand's image, bringing it closer to a diverse public, from the design to the narrative. The change of logo allows for better use and longevity of the icons, while the new typography brings a younger, bolder, and more fun feeling. It also improves its performance in graphic compositions.

The new look is more colorful, bigger, and easier to use. New graphic resources, such as illustrations and stickers, help to generate more coherent layouts across platforms and content levels. These design and strategic gestures help the brand adapt to the new digital era it is going through, where e-commerce, apps, and social media content are at the forefront.

Design/
Gastón García Aja

Collaboration/
Maher M. Mansour

Client/
Syra Coffee

Enjoy our summer coffees!
SYRA COFFEE

Guatemala / Washed
SAN CARLOS
Milk Chocolate, Roasted Almond, Pear and Brown Sugar
Variety Bourbon, Caturra, Catuai
Cupping Score 85,75
Altitude 1550 - 1900 msal.
Produced San Carlos Farm
Roasted for Espresso Methods
Roasted Date 25/04/2022
250 gr.

C100 M35 Y50 K13
R231 G214 B204

C20 M80 Y8 K0
R143 G83 B47

C0 M10 Y100 K0
R253 G192 B39

C35 M0 Y10 K0
R91 G36 B93

C20 M30 Y0 K0
R179 G137 B200

C68 M40 Y0 K0
R250 G180 B191

C0 M80 Y100 K0
R179 G137 B200

C75 M0 Y60 K0
R250 G180 B191

Pantone 3955 C
C4 M0 Y100 K0

Pantone 322 C
C97 M9 Y39 K34

Pantone 9285 C
C7 M9 Y9 K0

Pantone 123 C
C0 M19 Y89 K0

Pantone 172 C
C0 M73 Y87 K0

Pantone 2655 C
C54 M61 Y0 K0

Pantone 196 C
C0 M23 Y6 K0

Pantone 269 C
C80 M98 Y5 K27

Pantone 136 C
C0 M28 Y87 K0

Pantone 237 C
C6 M53 Y0 K0

Pantone 3275 C
C90 M0 Y52 K0

Pantone 2717 C
C34 M15 Y0 K0

Colham Red Packet 2023

Agency/
Frank Lo design studio

Client/
Colham Printing CO. Ltd

It is a set of red packets designed to celebrate the Chinese New Year and share blessings and joy with people. The design features bold colors and graphics that offer a fresh take on traditional Chinese aesthetics. The design team crafted those packets with the finest printing effects and paper to ensure premium quality for their festive goods.

Each box contains four unique red packet designs with four color variations. Each packet has a specific blessing, including Fortune, Happiness, Beauty, and Peace. They hope to spread joy during the difficult times and wish everyone the best.

HAPPY
HAPPY
FORTUNE
FORTUNE
BEAUTY

NEW YEAR
NEW YEAR
NEW YEAR
NEW YEAR

C0	M77	Y93	K0
R235	G91	B26	
C0	M24	Y29	K0
R250	G210	B180	
C60	M88	Y2	K0
R125	G54	B143	
C49	M47	Y95	K44
R101	G89	B24	

La Deseada

Design/
Isa Lloret
Pol Vila (Setze Studio)

Photography/
Enric Badrinas

Client/
La Deseada

With specialty coffees and artisan pastries as its flagship, La Deseada is making a name for itself in the Chamberí neighborhood of Madrid. La Deseada translates to "The Desired," an ambitious and unique name that reflects the founders' intention to turn their small establishment into a place where the sweetest and most discerning desires can be fulfilled.

The visual identity features a typeface with sharp serifs pointed like the thorns of a rose. It draws from photographs within the realm of coffee and pastries but from the floral world; every single origin (Ethiopia, Costa Rica, Papua New Guinea, and Nicaragua) coffee package identifies with its national flower and a hue from a botanical palette.

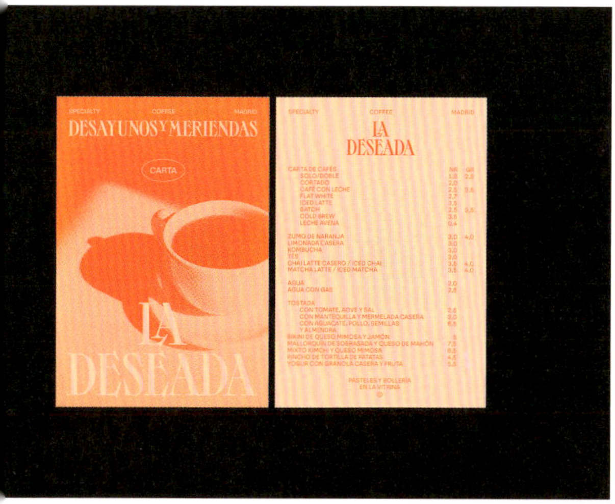
DESAYUNOS Y MERIENDAS
CARTA
LA DESEADA
LA DESEADA

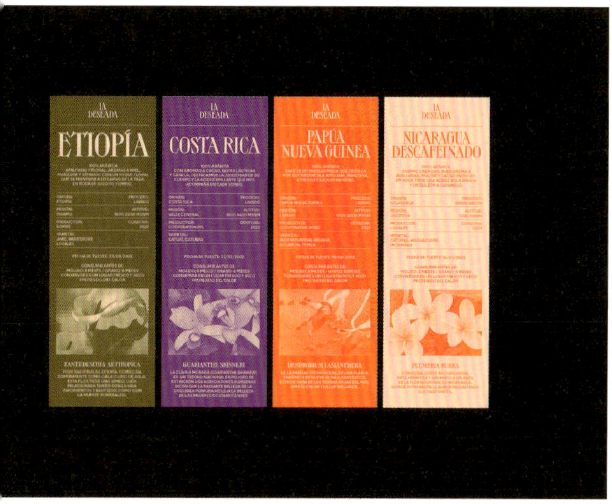
ETIOPÍA
COSTA RICA
PAPÚA NUEVA GUINEA
NICARAGUA DESCAFEINADO

PRÓXIMAMENTE
CAFÉS DE ESPECIALIDAD PROPIOS
EN LA DESEADA BUSCAMOS INCORPORAR UN@ REPOSTER@ EN NUESTRO EQUIPO
8→22.08
CERRADOS POR VACACIONES
LA DESEADA
DICIEMBRE
6→9 + 25.12.2023
CERRADO
EL OBRADOR DE LA DESEADA
BUSCA
AYUDANTE

ETIOPÍA
COSTA RICA
PAPÚA NUEVA GUINEA
NICARAGUA DESCAFEINADO

DESAYUNOS Y MERIENDAS
CARTA
LA DESEADA

SPECIALITY
COFFEE
MADRID
REPOSTERÍA ARTESANA Y CAFE DE ESPECIALIDAD
CALLE DE JOSE ABASCAL,
28003, MADRID

C/ DE JOSÉ ABASCAL
Nº 52, 28003
CHAMBERÍ, MADRID
SPECIALTY COFFEE
DESAYUNOS Y MERIENDAS
LA DESEADA
LUNES A VIERNES
8:30 A 19:00
SÁBADOS 8:30 A 14:00
EST. 2022
LA DESEADA

LA DESEADA
LA DESEADA
LA DESEADA

NICARAGUA
DESCAFEINADO
PAPÚA
NUEVA GUINEA
ETIOPÍA
COSTA RICA
GRANOLA
PISTACHO
MERMELADA
HIGO
MERMELADA
CIRUELA Y
FRAMBUESA

SPECIALTY
COFFEE
MADRID
LA DESEADA

SPECIALTY
COFFEE
MADRID
DESAYUNOS Y MERIENDAS
LA DESEADA

SPECIALTY
COFFEE
MADRID
DESAYUNOS Y MERIENDAS
DE LUNES A VIERNES:
DE 8:30 A 19:00
SÁBADO
DE 8:30 A 14:00
DOMINGO CERRADO
LA DESEADA

C0 R230	M90 G50	Y100 B20	K0
C70 R75	M20 G160	Y0 B255	K0
C10 R240	M10 G215	Y90 B20	K0
C70 R70	M0 G170	Y85 B65	K0
C60 R140	M80 G70	Y0 B185	K0

Change Festival

Agency/
Mistaker

Client/
Open City Roma

Change is a festival about architecture and climate change, a place to share ideas and create connections between architects, universities, and people. And it is a conversation to find resolutions and think about how much people impact their way of life.

Data is a tool for measuring changes, which is why Mistaker designed a variable data-driven identity system to show through an easy-to-understand visual system all the changes and their impact on everyday life. It is a visual identity to attract attention, raise awareness, and create participation.

Architecture.
Cities. Life.
CHANGE

JCDecaux
Architecture.
Cities. Life.
CHANGE

CHANGE
Smaltimento dei rifiuti della plastica
2015
Riciclata 19,5%
Incenerita 25,5%
Scartata 55%

CHANGE
Architecture.
Cities. Life.
24.09 — 31.10
MAXXI
changefestival.it
IL 40% DELLA PLASTICA NEL MONDO È DESTINATA A PRODOTTI USA E GETTA
CHANGE
Architecture.
Cities. Life.
CHANGE
Architecture.
Cities. Life.
24.09 — 31.10
MAXXI
changefestival.it
UN TERZO
DEI CONSU
DI ACQUA
È DOVUTO ALLE
ABITAZION
E ALL'EDILIZIA
CHANGE
Architecture.
Cities. Life.
NTRO IL 2050 SARANNO PIÙ DI 6 MILIARDI LE PERSONE CHE VIVONO IN AREE URBANE
CHANGE
Architecture.
Cities. Life.

C0	M16	Y84	K0
R255	G210	B66	
C0	M78	Y67	K0
R242	G83	B65	
C89	M0	Y7	K0
R0	G176	B229	
C0	M52	Y0	K0
R232	G132	B181	

Berlin Blendet Music Festival

Design/
Nina Carreiras

A visual identity project for a fictional pop-rock music festival held in two different venues in Berlin.

Berlin ✦ Blendet
Greta
PRESS
Berlin ✦ Blendet
Zachary
ARTIST
Berlin ✦ Blendet
Lisa Wagner
STAFF

Berlin ✦ Blendet
2021
Berlin ✦ Blendet
2021
Berlin ✦ Blendet
2021

Berlin ✦ Blendet
APRIL
–JUNI
2021
Lido Music Venue
EINE STADT.
2 KONZERTHALLE.
30 KÜNSTLERN.
VIEL MUSIK.
Berlin ✦ Blendet
APRIL
–JUNI
2021
SO36 Club

18. April
Gus Dapperton
Lido Music Venue
Doors: 19h.
SOLD OUT SOLD OUT SOLD OUT
Warsteiner
get your tickets at
www.berlinblendet.de

Berlin ✦ Blendet
APRIL
–JUNI
2021
Lido Music Venue
SO36 Club
ALASKALASKA
Das Moped
Glue Trip
Isolation Berlin
Yuck
Die Nerven
Swim Deep
Alvvays
Glass Animals
Karien
Wolf Alice
Still Corners
Marika Hackman
Lala Lala
Surf Curse
Declan McKenna
Ilgen - Nur
Clairo
Splashh
Panda Lux
Gus Dapperton
DIIV
Gurr
Cheatahs
Blond
Wild Nothings
Das Paradies
Jeremias
Warsteiner
BERLIN
get your tickets at
www.berlinblendet.de
BUS

C92 R0	M0 G158	Y97 B69	K0
C0 R231	M94 G41	Y100 B15	K0
C60 R85	M0 G195	Y2 B239	K0
C0 R255	M16 G216	Y89 B16	K0
C0 R236	M74 G100	Y85 B42	K0

Robertha Blatt - Conectando arte, psicologia e educação.

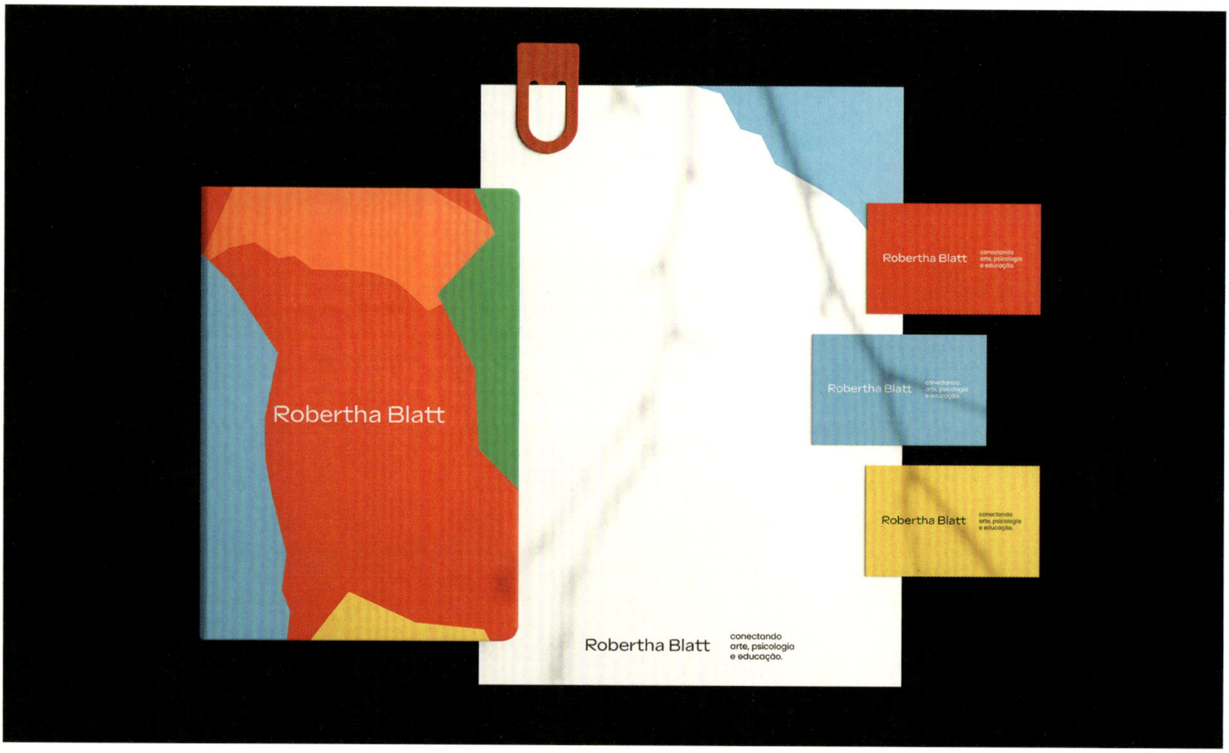

Design/
Jean Nicolas Guerreiro Dias

Client/
Robertha Blatt

Robertha Blatt investigates and works on the interaction between art, psychology, and education. For 15 years, she has been researching the articulation of therapeutic practices and artistic expressions, moving through the roles of child educator, family therapist, psychologist, mother, and artist. She specializes in family and couple therapy, cognitive behavioral therapy, positive psychology, and emotion-focused therapy. Her atelier provides several multisensory resources that enable other manifestations besides speeches.

Boa leitura!
Robertha Blatt

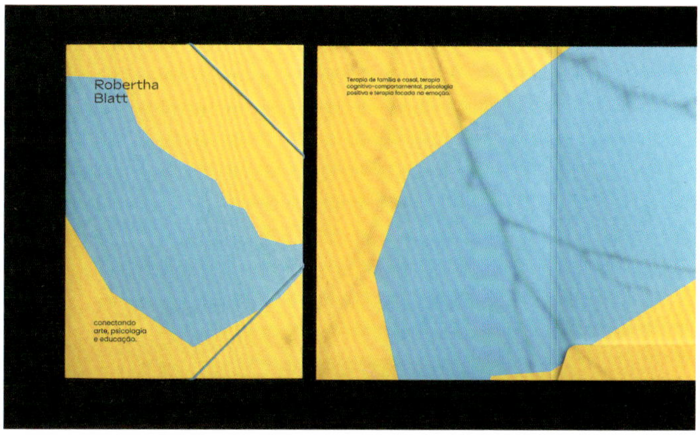
Robertha
Blatt
conectando
arte, psicologia
e educação.
Terapia de família e casal, terapia
cognitivo-comportamental, psicologia
positiva e terapia focada na emoção.

exposição
Robertha Blatt
como a arte
influencia na
psicologia?

@roberthablatt
Robertha
Blatt
conectando
arte, psicologia
e educação.
emoção
conexão
arte
família
movimento

Robertah Blatt
conectando
arte, psicologia
e educação.

C92	M0	Y100	K0
R0	G170	B79	
C0	M89	Y24	K0
R238	G67	B125	
C0	M24	Y100	K0
R255	G196	B23	
C84	M13	Y0	K0
R0	G164	B226	

Margarita Museum

The Margarita Museum is a visual identity that celebrates one of the most favored cocktails in the world, in a small-sized boutique museum. It merges the delightful ingredients of any margarita in vibrant bold colors that convey an energetic and celebratory atmosphere. From pink, green, blue, and yellow colors to an iconic logo symbol and a whole modular composition system, the Margarita Museum involves an immersive experience that is never just about drinking.

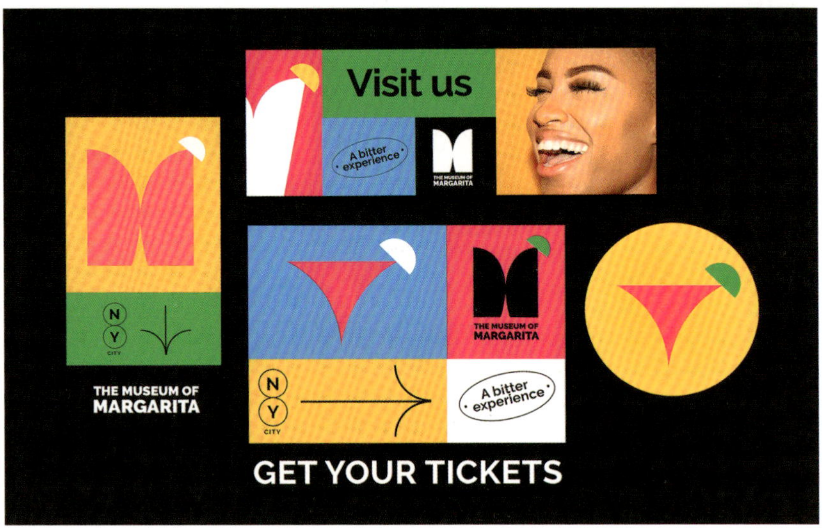

Design/
Nicole Rauen

Design Direction/
Anita Zeppetelli (SVA Continued Program)

A bitter experience
A bitter experience
THE MUSEUM OF MARGARITA

Margarita Day
It's not just about drinking
NEW YORK
A bitter experience
11 W 53rd st

N
Y
CITY
Celebrate & Visit us
THE MUSEUM OF MARGARITA
Enjoy & Learn
A bitter experience
THE MUSEUM OF MARGARITA
It's all about Margarita
Come & taste
THE MUSEUM OF MARGARITA

N
Y
CITY
Join us on 23th February
Free entrace on Margarita Day
THE MUSEUM OF MARGARITA
A bitter experience
THE MUSEUM OF MARGARITA
Visit us
NEW YORK
11 W 53rd st
A bitter experience
Learn & Taste

MARGARITA

Ticket
THE MUSEUM OF MARGARITA
$15
09.15.2022
everyone
00089

About the museum
Story
Map
Experience
Location
Shop
Get tickets

A bitter experience
Learn & Taste
Margarita Day
Celebrate & Visit us
N
Y
CITY

Entrance
A bitter experience
THE MUSEUM OF MARGARITA

N
Y
CITY
THE MUSEUM OF MARGARITA

THE MUSEUM OF MARGARITA
A bitter experience
N
Y
CITY
11 W 53rd st
Join this experience
themuseumofmargarita.com
It's all about Margarita

Come & join us for the weekend
themuseumofmargarita.com
THE MUSEUM OF MARGARITA
A bitter experience

C0 R255	M15 G215	Y95 B0	K0
C75 R0	M0 G200	Y15 B235	K0
C90 R30	M65 G75	Y0 B255	K0
C0 R255	M85 G65	Y30 B110	K0

Rede Santo Amaro

Rede Santo Amaro is a community organization located in the neighborhood of Santo Amaro, São Paulo, Brazil.

Design/
Ramon Santos da Conceição

rede—
-santo
amaro.

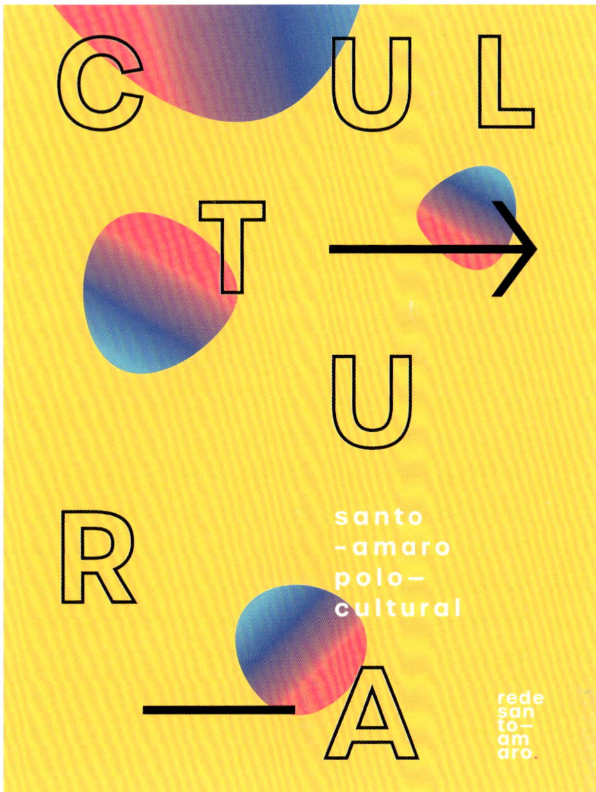
C U L
T
U
R
A
santo
-amaro
polo—
cultural
rede
san
to—
am
aro.

rede—
-santo
amaro.

rede—
-santo
amaro.

C0	M50	Y69	K0
R243	G153	B81	
C6	M0	Y70	K0
R247	G239	B99	
C44	M46	Y0	K0
R156	G141	B194	
C81	M89	Y15	K3
R71	G47	B120	
C92	M66	Y13	K1
R0	G87	B154	
C51	M0	Y7	K0
R124	G204	B233	

SweatMate

SweatMate is an India-based brand that develops products to assist athletes of all levels in preparing well, performing better, and recovering faster. It aims to empower individuals to lead healthier lives, whether they are professionals or amateurs, by enabling them to maximize their physical potential without unnecessary suffering. Its solutions offer clear benefits for pre-, during-, and post-exercise routines. SweatMate is the friend that motivates individuals to keep moving forward and live a healthier life.

Agency/
Brada

Art Direction/
Manuel Fernández del Campo García

Design/
Laura Silias
Manuel Fernández del Campo García

Photography/
Katherine Aguirre

SweatMate
ANTI-FRICTION CREAM
PRE WORKOUT
LONG LASTING
MOISTURIZING
ANTI BACTERIAL
NET WT
100ML

SweatMate
RECOVERY CREAM
POST WORKOUT
NET WT
100ML

WELL DONE!
TIME TO RELAX
WE GOT YOUR SKIN
NET WT
100ML

SweatMate™
PRE WORKOUT
ANTI FRICTION CREAM
LONG LASTING | MOISTURIZING | ANTI BACTERIAL
ENRICHED WITH SHEA BUTTER, TEA TREE OIL, LEMONGRASS OIL AND VIT E
NET WT
100ML
SweatMate™
DURING WORKOUT
NON DRIP SUNSCREEN
LONG LASTING | MOISTURIZING | ANTI BACTERIAL
ENRICHED WITH SHEA BUTTER, TEA TREE OIL, LEMONGRASS OIL AND VIT E
NET WT
100ML
SweatMate™
POST WORKOUT
RECOVERY CREAM
LONG LASTING | MOISTURIZING | ANTI BACTERIAL
ENRICHED WITH SHEA BUTTER, TEA TREE OIL, LEMONGRASS OIL AND VIT E
NET WT
100ML

C0	M100	Y100	K0
R255	G0	B0	
C0	M20	Y90	K0
R247	G199	B41	
C80	M0	Y95	K0
R5	G163	B80	
C45	M0	Y15	K0
R152	G227	B222	
C35	M40	Y0	K0
R163	G149	B200	

Selográfico

Selográfico is a design studio specializing in projects related to politics, art, education, culture, and socio-environmental issues. The vibrant colors used in these projects reflect the dynamic nature of the studio's works and embody their energetic approach.

Building upon the name "Selográfico," which in Portuguese "selo" can be translated as "stamp," the idea emerged to incorporate stamps into the graphics of this universe. It allows them to have various applications, such as creating patterns, photo masks, and text supports. With diverse applications, they ensure personality and flexibility, making them suitable for a variety of situations.

Design/
Carolina Lins

Client/
Selográfico Studio

estudioselografico.com.br
design que constrói relações
selo gráfico
selográfico
design que constrói relações
estudioselografico.com.br

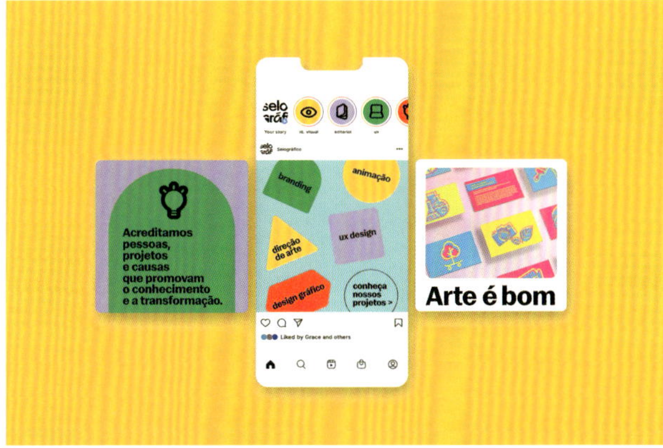
Acreditamos pessoas, projetos e causas que promovam o conhecimento e a transformação.
branding
animação
direção de arte
ux design
design gráfico
conheça nossos projetos >
Arte é bom

selo gráfico
Rio, 02 fevereiro
Lorem ipsum dolor sit amet, consectetuer adipiscing elit, sed diam nonummy nibh euismod tincidunt ut laoreet dolore magna aliquam erat volutpat. Ut wisi enim ad minim veniam, quis nostrud exerci tation ullamcorper suscipit lobortis nisl ut aliquip ex ea commodo consequat. Duis autem vel eum iriure dolor in hendrerit in vulputate velit esse molestie consequat, vel illum dolore eu feu.
Lorem ipsum dolor sit amet, consectetuer adipiscing elit, sed diam nonummy nibh euismod tincidunt ut laoreet dolore magna aliquam erat volutpat. Ut wisi enim ad minim veniam, quis nostrud exerci tation ullamcorper suscipit .
Att,
Lorem ipsum dolor sit amet, consectetuer adipiscing elit, sed diam nonummy nibh
design que constrói relações
selográfico
Natasha Gompers
selografico.com.br
@ selografico
+ 55 21 99992 0032
selográfico
design que constrói relações

design que constrói relações
selográfico
design que constrói relações
selo gráfico

estudioselografico.com.br
design que constrói relações
selo gráfico

C69	M0	Y52	K0
R63	G182	B147	
C7	M13	Y84	K0
R242	G216	B54	
C0	M57	Y91	K0
R239	G137	B28	
C0	M77	Y49	K0
R234	G91	B97	
C73	M71	Y0	K0
R91	G84	B161	
C72	M24	Y0	K0
R51	G155	B215	
C99	M92	Y9	K0
R23	G47	B135	
C0	M88	Y81	K0
R232	G62	B46	

9+ Wines

Agency/
Pràctica

Photography/
Enric Badrinas

It is a wine label redesign for 9+, the only winery in Catalonia—and perhaps in the world— whose name is a number, not a word.

This project presented the challenge of designing 15 labels, all under a global image but with different families: Base, Selection, and Sparkling.

It led the design team to create a naming and graphic system that orders and enumerates the wine bottles, not only to rationalize the wide range of products but to strengthen the winery's identity as well as to make it stand out from the natural wine sector.

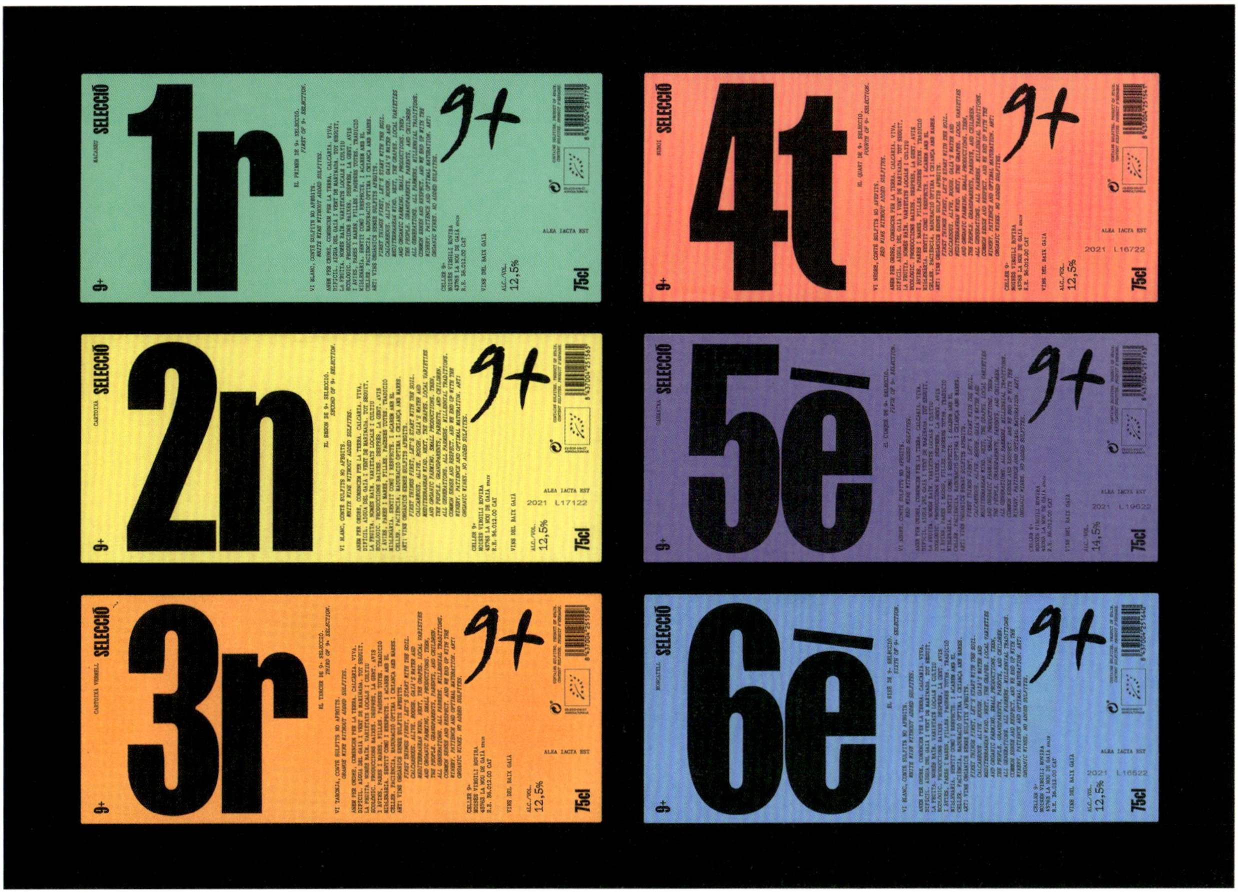
1r
2n
3r
4t
5è
6è
SELECCIÓ
9+
75cl

1r
2n
3r
4t
ESCUMOSOS
SELECCIÓ
BASE

C	M	Y	K	R	G	B
C85	M68	Y0	K0	R50	G84	B164
C3	M25	Y8	K0	R244	G208	B215
C74	M6	Y0	K0	R0	G174	B232
C78	M32	Y0	K0	R14	G139	B205
C3	M6	Y80	K0	R253	G232	B65
C0	M62	Y80	K0	R239	G127	B54
C0	M45	Y98	K0	R245	G162	B0
C0	M88	Y100	K0	R232	G62	B11
C50	M75	Y80	K70	R65	G28	B14
C5	M20	Y100	K0	R245	G205	B0
C85	M65	Y0	K0	R221	G209	B231
C87	M35	Y89	K28	R0	G103	B59
C65	M82	Y0	K0	R115	G66	B150
C8	M33	Y0	K0	R232	G189	B216
C40	M70	Y85	K50	R106	G57	B27

Denada Ice Cream

Denada translates to "It's nothing so like the ice cream itself; the design is stripped back of any additives." The ingredients are all natural with no surprises and the packaging reflects the same philosophy—something minimal, yet sophisticated. Throughout the design process, there was always a consideration of how the entire range looked on the shelf together and not just as individual tubs which stemmed from being a new product and needing a point of difference to have some impact in the marketplace. Inspiration and research covered everything from modern interior color design trends to retro Japanese medical packaging.

Agency/
Jo Cutri Studio

Photography/
Simone Ruggiero

denada
mango split
denada
sugar free 98%
mango split
ice cream

denada
sugar free 95.3%
caramel choc flake
ice cre*m
denada
sugar free 95.3%
caramel choc flake
ice cre*m
denada
caramel choc flake

denada
denada
sugar free 98.5%
caramel macadamia
ice cream
low carb. no added sugar. all natural 475ml

denada
sugar free 97.8%
milk choc choc chip
ice cream
low carb. no added sugar. all natural 475ml

C2 R244	M97 G8	Y78 B47	K0
C64 R2	M0 G221	Y38 B197	K0
C7 R254	M14 G223	Y88 B0	K0
C100 R0	M91 G30	Y1 B173	K0

2023 European Capital of Culture

DE_FORM presents a dynamic visual identity concept for Veszprém-Balaton 2023 European Capital of Culture. Their design reflects the event's key themes: community, regional development, openness, cultural diversity, meeting points, cultural education, and synergy. The graphic system serves as a starting point for the logo and offers versatile elements that can project onto various shapes and typography. With four vibrant colors in addition to black and white, the VI allows for varied and dynamic communication, capturing the essence of Veszprém-Balaton's transformational journey.

Agency/
DE_FORM

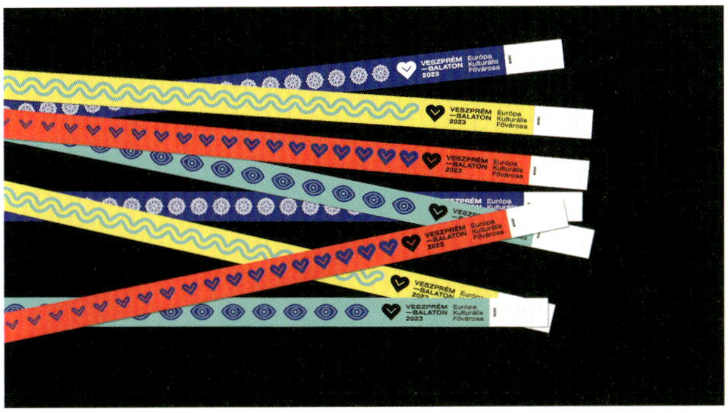

ARTIST
ARTIST
SZERVEZŐ
FOTÓS

VESZPRÉM
– BALATON
2023
EURÓPA
KULTURÁLIS
FŐVÁROSA
VESZPRÉM
– BALATON
2023
EURÓPA
KULTURÁLIS
FŐVÁROSA
VESZPRÉM
– BALATON
2023
EURÓPA
KULTURÁLIS
FŐVÁROSA

C90	M45	Y85	K60
R1	G59	B35	
C90	M32	Y100	K23
R0	G106	B49	
C84	M24	Y86	K8
R23	G129	B74	
C0	M0	Y35	K0
R255	G246	B189	
C0	M0	Y100	K0
R255	G255	B0	
C0	M60	Y100	K0
R242	G127	B7	
C15	M40	Y0	K0
R228	G171	B241	

Freyja

"All you need is love and hot water!" Freyja's cool hemp infusions and teas shake up the old tea-time codes to offer consumers a moment of well-being at any time of day because it's always time to take care of oneself. At a time when everything moves too fast, let's take the time to stop, observe, breathe, and infuse nature. With a world inspired by the 1970s, carefree and friendly, The design team is dusting off the image of herbal teas: acidic, tonic colors, geometric patterns, and typography with characters.

Agency & Photography/
STUDIO OUAM

Copywriting/
Salade Tomate Oignon

Client/
Freyja

FREYJA
FLOWERS POWER
VIVEZ D'AMOUR & D'EAU CHAUDE
THÉ DANSANT en infusettes
PANTOUFLES & ROBE DE chanvre

Chanvre VERVEINE MENTHE & TILLEUL

FREYJA
BON thé DIVIN
CBD

FREYJA
Chanvre VERVEINE MENTHE & TILLEUL
SOIRÉE RELAX & SEREINE
25 sachets
FREYJA
Chanvre ROOIBOS & TOUCHE DE VANILLE
JOURNÉE DOUCE & SAINE
25 sachets
FREYJA
Chanvre GINGEMBRE & CITRON
ÉVEIL PUISSANT & DÉTOX
25 sachets

●	C100 R4	M85 G5	Y0 B234	K15
●	C85 R43	M0 G179	Y92 B94	K0
●	C0 R251	M88 G67	Y98 B27	K0
●	C0 R248	M65 G125	Y0 B179	K0

Posters of the Japanese Cuisine Festival

Design/
Kristina Zotova

Maneki Neko is a summer festival of Japanese cuisine in Baku. Its goal is to immerse visitors in the atmosphere of Eastern culture and introduce them to Japanese food. The bright colors, emotions, and sensations evoked by macro photography and images of dishes from the world of Hayao Miyazaki

inspired the designer to create the identity. She used rich colors and simple shapes in the illustrations to whet the appetite and awaken visitors' desire to broaden their horizons by momentarily becoming part of Japanese culture.

	C	M	Y	K
●	C54 R141	M81 G64	Y0 B158	K0
●	C10 R214	M100 G0	Y10 B120	K0
●	C0 R251	M25 G202	Y85 B56	K0
●	C0 R242	M75 G94	Y85 B41	K0
●	C0 R246	M40 G174	Y60 B106	K0
●	C0 R239	M58 G140	Y28 B147	K0
●	C75 R71	M45 G120	Y0 B187	K0

JUMGO Rabbit Year Souvenir

At the end of 2022, to welcome the upcoming Year of the Rabbit, the design team made a series of cultural and creative expressions based on the theme of rabbits. In the Chinese New Year's blessing, it is often indispensable for idiom blessings from numbers. It has also become an indispensable part of the Chinese blessing culture. The design inspiration comes from this. First of all, they intercepted the symbols of "JUMGO" and "ORIG," and jointly formed a new rabbit logo to match the follow-up design. The concept of the blessing idiom of the rabbit logo to make a richer extension has also become the most direct presence of the entire vision. Different rabbit shapes extend to different geometric numbers, combined with six colors. Through creative and design language conversion, more open, diverse, and richer forms are presented.

Agency/
ORIG DESIGN

Design/
Zhu En

New Year
Of Rabbit
(癸卯兔年)
TRANSFER
I WANT TO
YOU
RABBIT
HAPPY YEAR OF THE RABBIT
2023·兔年喜樂·

JUMGO
EVERY
EVERY
TIME
(癸卯兔年)
DOWN
SECOND
RANSFER
WANT TO
YOU
RABBIT
HAPPY

C	M	Y	K
C85 R15	M37 G126	Y96 B64	K0
C68 R86	M35 G142	Y11 B189	K0
C4 R229	M78 G89	Y87 B39	K0
C14 R221	M37 G175	Y31 B163	K0
C0 R246	M40 G172	Y89 B30	K0

BEAN'S

Agency/
B&W Graphic Lab

Brewing in constant tumbling, the aroma slowly and thickly rises, and the rhythm constitutes a visual. The image of the Chinese character "豆 (Bean)" formed over time. The design team restored the scene of coffee beans when they are roasted, and disassembled them to form the graphics "豆" to express the unique flavor of the batch of coffee beans and the taste core from Yunnan, China.

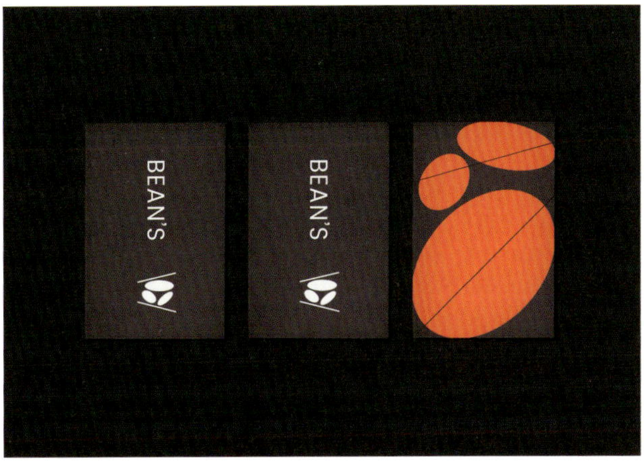
BEAN'S
BEAN'S

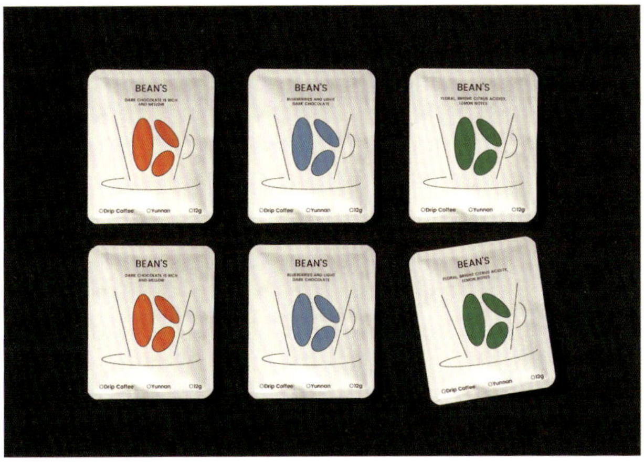
BEAN'S
BEAN'S
BEAN'S
BEAN'S
BEAN'S
BEAN'S

BEAN'S

BEAN'S
From:Yunnan
BEAN'S
From:Yunnan
BEAN'S
From:Yunnan

C	M	Y	K
C3 R252	M4 G247	Y18 B220	K0
C30 R201	M25 G186	Y88 B50	K0
C15 R223	M58 G134	Y60 B97	K0
C60 R112	M13 G182	Y44 B161	K0
C80 R78	M77 G77	Y16 B149	K0
C78 R27	M19 G159	Y70 B110	K0
C56 R133	M51 G124	Y50 B119	K0
C11 R229	M97 G16	Y91 B34	K0
C53 R132	M30 G166	Y6 B213	K0
C17 R220	M16 G213	Y17 B207	K0

A Very Local Brew

The design team decided to envision each product as a single house, which together makes up a whole neighborhood of Dalston! Each box has a colorful roof like the awning of the Dalston café where Borja first discovered specialty coffee. The designers even named the products after particular houses—"name of coffee" + "House." Each flavor is personalized with a distinctive color. Maintaining the brand's signature, planet-friendly green, they also added a warm red—a nod to the red brick houses of Dalston. Likewise, the logo was inspired by the typical brickwork found in this friendly London neighborhood: contained in two simple bricks and connected asymmetrically as if forming part of a wall.

Agency/
Ingrid Picanyol Studio

Creative Direction & Design/
Ingrid Picanyol

Illustration/
Lourenço Providência

Printing/
Gràfiques Copyset

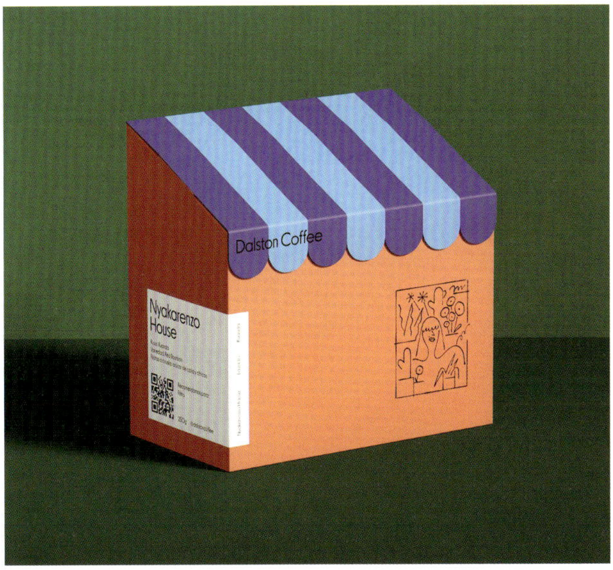
Dalston Coffee
Nyakarenzo House

Dalston Coffee

Masha House

Dalston Coffee
Las Brisas House

Dalston Coffee
Dalston Coffee

Dalston Coffee

C12	M13	Y15	K0
R229	G222	B214	
C2	M73	Y88	K0
R233	G102	B37	
C70	M0	Y61	K0
R58	G180	B130	
C77	M48	Y0	K0
R60	G117	B187	
C91	M79	Y62	K97
R0	G0	B0	

Berisso Museum

This project was developed as part of the Design III subject of the University of Buenos Aires, for the Berisso Museum in the town of Berisso, Province of Buenos Aires. The city is rich in history and diversity due to its immigrant heritage. It is in the museum that the community of Berisso seeks to recover everyday and living history. The designers aimed to capture this story in every detail of the editorial, web design, and digital pieces, thus connecting the public with the true essence of the city.

Graphic Design/
Melody Perco and Catalina Noya

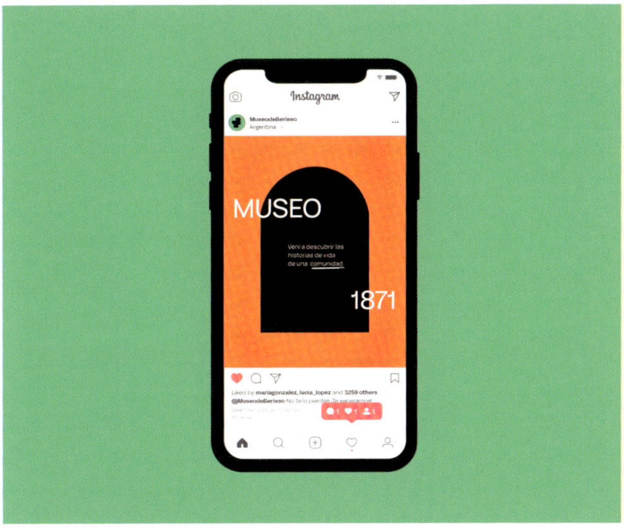
Instagram
MUSEO
1871

TALLERES
PUEBLO
RELATOS MIGRANTES
MUSEO
1871

Una comunidad organizada en busca del progeso social.

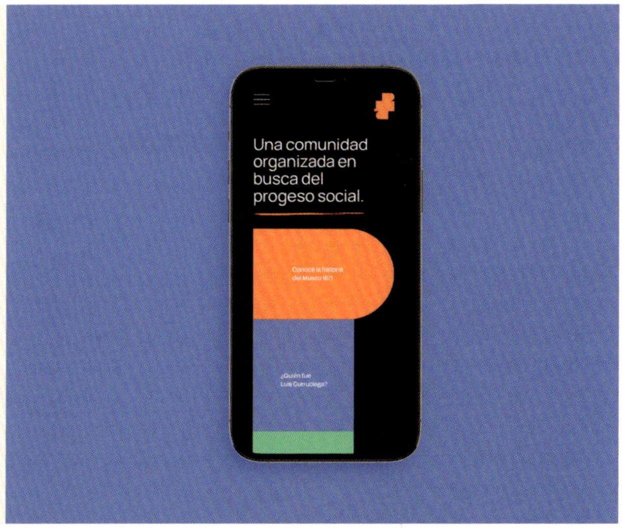
Una comunidad organizada en busca del progeso social.

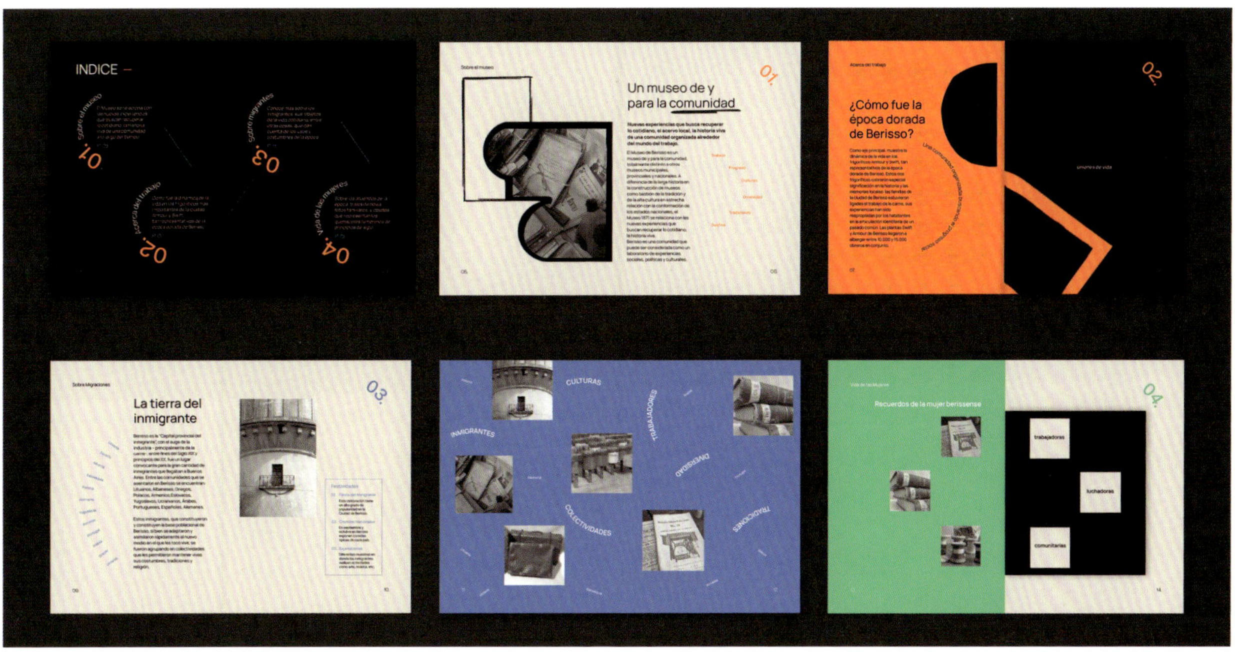
INDICE
Un museo de y para la comunidad
¿Cómo fue la época dorada de Berisso?
La tierra del inmigrante

C65 R146	M0 G213	Y100 B14	K0
C49 R166	M67 G118	Y0 B229	K0
C10 R230	M15 G221	Y19 B210	K0
C31 R213	M0 G243	Y60 B141	K0
C91 R21	M68 G52	Y99 B1	K53

Recargo

Recargo is a virtual fintech designed to optimize financial transactions in various projects. Offering innovative solutions, Recargo stands out in efficient resource management, making it the ideal choice for those seeking practicality and security in their financial operations. Whether for personal or business projects, Recargo represents the cutting edge of financial technology, simplifying and improving the user experience.

Design/
Taylor Shady

Recargo
Recargo
recargo.com
/recargo
recargo.com
/recargo

SOMOS O SEU COMEÇO.
Nunca foi tão fácil resolver o difícil.
Pedir agora

SEU RECARGO CHEGOU!
SOMOS O SEU COMEÇO.
Recargo

Recargo
Recargo
SEU PRESENTE CHEGOU
SEU PRESENTE CHEGOU
Recargo
SEU PRESENTE CHEGOU

FUTURO
recargo.com
/recargo

NÓS CUIDAMOS DE OBJETIVOS DIFÍCEIS
Recargo
recargo.com
/recargo

SOMOS O SEU COMEÇO.
Grandes
ideias
novas
conquistas
Recargo
CARGOCOIN
Navegue na onda da Recargo digital. Seu futuro financeiro ao toque das criptos!
AS IDEIAS
IDEIAS

SOMOS
O SEU
COMEÇO
Recargo
VISA
Grandes
novas
ideias
conquistas

SOMOS
O SEU
COMEÇO.
Grandes
ideias
novas
conquistas
Agora seremos referência em seus investimentos!
www.recargo.com
/recargo
somos uma fintech focada em fazer um novo mundo melhor de forma otimizada para lhe sobrar mais tempo!

C0 R255	M68 G116	Y99 B21	K0
C93 R0	M0 G172	Y100 B0	K0
C100 R28	M99 G28	Y9 B142	K3
C11 R255	M67 G105	Y0 B244	K0
C8 R230	M6 G230	Y7 B230	K0

TFR News

TFR News is an Indonesia-based online media agency that observes the way the creative industry works. TFR News reports what goes on behind the industry (professions, brands, companies, and culture). Entering its fifth anniversary in 2023, TFR News celebrated the occasion by refreshing its brand identity. As a media company that deals with mass communication, "scale" is the essence. The designer and TFR News were talking about amplifying the content to a bigger audience, thus the logo speaks volumes. The creative world is ever-expanding and it's growing bigger and better each passing day. People have become more aware of the industry, and creative communities grow larger every year.

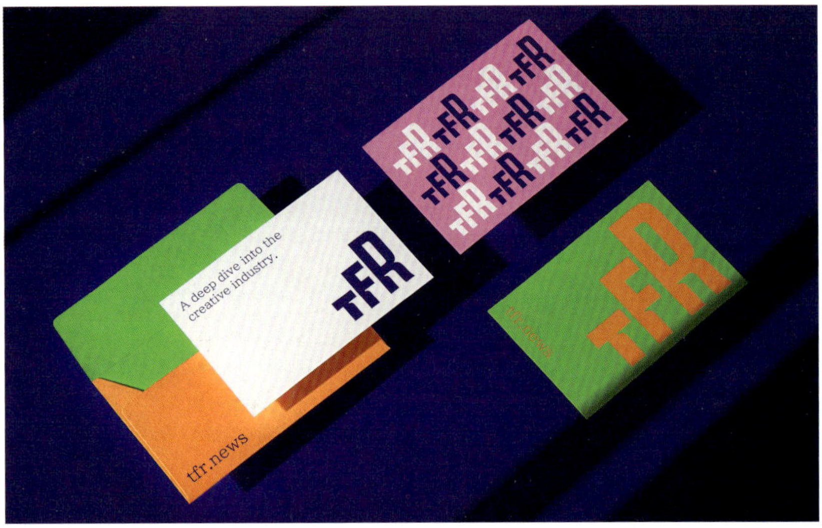

Design/
Evan Wijaya

Welcome to
The Finery
Report!
tfr.news

@tfrnews

C0	M42	Y100	K0
R242	G259	B21	
C0	M0	Y0	K100
R0	G0	B0	
C88	M28	Y85	K15
R0	G118	B70	
C90	M64	Y0	K0
R0	G91	B208	
C0	M86	Y74	K0
R232	G63	B60	
C18	M16	Y22	K0
R215	G207	B197	

Dose Podcast

Design/
Maria Alice de Sá Queiroz

Client/
Guilherme Ventura

Dose Podcast comes from three concepts: carioca slang, doses of alcohol, and access to hip-hop artists through interviews as if the public had "doses" of them. The main idea is to bring people who move the urban culture that would not be known in conventional interviews. The visual identity needed to be something that conveyed the brand's Brazilian and urban atmosphere. The colors were chosen precisely to translate these characteristics, through the strong and vibrant tones that refer to Brazilian streets and bars with all their peculiarities, such as plastic chairs and tables, beer boxes and bottles, etc.

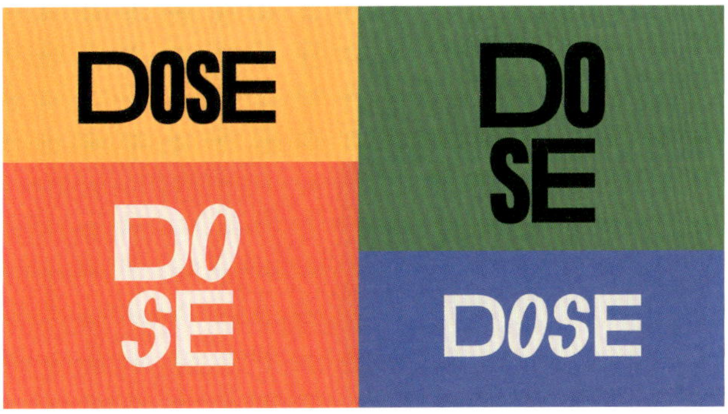
DOSE
DO
SE
DO
SE
DOSE

DOSE
@DOSEPODCAST
RIO DE JANEIRO - BRASIL

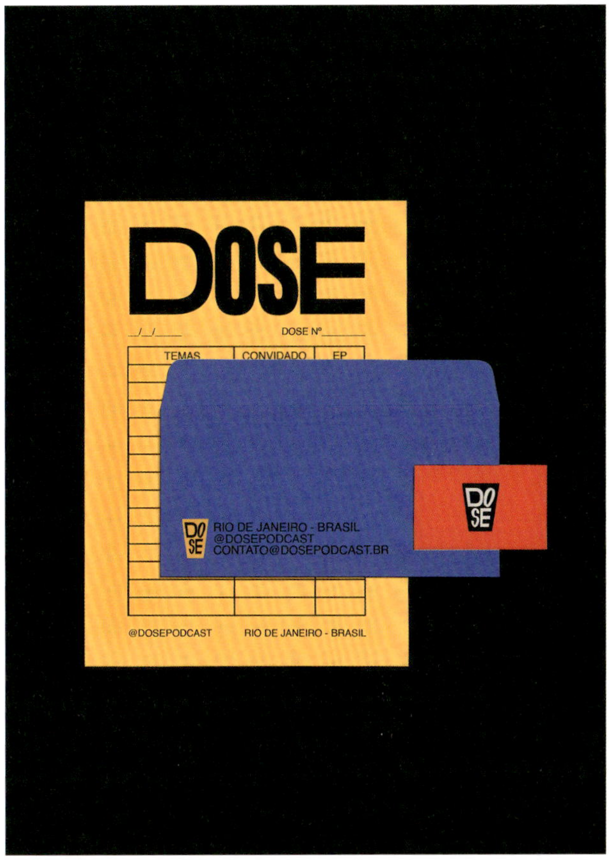
DOSE
DOSE Nº
TEMAS
CONVIDADO
EP
DO
SE
RIO DE JANEIRO - BRASIL
@DOSEPODCAST
CONTATO@DOSEPODCAST.BR
DO
SE
@DOSEPODCAST
RIO DE JANEIRO - BRASIL

TOME UMA
DO
SE
music
@DOSEPODCAST
RIO DE JANEIRO - BRASIL
eletromidia

DOSE
#01
EP. 01 – MARIA BETHÂNIA

● (blue)	C93 R9	M63 G91	Y0 B177	K0
● (orange)	C0 R232	M79 G80	Y100 B14	K0
● (black)	C0 R0	M0 G0	Y0 B0	K100

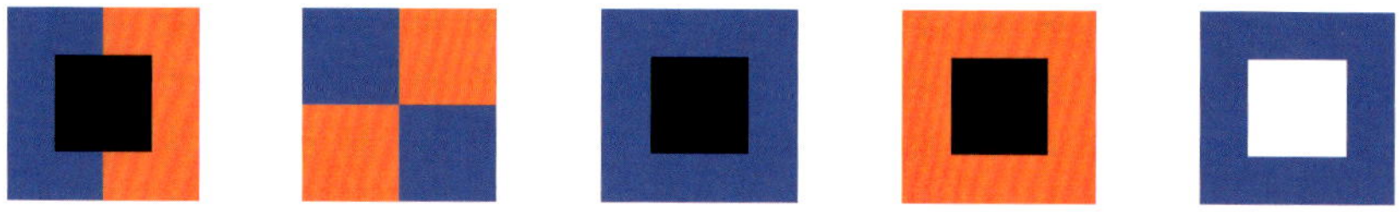

Studio Tangible

Tangible's new brand identity (BI) system is freely mixed with the upper and lower cases so that the overall length can be stretched and shortened flexibly. This flexibility highlights Tangible's ability to create stories and designs for various brands with no limits on categories, expressions, or target audiences. The BI represents Tangible's boundless visual perception through countless figures, frames, and images that align creatively. The main blue color symbolizes nature and cutting edge at the same time. It also expresses openness that can accommodate various perspectives. The orange sub-color represents adventure and positivity through the constant exploration of Tangible's aims.

Agency/
Studio Tangible

Design/
Allen Shim, Somin Lee, Seohee Min

Index

delight, making connections with people.

P250

Brand Brothers

brandbrothers.studio

Founded in 2010 by Johan Debit and Jean-Rémi Massery, Brand Brothers is a branding studio specializing in strategy, graphic, and typographic experimentation, branding, and visual identity. They regard their projects as functional and useful systems that combine high standards and honesty of content and form.

P212

BRUTTO

brutto.studio

BRUTTO was founded by Marco Oggian in 2020. BRUTTO is an Italian-Galician studio based in northern Spain that creates branding, images, videos, objects, and more. "Brutto" means "ugly" in Italian. So they are.

P104

BY-ENJOY DESIGN

by-enjoy.com

BY-ENJOY DESIGN, established in 2017, is an unconventional and intriguing design studio. They have a long-standing commitment to exploring and implementing the value of design in various fields, including commercial consumer brands, local traditional industries, and contemporary art and culture. Their approach emphasizes the use of visual functionality to drive brand communication, with a strong focus on brand identity design, visual system development, and creative product packaging. These areas serve as the core pillars of their creative work and projects.

P136

Carolina Lins

carolinalins.myportfolio.com

Carolina is a Brazilian graphic designer based in Rio de Janeiro, Brazil. With a career specializing in branding, she believes in working with creativity and strategy together, always seeking innovation and visual impact. Her work visually narrates stories to establish a strong presence in the market.

P252

CB Design

behance.net/cb625

CB Design is a graphic design studio founded in 2016 by Jackie Price. Nestled in Shenzhen, China, they offer a range of design services with a focus on branding and visual identity. The team consists of passionate designers who are dedicated to the art of design and take pride in being designers. They believe in collaboration and mutual respect for ideas to create outstanding results. Their slogan "Let's create something awesome together" reflects their dedication to working closely with the clients to bring their visions to life.

P040

CULTO CREATIVE

behance.net/culto_creative

Founded in 2010 by Daniel Duran, CULTO CREATIVE is a design studio that practices branding and creative direction. They think of their projects as functional and useful systems that combine high standards and straightforwardness of content and form.

P114, P224

Danara Khurgunova

behance.net/danarakhurgun1

Danara Khurgunova is a Belgrade-based art director and graphic designer with a background in marketing and advertising. She focuses on crafting compelling visual identities and graphics that evoke nuanced emotions through intricate metaphors while maintaining strong commercial appeals.

P130

Daqing, KimYeonhee

behance.net/da-qing
behance.net/yeonheee

Daqing is a grpahic designer from Shanghai. KimYeonhee is an art director in China.

P044

DE_FORM

de-form.hu

With more than ten years of experience in design, DE_FORM is developing design strategies to help institutes and companies in the cultural field through consulting and developing branding. They have designed visual identities and installations for more than 100 exhibitions and cultural events and are responsible for the overall branding of several major cultural institutions. DE_FORM represents multidisciplinary design thinking, constantly inspired by team thinking and collaborating with other professionals, curators, and artists.

P258

Diego Bellorin

empk.net

Diego Bellorin is an art director and freelance graphic designer originally from Maracaibo, Venezuela. Diego Bellorin's works are minimalist, often characterized by lines and dots, repetitive shapes, and overlapping layers, as well as the use of color and collage. His work is influenced by architecture, mathematics, and geometry. He currently resides in Mallorca, Spain.

P156

Dima Nislin

instagram.com/dimanislin

Dima Nislin is a graphic designer based in Moscow.

P146

Eduardo Nolasco

behance.net/eduardonolasco

Eduardo Nolasco is a Brazilian graphic designer with a mission to infuse intelligence, functionality, and efficiency into every project he undertakes. He believes his work benefits both businesses and individuals, creating a brand experience that is both unique and impactful. His approach goes beyond aesthetics, delivering visual solutions that connect and leave a lasting impression.

P170

errorerror.studio

errorerror.studio

They are a creative studio working on brand identity, photography, graphic design, typography, and communication campaigns.

P176

ESTUDIO ALBINO

estudioalbino.com

ESTUDIO ALBINO is a creative studio specializing in the development of distinctive branding, solid graphic identity systems, art direction, creative direction, and packaging experiences. They explore ways to tell stories and create strategies; finding beauty means transforming ideas into concepts that adapt to any expression.

P094, P148

ESTUDIO CRU

estudiocru.com

They are a Brazilian graphic design studio specializing in building visual narratives. Their works focus on developing strategies and identities for cultural, commercial, and experimental projects. They believe that intelligent design contributes to the advance of critical thinking at all levels of society.

P036

Estúdio Kuumba

estudiokuumba.com.br

It is a digital design studio that develops brands and packaging that connect with people. They combine simplicity and modernity to create strategic, functional, and timeless visual concepts, focusing on brand strategy, visual identity, and packaging.

P110

Evan Wijaya

behance.net/evanwijaya

Evan Wijaya is an Indonesia-based graphic designer with a passion for graphic design for films and real life. His work spans a wide range of disciplines, from films, fashion, and tech to the F&B industry. When it comes to design, he appreciates great attention to detail.

P276

for&st

for-st.co

for&st is an award-winning design studio, established with the moral—"design for story," believing design is not just purely aesthetic but to construct the experience. The name for&st extracted from "form & structure" / "forward & stand" / "for & story." They craft the aesthetic form and also the information hierarchy; to make ideas forward and stand.

P124

Forma

forma.co

Forma is a graphic design and illustration studio based in Barcelona, Spain. They help people, companies, and institutions to create or enhance their images. They always work with ideas as a starting point, using a clean and bold aesthetic.

P058, P160, P178

Forth+Back

forthandback.la

Forth+Back is a cross-disciplinary creative studio working with both cultural and commercial brands. Their capabilities are broad and span from creative direction, identity design, art direction, and photography to all levels of print and digital design. Forth+Back was founded in Los Angeles by Nikolos Killian and Tanner Woodbury.

P208

Frank Lo design studio

franklo.hk

Frank Lo design studio is an independent design studio based in Hong Kong, China. Their works across brand identities, packaging, print matters as well as digital products. They see visual as a communication tool and strategy. They care about functionality, yet wouldn't forget the humanistic touch-up. They help to extract the essentials from chaos and simplifying the complexity. They design the solution suit clients the best.

P232

Frank Wo

frankwo.com

At Frank Wo, the designers specialize in visually stunning designs with a focus on simple yet sophisticated aesthetics and thoughtful use of space. The studio brings a fresh and contemporary approach to every project, infusing it with creativity and elegance.

P164

Gastón García Aja

sajismo.com

Gastón García Aja (SAJA) is an Argentinian graphic designer and publicist who works in different areas of graphic design, especially in visual identities, focusing on concept, strategy, and aesthetic resolution, based in Barcelona, Spain. Without a specific style, the synthesis and austerity go through all his work, adding a particular and sensitive way to connect messages with real people.

P230

Humana Studio

humanastudio.com

Humana Studio is the work of Ana Abreu and Tiago Narciso. They do brand artistic direction, identity design, and print collaterals for people who don't mind being different.

P122

Ingrid Picanyol Studio

ingridpicanyol.com

Founded in 2014 and led by internationally award-winning creative director Ingrid Picanyol, the studio is based in Barcelona, but it works with clients and collaborators throughout the world. Strategically, the studio thrives off being a team that deeply understands the needs of a client by bringing a cohesive brand ecosystem: branding, packaging, photography, and web design. For the studio, the only way to win the attention and hold the affection of an audience is by meaningfully crafting a brand across all touchpoints in a holistic manner.

P268

Isa Lloret

behance.net/isa_lloret

Isa Lloret studied graphic design in her hometown, Valencia. She moved to Milan after completing her degree to pursue a master's in Visual Design at the Scuola Politecnica di Design. After gaining experience in various studios and cities in Italy, she returned to Spain to continue working and learning in Madrid and Barcelona. In Barcelona, she met Pol Vila, with whom she decided to co-found Setze Studio. Currently,

Isa Lloret continues her career independently.

P234

Isabelle Lin

behance.net/linhsi

Isabelle Lin is a graphic designer currently living in Sydney and Auckland.

P070

Jean Nicolas Guerreiro Dias

jeanguerreiro.com

He is a Brazilian graphic designer with over six years of diverse design experience. His current field of expertise revolves around visual identity and branding for companies and freelancers. As a designer, his objective is to strategically and aesthetically tackle challenges, seamlessly blending form and function in the execution of projects.

P242

Jo Cutri Studio

jocutristudio.com

Jo Cutri Studio is a multi-discipline design studio working with brands all across the world. They specialize in branding, packaging, and web design.

P256

Kate Zest Studio

katezest.com

Kate Zest Studio is a branding studio with a zest. The founder Kate is from Saint Petersburg, based in Amsterdam. She is a certified fine artist and a branding expert with a business degree obtained in Finland and Italy. She uses her view to convert products and services into authentic niche brands.

P030

Koen Tan, Vicky Zhao

behance.net/22501512661b6b
behance.net/1095559172f0d5

Tan is an interesting design lover from Qingdao. Zhao is a designer from Hong'an.

P098

Kristina Zotova

behance.net/chriszotova

Kristina is a freelance designer and digital artist from Russia. She specializes in branding development and UX/UI design. In her work, she explores the influence of color and form on human perception. Each project is an opportunity for her to bring unique ideas to life and visualize the world around her through recognizable images based on people's experiences.

P262

Leste

lestebr.com

Leste is a creative content studio based in Brazil, composed of a great team specializing in graphic design, illustration, motion graphics, animation, and cultural productions.

P154

Liam Nguyen

behance.net/liamd197

Liam Nguyen is a self-driven freelance graphic designer based in Ho Chi Minh City, Vietnam, who shares a huge passion for brand identity, especially for small start-up companies. As a graduate with a business degree obtained in 2020, Liam has started self-learning graphic design and created various projects with unique tones and styles.

P174

LMD

lucas-machado.com

Operating in Brazil, LMD is a global graphic design studio collaborating with clients on different scales. Their methodology is meticulous, emphasizing the use of typography and grid systems to generate impactful visual solutions. This approach, combined with strategic planning, ensures that they deliver tailored solutions that align with their clients' needs and the ever-changing contexts they navigate. With a diverse portfolio encompassing brand identities, editorial design, and signage, they serve clients across the architecture, culture, design, and art industries.

P138, P192

Lorenzo Tre

behance.net/lorenzotiemme

Lorenzo Tre is an independent graphic designer from Northern Italy. Operating across the commercial, cultural, and art sectors, his creative process aims to be both contextual and experimental, and in line with partners promoting inclusivity and sustainability.

P216, P220

LOTIPA STUDIO

lotipa.com

LOTIPA STUDIO is a Brazilian studio with Antoniel Felaînne.

P028

Lucas Barreira

lucasbarreira.me

Lucas Barreira is a Brazilian designer specializing in visual identity with more than 100 projects approved in six countries, including South Africa, the United States, Holland, and England.

P034, P082

Mano a Mano Club

manoamanoclub.com

Mano a Mano is a new graphic design club with two major fighters: Rajoy and Sanchez.

P088

Maria Alice de Sá Queiroz

behance.net/alicesaqueiroz

Maria Alice is a design student and freelance designer, passionate about design forever. She seeks to show simplicity and versatility. Her Latin roots in her work through colors, shapes, and types. Being from a small town in the countryside of São Paulo, design has become a form of self-expression as well as a tool to survive and fight against conservatism. She is not afraid to explore the many possibilities within design, which is why her work is colorful, vibrant, and conceptual.

P278

Mariia Terebenina

behance.net/marieter

Mariia Terebenina is a freelance graphic designer specializing in branding and packaging. Born in Russia, she currently lives in Turkey and works with clients from all over the world.

P050

Matteo Simonetti

behance.net/matteosimonetti

Matteo Simonetti is a visual designer from Rome, Italy. He studied Design at the Sapienza University of Rome, and he focuses on branding, editorial projects, wayfinding, and icon systems. Now he is working as a freelancer to continue his studies in visual communication and improve more and more.

P080

MAUM STUDIO

maumstudio.co.kr

MAUM STUDIO is a communication design studio that presents the value of heartfelt design through VI design, space design, and product projects. They are apt at conveying the warmth and fun of a brand with bright colors and simple graphics in the space.

P190, P194, P228

Melody Perco

behance.net/melodyperco

Melody Perco is a graphic designer graduated from the University of Buenos Aires, specializing in digital design and identity projects. She seeks to create significant visual solutions that connect the public, adding value through a strategic and functional approach. She is a lover of details and typography.

P270

Michelangelo Greco

behance.net/dudegraphic

The multifaceted nature of each different reality has allowed him to develop an extremely elastic and diverse approach to design in which each element while maintaining its consistency, can be a cue for new worlds and new ways of conceiving the project itself by ensuring that the interdependence of different factors creates connections that are each time different and never taken for granted.

P054

Mistaker

studiomistaker.com

Mistaker is an independent multi-disciplinary studio based in Rome founded in 2016 by Martina Tariciotti and Riccardo Casinelli. They focus on visual design, infographics, editorial, and motion graphics. They believe in research, simplicity, and details as the foundations of their creative process in aim to work with various clients, from big to independent. Since 2016, they have worked as information designers at La Repubblica and L'Espresso. They teach infographics and basic design at Istituto Europeo di Design in Turin and Rome.

P238

ModiFox Creative Agency

behance.net/modifoxcreative

ModiFox Creative Agency, a distinguished creative agency specializing in graphic design, is dedicated to designing, building, and developing brands in Vietnam. Comprised of a team of young and enthusiastic individuals, alongside founders boasting extensive experience, they have garnered a reputation for creating numerous unique and successful brands that thrive within the Vietnamese market.

P084

Monograf Studio

monograf.studio

Monograf Studio is a branding and design studio with experience in art direction and advertising. They believe in the importance of concept and visual communication in each project, finding inspiration in art, music, stories, and everything that connects people. They know that creating projects with simple language makes it easier for people in a visually saturated world.

P134

Monumento Co.

monumento.co

Monumento is a creative office focusing on tailored concepts for premium brands. It is also a design consultancy specializing in branding, art direction, editorial and print design, websites and digital platforms, space creation, and creative strategy for clients that strive for modern culture. Their design process is founded on research and strategic thinking. They use branding and design as tools to build projects that are not only beautiful but timeless, functional, and unique.

P222

Murri Studio

murri.studio

Murri Studio is a graphic design studio known for having a strong conceptual component in their works.

P076

Nastia Butkevich

behance.net/nakukux

Nastia Butkevich is an artist and graphic designer. She strives to combine design and art, creating work that is not only beautiful but meaningful.

P158

Nathalia Ultramar

behance.net/nathaliaudesign

Nathalia Ultramar is a designer passionate about colors and creating solutions for brands. She specializes in branding and packaging. Her goal is to translate the truth of each brand into strategic visual solutions that connect people.

P052

Nelson Balaban

nelsonbalaban.com

Nelson Balaban is a Brazilian graphic designer and art director with over two years of experience working within a wide range of disciplines for local and international brands while also teaching at international art & design schools.

P106

Nicole Rauen

behance.net/nicoleraue026b

Nicole Rauen is a Brazilian graphic designer based in São Paulo. She is passionate about typography, branding, and illustration. Her work applies strategic thinking to create engaging and stunning visual solutions across a range of projects through a deep act of exploring, researching, and being empathetic.

P244

Nil (Denilson Carvalho)

nildesigner.com

Nil is an independent designer dedicated to branding projects, unifying design with strategy.

P090

Nina Carreiras

behance.net/ninace

She is a graphic designer and illustrator based in Madrid, Spain. The use of bright and bold colors gives her work a unique and eye-catching quality.

P240

Nord Brands

behance.net/pamela-picoli

Nord Brands is a studio specializing in design, branding, and packaging, located in Brazil.

P072, P108

ONNFF™

behance.net/onnff

ONNFF™ comes from "ON AND OFF" and represents two extreme states of things. They are keen to dig out the appearance of things and hope to make thoughtful designs. They use graphic design as the main means to discover the beauty of the details in life. They hope that every "extreme" treatment can infinitely collide with new ideas and inspiration.

P026

ORIG DESIGN

ooorig.cn

ORIG DESIGN is a brand-strategy leader who regards inspiration as their source. It is creativity that makes their blood boil with indignation. Then they persevere in designing. They create with heart and enjoy working with client's trust. Because they know the only way to lead to success is to be original.

P264

Papanapa

papanapa.com

They are an independent branding studio based in São Paulo, Brazil. With over a decade of experience, they have worked with well-known brands, small businesses, and startups at different stages of their journeys. From launching new products to conquering new territories, obtaining investments, or discovering the best way to reinvent themselves for the world, they use the power of narrative and design to build consistent, authentic, and long-lasting brands.

P132, P186

Parco Studio

parco.studio

Parco is a graphic design studio based in Milan, founded by Loredana Bontempi and Emanuele Bonetti. Since 2010, they have been designing communication systems and visual strategies to shape the contents of their clients, with particular attention to socio-cultural issues and constant research for possible interactions with contemporary visual culture. They firmly believe that imagination is the best tool to shape the future.

P182

Pràctica

practica.design

Pràctica is a full-service design studio based in Barcelona and New York. They produce work that aims to be meaningful and distinctive by working closely with a selected network of collaborators.

P254

Puro Diseño

purodiseno.mx

Puro Diseño is an agency passionate about design, specializing in the creation of branding projects that transcend an infinite number of areas of daily life. Their inspiration comes from shapes, colors, textures, and trends; always focusing on the fusion of details since they believe that they are the essence of each design Puro Diseño creates. They are located in the city of Merida, Yucatan, Mexico. They work every day to fulfill their objective, to communicate graphically and functionally.

P128

Ramon Santos da Conceição

behance.net/ramonsantosc

He is a Brazilian graphic designer focusing on visual identities and techniques in visual communication.

P248

Réka Neszmélyi

behance.net/rekaneszmelyi

Réka Neszmélyi is a graphic designer from Budapest, Hungary.

P144

Sérgio Fonseca Studio

sergiofonseca.com

Sérgio Fonseca Studio designs visual identities for specific projects. Focusing on simplicity, clarity, and timelessness, the studio's passion is to turn ideas into timeless realities. They always believe that good design helps brands grow.

P068

Spatio Studio

spatio.studio

Spatio Studio is a small creative agency that specializes in creating brand identities with a focus on meaningful and conceptual design. The agency's designers align themselves with clients by sharing common values and principles of synergy. They strive to create products that reflect the personality and values of brands and companies. While Spatio Studio initially started its operations in Ukraine, the creative group has expanded its work to Poland, catering to the international market.

P100

STUDIO OUAM

studioouam.com

STUDIO OUAM creates a colorful, story-rich world around brands so that the client's tale leaves a lasting impression on the minds of those who discover it. The team consists of a core group of two complementary art directors—Alice Bouchardon and

Maxime Pirot—and a dream team of talents called in on a case-by-case basis to create the best team for each project.

P116, P260

Studio Romanes

ryanromanes.studio

Studio Romanes is the independent design practice of Ryan Romanes and his collaborators. With ties to New Zealand and Australia, they work with clients globally across various disciplines to realize their unique creative voice.

P032

Studio Tangible

tangiblebd.com/work

Studio Tangible is a branding agency based in Seoul that collaborates with international clients to deliver innovative design solutions. The studio offers a comprehensive range of services, including developing brand concepts, designing brand identities, packaging, visual identity systems, naming, and spatial design.

P280

Studio Xico Liborio

xicoliboriodesign.com

Studio Xico Liborio was founded Xico Liborio. He is an independent graphic designer, specializing in creating visual identities. He always seeks to apply concepts that give life to brands and thus connect people through their looks. The inspiration, idea, and implementation processes are present in all projects so that people obtain good market results.

P078, P198

Tanya Devaeva

behance.net/devaeva

She is a communication designer and artist specializing in visual identities, illustrations, and digital projects.

P226

Taylor Shady

behance.net/taylordsgn

Taylor Shady is a creative director and brand designer based in Rio de Janeiro, Brazil.

P272

The Woork

thewoork.eu

The Woork designs brands that matter. They are a team of specialists in brand creation and management with many years of experience working for multinational brands and start-ups. They have their own work methodology, which they adapt to the size of the client's project.

P218

Tiquismiquis.club

tiquismiquis.club

They are a graphic design duo based in Málaga, including Roberto Espartero and Juan Martín, specializing in visual identity and editorial design. Typographic play and editorial compositions are the hallmarks of their works, which they develop in collaboration with other creative profiles to offer tailor-made solutions with a unique identity.

P096, P168

Toormix

toormix.com

Created in 2000 in Barcelona by Ferran Mitjans and Oriol Armengou, Toormix is a mix of a brand consultancy, a design studio, and a digital creative agency. They use strategic thinking and design to create innovative brand experiences across physical, digital, or spatial media with a clear focus on user's needs. They also understand the business challenges and objectives. Their over 20 years of experience in all types of projects and disciplines, together with their team and network of specialists and external collaborators, allow them to face any challenge.

P202

Transform Design

transform.tw

Transform Design is a comprehensive design company specializing in branding construction and visual strategy. They are committed to transforming the intangible concept into a precise and unique visual identity. Navigating between imagination and practicality, they establish appropriate perspective and vision. Design embodies life experiences and is the reflection of contemporary society. Transform Design believes only through constant improvement and revolution can they really develop the most unparalleled value for each distinct project.

P060

Vanessa Rudger

behance.net/vanessarudger

Vanessa Rudger is a graphic designer and passionate about the field of design. She works as a freelancer, providing services in visual identity and branding, social media management, and creating designs for t-shirt prints.

P180

Victor Mazariegos

victormazariegos.com

Victor Mazariegos is an independent art creative director based in Barcelona.

P206

XXD DESIGN

xxddesign.com

It is a young visual design company established in Shenzhen in 2021. The founders Xiao Qiyuan and Xu Yuqing graduated from the Sichuan Academy of Fine Arts and Hongik University in South Korea. XXD focuses on the field of new consumer brands and is keen on creating and pursuing experimental and exploratory thinking. Through conceptual innovation and new visual experience, XXD assists customers in creating unique market value and provides design services such as brand design, visual identity, product packaging, and graphic illustrations.

P142

Acknow-ledgements

We would like to express our gratitude to all of the designers and agencies for their generous contribution of images, ideas and concepts. We are also very grateful to many other people whose names do not appear in the credits, but who have made specific contributions and provided support. Without them, the successful compilation of this book would not have been possible. Special thanks to all of the contributors for sharing their innovation and creativity with all of our readers around the world.